Reflections of Hope

Daily Readings for Anyone
Affected by Another Person's
Sexual Behavior

S-ANON
International

Family Groups

Reflections of Hope
Daily Readings for Anyone Affected by
Another Person's Sexual Behavior
© S-Anon International family Groups, Inc., 2008

P.O. Box 111242
Nashville, TN 37222-1242

Library of Congress Control Number: 2007909421
ISBN # 978-0-9676637-3-9

S-ANON
International

Family Groups

S-Anon Conference Approved Literature

For information and a complete listing of literature,
contact the S-Anon International Family Groups office:
    S-Anon International Family Groups, Inc.
    P.O. Box 111242
    Nashville, TN 37222-1242
    Phone: 615-833-3152 or 800-210-8141
    E-mail: sanon@sanon.org
    Web site: http://www.sanon.org

Forward

S-Anon members have longed for the day when we could open a daily meditation book and have it speak to our own experience. We wanted the ease of reading helpful words without the awkward substitution of the word *sexaholism* for *alcoholism*. As early as 1995, the S-Anon Literature Committee made plans for such a book. In the year 2002, the Board of Trustees* acknowledged the *expressed need* of our fellowship, which set in motion this long-awaited project.

Reflections of Hope is a fitting name, not only for this collaborative effort, but also for the Conference Approval process through which the book was written. Hundreds of S-Anon members stepped forward and participated in making this dream become a reality. *Reflections of Hope* embraces the voices of S-Anon men, women, and teens, all touched by the effects of another person's sexual behavior. These readings reflect the hope that comes from the experience of banding together to solve our common problems. It reflects the hope that comes from the new understanding of ourselves that we gain through working the S-Anon program. It also reflects the hope we gain through achieving a new perspective about the disease of sexaholism and the far reaching effects it has on our families, friends, and communities. Finally, *Reflections of Hope* reminds us of how important it is to accept our past, not to fear what might happen tomorrow and be open for the joys and miracles of what can happen in our lives today.

* In 2003 the S-Anon World Service Conference was formed. S-Anon literature needs are now expressed through our World Service Conference.

Acknowledgments

We gratefully acknowledge Alcoholics Anonymous and Al-Anon Family Groups, who both took the initiative to write daily readers for their respective fellowships. Many of us in S-Anon have gained tremendous help and insight form the experiences expressed in the Conference Approved Literature of the AA and Al-Anon fellowships.

The materials excerpted from *Alcoholics Anonymous, Twelve Steps and Twelve Traditions, As Bill Sees It,* and *Daily Reflections* are reprinted with permission of Alcoholics Anonymous World Services, Inc. (A.A.W.S.) Permission to reprint these excerpts does not mean that A.A.W.S. has reviewed or approved the contents of this publication, or that A.A. necessarily agrees with the views expressed herein. A.A. is a program of recovery from alcoholism only – use of these excerpts in conjunction with programs and activities which are patterned after A.A., but which address other problems, or in any other non – A.A. context, does not imply otherwise.

Excerpts from Al-Anon Conference Approved Literature are reprinted with permission of Al-Anon Family Group Headquarters, Inc. Permission to reprint these excerpts does not mean that Al-Anon Family Group Headquarters, inc. has reviewed or approved the contents of this publication, or that Al-Anon Family Group Headquarters, Inc. necessarily agrees with the views expressed herein. Al-Anon is a program of recovery for families and friends of alcoholics – use of these excerpts in any non Al-Anon context does not imply endorsement or affiliation by Al-Anon.

Grateful acknowledgment is made for permission to reprint the following:

Excerpts from *Alcoholics Anonymous,* Copyright 1939, 1955, 1976, 2001 by Alcoholics Anonymous World Services,

About This Book

We hope *Reflections of Hope* will be a helpful tool in your recovery.

Each meditation includes the following features:

- **Title.** The title reflects something you will find in the reading.

- **Page number, day and month** These are for your reference.

- **Daily Reading.** We tried to include spiritual principles found in our Steps and Traditions, which have helped many of us to find hope and even happiness as we recover from the effects on us of another person's sexaholism. These readings are based on sharings from members of our fellowship. Though they indicate a gender or specific relationship, the principles are applicable to each of us. The use or mention of Higher Power in terms of God or He is not meant to be offensive or suggestive. It is consistent with our Conference Approved Literature (CAL).

- **Further Reflections.** The majority of the quotes used were taken from our own S-Anon literature. Some quotes were also taken, with grateful permission, from Alcoholics Anonymous and Al-Anon. All the quotes are Conference Approved for use in this publication.

...I am learning to trust myself to rise to the occasion as a problem presents itself. I will have the resources when I need them. I don't have to control the outcome but can learn to trust the process. This allows me to be less afraid of the future. I am learning to accept change and not automatically see it as the end of the world or negative, but rather an opportunity for growth.

Working the S-Anon Program, p. 42

Meditation Titles

The Serenity Prayer

God grant me the serenity

To accept the things I cannot change,

Courage to change the things I can,

And wisdom to know the difference.

Learning to Let Go!

I have been attending S-Anon meetings for a few months, so I'm in the early stages of my recovery. I'm beginning to work on the Steps and starting to let down the walls around me that I had built over the past six years of my marriage. I discovered that when I admitted I was powerless over the disease of sexaholism, it allowed me the freedom to begin to see myself.

I slowly recognized the endless hours I had spent planning and scheming, in hope of controlling the sexaholic. I had given everything of myself and was bankrupt in my marriage, emotionally and spiritually. I was shocked by this revelation, as I attended church on a regular basis and prayed every day for the craziness to go away. I realize now that I was not willing to surrender and turn my life over to God, only willing to give up bits and pieces. I held on tight to my fear and pain.

Today I am slowly making deposits back into my spiritual bank by placing God first and foremost in my life. When I ask God to help me, I have to ask: Am I truly surrendering and trusting in my Higher Power? Today, I know the answer for me has to be yes; otherwise I will try to manipulate and control my life as I once did with the addict.

Further Reflections...
"The phrase 'came to believe' reminds me that faith is a process, not an event, from which sanity arises."
[Al-Anon] Hope for Today, p. 32

I Changed

When I was in a relationship with an active sexaholic, I spent my time waiting for him to change. I focused all my efforts on making that happen. I grandiosely thought he was the only one who needed to change. I also knew exactly what the changes needed to be and how they needed to come about. I was just sure that if he changed, I would be happy.

Even though I tried to orchestrate all of this change in him, nothing actually happened until I realized I was the one who had to change. Through working the S-Anon program, I stopped blaming the sexaholic for my unhappiness and started focusing on changing myself. With a lot of help, I set boundaries for myself. I stopped my compulsive controlling and left all outcomes to God. Surrendering control over others has become the most profound aspect of my program.

As I changed, the sexaholic decided to leave the relationship. While I was not able to experience the relationship with him I had hoped for, my relationship with myself and my Higher Power has improved significantly. I have become honest with myself, and I am physically healthier. I have peace in my life and I am doing things that are fulfilling and enjoyable for me. Many good things have come my way since I realized that I am the only person I can change.

Further Reflections...
"We learn that it is not our responsibility to keep the sexaholic sexually sober. Instead, it is our job to manage our own lives, whether or not the sexaholic chooses sobriety."
S-Anon Twelve Steps, p. 2

Eyes and Heart Open

During my divorce from my sexaholic spouse, we developed a joint custody visitation plan to define the time our one year-old daughter would spend with her father and me. I knew it was important for my daughter to have time with her father, yet I had a lot of fear about the effects of my soon-to-be ex-husband's sexaholism on our daughter. Particularly, I worried about him sexually abusing her, although there was no indication this had ever happened in the past or that he had any inclinations toward children.

My husband and I met with a therapist to discuss the pros and cons of each situation. The therapist helped me to understand the signs and symptoms of child sexual abuse. My daughter had never displayed these in the past. We also discussed getting books from the library for children in order to facilitate age-appropriate talks with her about sexual boundaries. We discussed the importance of continuing to talk openly with her about body parts and functions so she would have a vocabulary to use, if needed. We talked about the importance of promoting open discussion of feelings and discouraging the keeping of secrets.

With my awareness raised from factual information and with the communication lines open, I felt that the benefit of our daughter having a loving relationship with her father outweighed the future risk of sexual inappropriateness. I went ahead with the co-parenting plan, and I continue to use the tools of S-Anon to keep my eyes and my heart open.

Further Reflections…
"There are times that I am not parenting, but acting out my own fears through controlling others."

Working the S-Anon Program, p. 91

❖　❖　❖

Help for Families of Sexaholics

During the many years of my troubled marriage, I tried everything to solve our problem: couple's therapy, courses to improve myself as a wife, dressing to please him, catering to his moods and wishes... Nothing worked.

My husband's sexaholism escalated when we purchased a home computer. His sexaholism found a new venue and his acting out spiraled. My emotions see-sawed out of control; I feared he would use up our savings, because he wasn't working or even looking for work. I imagined losing our home and our family. I obsessed about him possibly being arrested for illegal online activities.

Fortunately, I was told about help for families of sexaholics. I found an S-Anon group and, in that group, I found the help, unconditional love and support I desperately needed. I let go of the uncontrollable through letting my God guide me, one minute at a time. I placed my marriage in God's hands and felt a new freedom in focusing on myself. I learned about my talents and gifts and used them to find solutions to my problems. I found hope for myself, even though I didn't know if my marriage would survive or if my spouse would find sobriety.

That was years ago, and I am still a grateful S-Anon today, enjoying the serenity I regained and giving back through service the hope I was given.

Further Reflections...
"Each S-Anon Family Group has but one purpose: to help families of sexaholics. We do this by practicing the Twelve Steps of S-Anon, by encouraging and understanding our sexaholic relatives, and by welcoming and giving comfort to the families of sexaholics."

Tradition Five

Regaining Serenity

Once my husband's sexaholism was confirmed, I started losing many things I thought I was able to control. I lost my temper, my self-respect, and respect for my husband, my ability to focus at work, and any patience I thought I might have had. I had young children at home at the time, and I knew it was particularly important for me to do what I could to find serenity.

In S-Anon I stared to feel less anxious, and to find more patience with myself and others. I learned to take my eyes off my spouse, and to focus on my own recovery. I began to recognize I did not cause my spouse's sexual acting out and that I could not cure it or control it. I could be supportive of his efforts around recovery, but not force outcomes. I educated myself about the disease of sexaholism, and I looked at patterns in my own life that played a role in this family disease.

Working the S-Anon program has given me hope and faith in myself and in my Higher Power. By following the example of other S-Anons, I have come to believe that I can be O.K., no matter what my spouse chooses for himself. This belief in and of itself brings serenity to me.

Further Reflections…
"The Serenity Prayer points out that our Higher Power guides us in our recovery process and that powerlessness is not the same as helplessness."

Working the S-Anon Program, p. 41

A Fellowship of Equals

Until I arrived at S-Anon, I struggled with the feeling of not belonging anywhere. I was carrying around a secret: I was living with a sexaholic. I was afraid to tell anyone, even the S-Anon members in my first meeting. By the time it was my turn to share, I felt safe because I heard the other members sharing parts of my story. They knew what it was like growing up and living with sexaholism.

I was still concerned that someone was going to tell me to leave my marriage. I knew if they did, I would never come back, because I was there to save my marriage. At that point, I didn't know that in S-Anon, we are asked not to give advice. I also learned to my relief, Tradition Two reminds us that there is only one authority: a loving God as he may express Himself in our group conscience.

It was the principle of anonymity that kept me coming back. Anonymity means S-Anon is a fellowship of equals where everyone belongs. By maintaining anonymity, we leave our other identities outside the meeting such as our professions, educational backgrounds, and religions. One way I personally practice this principle is by not sharing the length of time I have been working the S-Anon program during my initial contact with a newcomer. I simply share my story and the positive changes in my life, since I started working the S-Anon program. Until newcomers understand that we are a fellowship of equals, they might assume that a long-time member is an "expert" on working the program.

Further Reflections…
"By maintaining anonymity, we are practicing humility in our recovery."

Working the S-Anon Program, p. 37

Overcoming My Fears

As a man going to my first S-Anon meeting, I was embarrassed, ashamed, nervous, and fearful. I thought of all kinds of reasons to be afraid. I feared the women there would consider me as part of the enemy. I had no experience in sharing my feelings and fears. I thought that as a man I was not supposed to be powerless over anything, and I felt ashamed to have a spouse who had acted out.

I also knew I was at the end of my rope. Physically, I had ulcers from my obsessive thinking and the constant shame and isolation I was feeling. I went to my first meeting, in spite of my nervousness. I was the only man there and thought that surely some of the women there were uncomfortable with a man being in their meeting. However, once they read the Traditions, I knew I belonged. After hearing the sharing, there was no doubt I was one of them. (I have since met other men in the S-Anon Fellowship.)

As time went on, I became more and more comfortable in the meetings. I was able to share openly, without fear. I was able to hear experience, strength and hope and apply the Twelve Steps and Twelve Traditions in my life. I am grateful that I was in so much pain that I was willing to walk through my fears, and attend the meetings. S-Anon gave me a new life.

Further Reflections…
"We couldn't have imagined when we first came to S-Anon that our lives would one day be filled with joy, serenity, and peace, but that has been the experience of countless S-Anon members. Without hesitation, we invite you to join us on our journey of recovery."

Working the S-Anon Program, p. xiv

❖   ❖   ❖

Clear Path to Serenity

On a cold and rainy evening — I trudged from my car to the meeting room. With anger and frustration I thought, "I've been doing this for a year now and nothing is better." I was angry with my spouse, the program, God, and myself. I wanted the pain and the stress to be gone. I wanted peace in my marriage and within myself. I wanted to feel joy.

Taking a seat, I waited for the meeting to begin. Lost in frustration and self-pity, my thoughts drifted. I imagined myself driving a car with gray mud all over the windshield, so thick it was impossible to see. The more I tried to clean the mud off with the windshield wipers, the messier it got. Then a thought emerged: Perhaps it is time to pull over and rest a bit. If I just let the rain fall and stop trying to make the wipers do the job, the windshield will clear.

After the meeting, as I drove home, I noticed my mood had improved. Turning on the windshield wipers, the image of mud and muck returned. Then it occurred to me: I had been pushing my spouse and myself to move ahead without trust, just to make something move. With the clarity provided by the meeting, I knew I needed to let go of the anger and sadness — to just "let it rain" because the way would eventually become clear for me. The S-Anon fellowship provides a clear path to serenity, if I am willing to trust the process.

Further Reflections...
"In fact, we have found we are most able to be helped when we realize that our power is limited and we really need help."

Working the S-Anon Program, p. 41

When I Lighten Up, I Can Better Solve My Problems

When my humor about my struggles in recovery is intact, I know I am doing something right. I live with a recovering sexaholic who continues to have occasional slips. The other day, after learning of one of his slips, I found myself very angry and unable to contain my anger and indignation. I impulsively scooped up a handful of dust bunnies from the dust pan I was using to clean, and sprinkled them on his computer keyboard.

Horrified by what I'd done, sanity started to return, and I called my sponsor to report my own relapse. After listening to my dust bunny story, she humorously pointed out my actions were "just in time for spring cleaning." We both had a good laugh and I regained my perspective. I was reminded of something that has been a key for me; his sobriety is not my responsibility or mission in life. I got off the phone and removed the dust bunnies. I now see that when I lighten up, I can solve my problems much more easily and can avoid creating more suffering for myself, and others.

When I shared my dust bunny experience at a meeting, I got a room full of nodding heads and chuckles. This reminded me that I am not alone in my occasional insane reactions to sexaholism, and that life works better for me if I don't take myself too seriously.

Further Reflections...
"Taking ourselves too seriously won't solve a problem any quicker... A good laugh may be the best tool available to help us let go..."

[Al-Anon] Courage to Change, p. 91

Letting Go of My Need to Control

S-Anon is helping me to see that just as lust is a serious problem for the sexaholic, my need to control is also a serious problem for me. When that character defect of being controlling is active in my life, I want things done my way at any cost. I want my husband to be just the way I want him to be.

Today, when I sense myself becoming anxious and controlling, I ask my Higher Power to help me see the other person (usually my husband) as a capable adult person, not wanting or needing my control. That person is a human being, a child of God, and I owe that person the dignity of making his or her own choices.

I am also grateful that through the gifts of my husband's recovery, he now is able to alert me gently when I have over-stepped his boundaries. Little by little, our Higher Power is removing character defects from both of us.

Further Reflections...
"I had a spiritual renewal as I humbled myself and realized I was really no better or worse than anyone else..."
                                Working the S-Anon Program, p. 4

Focusing on Myself

I have noticed a huge spurt in my emotional growth since attending a recent S-Anon International Convention. I drove away from the convention with a big awareness: I must focus on my behavior rather than anyone else's. I have always known that focusing on ourselves is a key principle of the S-Anon program, but I didn't have the insight into my own behavior until the convention.

This awareness has helped me change my behavior toward my sexaholic family member. I no longer try to manipulate by making "helpful hints". I do not make sarcastic remarks, putting down the sexaholic for his behavior. I see the insanity of my thinking and behavior. I thought if I acted mean and said hurtful things, this would cure or control the sexaholic from acting out in his disease. Instead, I am now asking myself, "What's going on with me when I feel that "urge" to put others down?" How is my behavior helping or hindering my serenity? Can I feel compassion for myself and others?

My behavior has changed with other family members also: I am no longer pushing myself on my adult children. If they don't want my input on something, or if they have a change of plans and are unable to visit me, I use my program tools to work through how I am feeling. I can then make a plan to get on with my day. By changing the things I can, I have a better understanding of why we call this a "family disease" and my part in it. This new awareness has done wonders for my serenity!

Further Reflections...
"The way out of... frustration is to begin to put the focus on ourselves and our own actions and reactions."
Working the S-Anon Program, p. 45

A Message of Hope

When I first discovered the sexaholic behavior of my spouse, I was angry enough to implode. I became so overwhelmed that I used a survival technique learned long ago: distracting myself with busyness to numb my feelings. Months later, my fear and anxiety re-surfaced, and I became very ill. I could no longer deny the reality of my situation. My illness was a wake-up call, helping me realize how severely I had been affected by the sexaholic behavior of not only my spouse, but three other intimate partners previous to my marriage.

Fortunately I made a phone call to the local S-Anon hotline. After I poured out my story to the person who answered my call, she read "The S-Anon Problem" from the booklet *We're Glad You're Here...Helpful Information for the Newcomer*. I could relate to every word! Hearing that reading profoundly changed my life.

I attended my first meeting and in the midst of my pain, I knew S-Anon was where I belonged and that it would be the source of my healing. Now I keep our booklet for newcomers close to the phone so when anyone calls out for help, I can choose a section to read to them. I, too, can carry the S-Anon message of hope.

Further Reflections...
"We try to carry the S-Anon message by sharing our experience, strength and hope with others, and we have found our joy and gratitude growing when we see the attitudes of other woman and men change from despair to hope. We have seen that we can be uniquely helpful to those who are still suffering from the effects of sexaholism."
                                                                Working the S-Anon Program, p. 28

S-Anon Is For Me

I went into a tailspin when my husband began to question whether or not to continue going to SA meetings. I wanted to nag him to go to meetings and other program functions with me and to tell him he'd never make it alone. Using program tools, I detached as best I could.

Eventually my spouse stopped going to meetings altogether. Detaching with love and compassion was difficult for me. I made lots of telephone calls. I consistently heard that I was powerless over whether or not my husband had a program. I was so entangled in our relationship; the thought of losing my husband scared me to death! I did everything with him and for him.

It was very difficult for me to continue to work a program without him. I had to "act as if" going to meetings was just for me. In truth, I was going to meetings to get back at him for the resentment I felt, trying to show him up, as if I were better than him.

Yet God worked with me, even through my misguided ulterior motives. As I continued to go to meetings, I came to believe that recovery could help me find the courage to make the one decision I never wanted to face – whether or not to stay in my marriage. I finally understood what detachment really meant for me – working my program just for me.

Further Reflections...
"We realize we cannot find serenity for ourselves if we continue to focus on someone else's recovery, so we commit ourselves to our recovery."

Working the S-Anon Program, p. 119

My Program Is Back in Place

After my husband had nearly 14 years of sobriety, evidence of his relapse was revealed to me on three separate occasions. My responses have been interesting.

The first – finding pornography in his car – was a devastating shock. Initially, I denied that this was his. Working with my sponsor, my S-Anon program kicked in, and I accepted that it was his. After reflecting and talking with others in the program I realized my focus still was on how to get "him" or "us" back on track. I was redirected to look at my own program, and determine if I was taking care of my physical and spiritual needs.

The second instance, a few months later, involved stumbling onto him viewing pornography on a public access computer terminal. I was hurt and I withdrew emotionally by having minimal direct contact and overtly expressing my indifference. I worked the Steps around my own behavior over the year leading up to and during his relapse. It became clear to me that he was not the only one who had been in relapse.

The third instance, again involved finding pornography in his car. There was no devastating shock and no emotional withdrawal. I stayed in the present, leaning on my Higher Power and using my tools. I instituted boundaries for myself and communicated honestly with my husband. I took time for myself, yet met my responsibilities at home and at work. I don't know how this will turn out, but I do know God is with me and I will be O.K. My program is back in place.

Further Reflections...

"When I am sober in this program I take control of my own actions and change what I can about myself..."

Working the S-Anon Program, p. 56

Staying Out of "What Might Have Been"

In a recent meeting, the topic for discussion was: feelings of inadequacy. I shared I had wanted more from my life than what my upbringing prepared me for. I spoke of how I would look around at others and think they had been given better guidance than what I had been given. I admitted I spent a lot of my energy and time brooding over "what might have been" – or as I've heard it described, "Comparing my insides with others' outsides."

I listened to the sharing of others in the meeting, and I was reminded that I was not alone. Almost everyone expressed having felt inadequate at one time or another. I realized that while I might have missed some important preparation for life, getting stuck in regretting "what might have been" has only acted as a block on my ability to rise from my problems and find happiness.

I am working with my sponsor to turn my negative thinking around. I am learning to focus on the assets I have today, such as being a good mom. I am learning I can start my day over as often as I need. I'm coming to believe that I have exactly what I need to have a good life today. I have the guidance of my Higher Power and the S-Anon program.

Further Reflections...
"We gain so much for our own recovery when we share our experience, strength and hope with others. In fact, most of us feel that we have received much more help than we have been able to give."

Working the S-Anon Program, p. 103

The Way to Joy

Discovering that my spouse was a sexaholic was life-shattering for me, so it seems ironic to write about joy now. After I got into recovery, my spouse chose to turn away from his own recovery program. He left me for another relationship and ended our marriage. These were devastating losses and very painful for me. I found it very difficult to experience anything remotely like joy through this time.

I've learned, through working this program and listening at meetings, that the way to joy is to stop sidestepping pain. There haven't been any shortcuts or quick fixes for me. I have worked the program head-on, and over time I have reached the other side of my deep pain. As I worked my program, the Gifts of the S-Anon Program slowly started to come to me – even "We will recover the feelings of joy."

My journey has been often trying, with a lot of soul-searching. It became easier when I realized that God has a treasure hidden in all my experiences; it's my job to search for the gift, wrapped just for me. Once I find the gift, I get the joy of opening that gift, accepting it and owning it. It may be a kind word, a smile, a new friendship, an accomplishment or opportunity. These moments of joy are all gifts. While I still feel some grief for my losses, there is now joy in my life, as well.

Further Reflections...
"One definition of a spiritual awakening is the ability to do, feel, and believe, through God's power, that which a person could not do before with his or her own power."

Working the S-Anon Program, p. 28

Gratitude for the Blessings of Relationships

An overwhelming feeling of gratitude for people in my life washed over me on my way to work one day. I thought of people in the S-Anon program, my family, and my acquaintances at work. All these relationships enrich my life by adding texture and meaning. Even people I find difficult to be around offer an opportunity to learn something about myself. These relationships allow me to practice my program by working Tradition Twelve and "principles above personalities."

The warm feelings of gratitude lasted that whole day. Everyone I came in contact with seemed new and precious to me. While that day is done, I pray that I am able to take this new perspective of gratitude with me from day to day.

Today, my prayers are often about asking for the willingness and strength to do God's will. I pray that the people I meet on any given day and those people I love and care about, will have God's blessings. When I remain open to the concept of Higher Power's will, I feel better about myself and spend less time worrying about things I really have no control over anyway.

Further Reflection...
"We see that each relationship is a necessary part of our growth and learning."

S-Anon Twelve Steps, p. 94

Road to Recovery

The longer I am in S-Anon, the more I see how impatient I am. This character defect is evident especially when I am driving. Recently through prayer and meditation, I got the message to try driving in the right lane only. I decided to "yield" to Higher Power, thinking that I might learn something valuable for my recovery. So my driving slogan became "stay right with God." Driving in the right lane meant making changes. I slowed down and drove more consistently. I had to be patient with those who were not driving as fast as I thought they should drive.

This experience is helping me see just how much I want things my way. I am reminded of how I tried to control the sexaholic behavior, over and over again. I would surrender control of the sexaholic to God, inevitably taking it back again as I grew impatient with the pace of the sexaholic's recovery. I wanted to go at my pace instead of His. I now see that the right lane symbolizes doing things God's way, and the left lane symbolizes doing things my way. Taking the Third Step every day reminds me that turning my life over to the care of God and letting go provide a smoother road to recovery. Faith in my Higher Power can keep me in the correct lane—following Higher Power's will for me keeps me right with God.

Further Reflections…
"Simply having faith in a Higher Power is not enough. We have to surrender our will and our lives over and over again."

S-Anon Twelve Steps p. 29

Self-Honesty

S elf-honesty is not about looking in the mirror to see what the world sees. Self-honesty is a commitment to the truth about my feelings and what is actually going on in my life. When I first came to S-Anon, I was focused on looking at the glaring defects of my spouse. I thought whatever defects I might have could not compare to the hurt-producing ones my sexaholic spouse had.

Through working my program I have learned that I can only work to know myself and I can only uncover my own part in this family disease. My Higher Power revealed an important connection for me: my unhealthy behaviors hurt me and the people who interact with me.

Today, I can face my character defects with the knowledge that God can and will change me if I continue to do my own work.

Further Reflections

"As I connect at a deeper level with my Higher Power's love for me, I feel a greater ability to be honest, to know myself, and to let myself be seen and heard by others."

Working the S-Anon Program, p. 49

Staying Connected with Reality

At my first meeting, it was comforting to hear I was not alone in my problem of living with a husband who admitted to being a sexaholic. I thought I was the only one who experienced such fear, anger, and the need to control. I was relieved to find there were others like me. Even though I grew up in an alcoholic home, not a sexaholic home, my beliefs were just like those of so many other members. I thought I could control people around me through my actions and words. I believed it was my fault that my parents fought. I felt I deserved whatever I wanted. I believed sex was the most important thing in a relationship, and that I would gain approval and acceptance, if I provided pleasure through sex. I believed God did not exist and certainly was not going to help me, or forgive my transgressions.

It is now clear to me, that those beliefs were not based in reality, but were a product of our family disease. Coming to S-Anon meetings is how I discovered reality, and it is how I continue to stay connected with reality. Listening to others share their experiences helps me cope with my own. I get pieces of information I can adapt to my own situation. If I miss meetings, not only do I lose contact with the people I have grown to love, I also get trapped by my own unrealistic thinking. Meetings help keep me in reality and help keep me sober.

Further Reflections...
"For those of us who have access to them, regular attendance at meetings is an important tool in working the program and staying 'sober' in S-Anon."

Working the S-Anon Program, p. 3

Powerless, Not Helpless

When I first began working the Steps, I struggled with several key concepts including powerlessness, my Higher Power, and surrender. I reasoned that I have certain talents, abilities, and skills. Obviously I was intended to use these and have "power" over some things. Why was I supposed to surrender everything to my Higher Power? This confusion led to my initial interpretation of Steps One, Two, and Three, and I was left feeling small with shame. I did not want to admit my needs or ask for help, from a Higher Power whom I believed loved me based on my performance. My performance was not very impressive.

Later, I realized that admitting my powerlessness did not mean that I was helpless. Rather, powerless meant that I was the recipient of gifts that my Higher Power wanted me to use to the fullest. Surrendering my will and the care of my life to my Higher Power has resulted in wonderful and unexpected outcomes that I alone could not have caused.

I understand now that part of my spiritual growth involves surrendering not only my fears, shortcomings, and lack of faith, but also how I use my talents, skills, and abilities. My Higher Power unconditionally loves me and is able to miraculously transform everything I surrender into more opportunities for progress for me and my fellows.

Further Reflections...
"Admitting our powerlessness may make us feel defeated, but it is really the first step toward rebuilding our lives. We now know we need help."

S-Anon Twelve Steps p. 15

Dancing to a New Tune

In a stormy period before recovery, my sexaholic husband and I attempted to take dance lessons. After three sessions we stopped speaking to one another. That was the end of dance lessons. We did what we often did back then – quit rather than work through the problem.

A few years into recovery, we found ourselves at a restaurant that had dancing. Our relationship was in a good place and we decided to dance. We laughed because we had forgotten everything we had learned in those few lessons years before. We were not a pretty sight, but the difference between what we were like before recovery and what we were like after just a few years in our respective programs was striking. We actually had a good time!

Now it is years later and soon we will be taking a cruise to celebrate our twentieth wedding anniversary. There will be dancing, so I dared to suggest that we take a few lessons before going. My husband agreed and admitted he was nervous because of our previous dance lessons. I shared with him my awareness that I was the one who had caused a great deal of the problem in those first lessons because I had been so focused on how he was doing and trying to lead him, that I had made cooperation difficult.

Today I am aware that I no longer need to be in control. I can follow a lead.

Further Reflections...
"We had to quit playing God. It didn't work. We decided that hereafter, in this drama of life, God was going to be our Director. He would be the Principal; we, His agents."

Alcoholics Anonymous, p. 48

Extending My Hand in Fellowship

Often I hear newcomers say they don't understand why so many people continue going to S-Anon meetings if they have found the serenity to deal with the sexaholics in their life. I thought about where I would be if S-Anon and its members weren't here for me when I first walked through those doors. I remembered I felt lonely and afraid; I wanted desperately to connect with someone else who understood my pain.

When I hear someone share from their despair, I am reminded of where I was, and also of how far I have come. I am grateful for the hope I hear from those members who continually work this program and show up week after week. They share what this program has offered them, and how their lives have changed. They remind me that I may be powerless over the disease of sexaholism, but I am not helpless to make healthy changes in my life.

I keep coming back to extend my hand in fellowship. I always find that I receive so much more in return. ..."Let the hand of S-Anon and S-Ateen always be there, and let it begin with me."

Further Reflections...
"Another way we work the Twelfth Step is to do service work in our "home' group. (This is the group we attend regularly – the one in which we feel most comfortable.) We can help set up the chairs and literature before the meeting, act as the meeting leader, contact people who inquire about our program, or volunteer to be a trusted servant such as the group secretary or treasurer. Any activity that makes it possible for the meeting to take place and to be a source of hope and recovery for a newcomer is Twelfth Step work."

Working the S-Anon Program, p. 98

I Do Not Need to Be Afraid

For as long as I can remember, I have sought the approval of others. Sometimes out of fear and sometimes because I felt less worthy than certain individuals or groups. Either way, I tried to conform to the rules of others so I could "fit in." I thought others' opinions of me mattered more than my own opinion.

In S-Anon, I am learning that what others think of me is none of my business. Instead, I am learning simply to seek the will of a Higher Power. If someone is not happy with something I have said or done, rather than reacting by trying to fix their feelings out of fear of losing their approval, I ask myself some questions: What is God's will for me? Can I accept myself as I am? Do I have an amend to make? Am I focusing on another's path instead of my own?

At this point I check in with someone in S-Anon (usually my sponsor) to discuss my options. By using tools like self-examination and telephone check-ins, often I find that my own actions and expectations are what is actually causing me discomfort. When I walk my path with openness and listen for the will of God, I do not need to be afraid of what others think of me.

Further Reflections...
"We will no longer depend on other people to provide us with an identity or a sense of self- worth."
Gifts of the S-Anon Program

Letting God Help

I have learned that in order to be emotionally healthy, I must not obsess about those things over which I have no control. For example, I cannot stop my husband from lying. I feel pain, anger, sadness, betrayal. and deep sorrow when I think about his actions and lies. Wallowing in these emotions won't change the facts and may even slow my progress toward finding joy. For my own sanity and serenity, I must surrender my husband and the life he chooses to live to his Higher Power.

The S-Anon slogan "Let go and let God" is a helpful tool of surrender for me. Another tool is writing. I am journaling about the events that have brought me to today. Sometimes my writing brings up pain over the betrayal of my trust. I feel the pain, and then decide to turn over these feelings to my Higher Power and to ask for his care and healing in my life. I also ask my Higher Power's help to increase my willingness to forgive my husband and myself for the past, as well as help to make choices about the future of my relationship and help with the details of the present.

Through my commitment to recovery, I know I will make better choices for myself in the future. I am beginning to trust my Higher Power's plan for my life.

Further Reflections...
"Step Three told me that I was not alone and that regardless of circumstances, I would be O.K. I could trust that my Higher Power had a plan for me that was better than I could imagine."

S-Anon Twelve Steps, p. 31

Destruction and Construction

I've heard it said that "change is necessary" and "the only constant is change." To take that leap of faith and make a decision to change my life in a profound way is very difficult, particularly to make a decision that could change my belief system or my relationships.

Making a change can still feel like I am falling off a cliff or diving into the unknown. I think this is because change usually involves an ending, which often brings up fear or grief. Sometimes I try to block these emotions by staying in a holding pattern and avoiding making decisions that bring about change. When I don't take action, I stay stuck and suffer anyway.

My sponsor is encouraging me to view change in a new way. She says that some form of destruction must take place before something new can be constructed. For example, during a renovation, demolition takes place; land is cleared before a new building can be built. Change involves the process of destruction and construction, and, while I might not notice it, these things are taking place all of the time.

I am learning to actively work Step Three during transitions in my life. I am beginning to see that I can trust God to be with me, and that I can leave outcomes to my Higher Power. When I do this, things seem to work out just the way they are supposed to, no matter how large or small the change is.

Further Reflections...
"If I knew that a Higher Power was truly in charge of my life and that everything happening now would work out for the best, how would I feel and act?"

S-Anon Twelve Steps, p. 37

Learning to Live by Spiritual Principles

When I came into S-Anon, my motto was Life isn't fair. For many years I wanted to "make" life fair according to my definition of fairness. People, places and situations had to play by my rules — but I never told anyone what my rules and conditions were. I created the illusion of control through keeping an account on everyone and when they did something to upset me, I mentally scored them with a "strike" or a "foul ball." Needless to say I had very little joy and lots of pain in this game I played. In S-Anon I learned that as long as I expect others to follow my unstated "rules" in search of fairness, I will have no serenity.

Today, when I think that life is being unfair to me, or to others, I look to my Higher Power and surrender the situation. I know I have a limited understanding about the meaning of "fairness" in my life or the lives of others. I may not know what results will come from surrendering, but I trust God does. Through this act of surrender my old "rules" have been replaced with the spiritual principles of the Steps and Traditions. I am experiencing joy – something I never thought was possible.

Further Reflections...
"I have begun to trust in the experiences of others and have surrendered my need to control every situation to protect myself from nameless, faceless, countless dangers. I have seen that this Power can be trusted..."

Working the S-Anon Program, p. 39-40

Slowly Discovered My Faulty Thinking

My life changed forever the day my spouse told me he was attending meetings for recovering sexaholics. He expressed his enthusiasm for his new found freedom from lust and explained a little bit about what that was like for him. He concluded by letting me know about S-Anon, and by asking if I was interested in going. As I was already working an Al-Anon program, I understood how important it was to see what S-Anon was all about.

I actually came to my first S-Anon meeting feeling jovial – I was happy he was finally admitting he had a problem other than me! As the weeks passed, those jovial feelings gave way to a painful awareness of how I had been affected by sexaholism. Fortunately I already had a foundation in the Twelve Steps, and the support of my sponsor in the other program. That support – along with my S-Anon meetings and new S-Anon friends – became the glue that held me together, as I slowly discovered just how deeply ingrained my faulty thinking was, regarding "how my life was supposed to be."

That was many years ago, and S-Anon continues to hold a very special place in my heart. Without this program, I would not have been able to hang in there with my spouse or to find healing from the effects of this terrible disease. I continue to go to meetings, to work with my S-Anon sponsor, and to volunteer in service. I have been given so much – to give back is a pleasure.

Further Reflections…
"Day by day, week by week, my vision cleared. I began to see who I really was."

S-Anon Twelve Steps, p. 42

No Longer a Snooper

I used to spend a lot of time searching the sexaholic's house and reading his journals looking for "evidence" against him. Back then I believed that any "evidence" I found defined me as a woman, either proving or disproving the sexaholic's love for me. I was desperate for him to fulfill my need for love.

I now know that no one person could have filled me up, because deep down I believed I was unworthy of love. The only thing I accomplished by my obsessive searching was the loss of my time, serenity and emotional sobriety. By working the Steps in S-Anon, I now seek love from my Higher Power. I replace the fear of not getting enough love with the courage to trust that my Higher Power will put people in my life who love and support me in a healthy way. The Steps have helped me to learn to love myself and trust that I do have the ability to make healthy and appropriate choices for myself.

Thankfully my urges to snoop are being replaced by urges to read literature, write in my journal, and check in with my sponsor and other S-Anon members. I am doing what I can to improve my relationship with the sexaholic. Today I am finding that God provides me with the love I need.

Further Reflections...
"Now we can really do something! We can trust God to do what we cannot do for ourselves."

S-Anon Twelve Steps, p. 16

How Important Is Service Work?

When I used to hear the word "service" in S-Anon, I would tune out. I was not interested in all that hum-drum stuff. I was too overwhelmed with needing to fix my marriage, to be bothered with those trivial details. As I've progressed in my program, I've become more aware of how important service work is.

If someone hadn't decided to start a meeting, I would-n't have a group to attend. If someone hadn't staffed a phone line and gently returned my first tenuous phone call for help, I wouldn't have learned to trust enough to contin-ue to reach out, and I certainly would never have found my first meeting. If someone hadn't donated a few hours of their time to be an Intergroup Representative for our group, I wouldn't know about the needs and activities of S-Anon as a whole. If someone hadn't spent some time and energy to organize local marathons, international conven-tions and open meetings, I wouldn't have met some peo-ple who have had a very positive influence on my recov-ery.

How many people, many of whom I will never meet, have given something of themselves so that I may benefit? How can I thank the invisible hand of S-Anon that has cra-dled my growth? As I grow and better understand this program, I too am able to help the newcomer, so that S-Anon will continue to be there for those who still suffer. I see my willingness to do service as evidence of my recov-ery for which I am eternally grateful.

Further Reflections...
"It's wonderfully rewarding to be able to contribute to the growth of our fellowship and to be part of the group con-science working for S-Anon as a whole."
Working the S-Anon Program, p. 100

I Had an Epiphany

Some of my friends repeatedly used to ask me, "What are you doing to take care of you?" I couldn't understand why they asked me that. I thought I was taking care of myself by focusing on my sexaholic husband and what he should be doing to change. After all he was the problem!

Years of focusing on "the problem", with no results, wore me down. One day I realized that no matter what I said or did, I could not control my husband's sexaholism. I had an epiphany: "My life is a mess; I have no control over my husband's behavior, and I am going to go into deep depression if I don't get help fast." Clearly, I had to start learning how to take care of myself. I looked in the phone book, hoping to find something like Al-Anon for people who were involved with sexaholics. I was so relieved to discover S-Anon.

I went to my first meeting and heard Step One read aloud, I knew I was in the right place. I felt a heavy weight being lifted from my shoulders, as I heard how so many others faced similar problems. They were learning to deal with life and take care of themselves on a day-to-day basis and it gave me hope that I could too — one day at a time.

Further Reflections...
"We become willing to accept responsibility for our own lives, and we begin to achieve our goals."
S-Anon Twelve Steps, p. 3

Reconciliation and Healing

One of the first things I had to deal with in recovery was my overwhelming shame and guilt over how my part in this disease affected my children. Their father was not a sexaholic, but my disease was fully present when I was married to him, and grew worse over the years. The best of my efforts and attention were always focused on my partner, and I neglected my children emotionally and physically.

When I felt ready to face the possible rejection, I told my children as much as they wanted to know about the past, and their reactions were as individual as they are. My current husband's involvement in SA was mentioned in passing, but the details of his old behaviors seemed irrelevant as far as they are concerned. It was my obsession with him that affected them.

As the years have passed, I have sensed our children's growing respect for my husband's and my recovery. It fills me with joy to realize that we have become the kind of parents to whom they can turn with their problems, knowing that we have faced and overcome some really tough issues, one day at a time. Today, even the problems related to my children [and grandchildren!] are a luxury that at one point in my life I believed I would never enjoy. I also know that the most valuable gift I can give them is my ongoing, one day at a time S-Anon recovery.

[Excerpt from *Working the S-Anon Program*, p. 90]

Further Reflections...
"Our ability to give and receive love will expand tremendously, and will become increasingly available for loving relationships with others."

Gifts of the S-Anon Program

My Spiritual Path

Through my S-Anon recovery, I've learned that I need to seek intimacy with God and people. I don't want my relationship with God to exclude relationships with others. I am learning to find a healthy balance.

Based on my history, finding balance has been difficult for me to do. I have had a number of betrayals and disappointments when I've established relationships with people whom I thought of as spiritual leaders. I became attracted to one of these spiritual leaders and began a relationship with him. I allowed him to be my connection to God and was devastated when his sexual behavior betrayed my trust. In recovery I am learning about the disease of sexaholism. It is through my recovery that I have started living in reality.

Today, I have my own relationship with a God of my understanding. Consequently I have become more observant and cautious when around those I identify as spiritual leaders. I no longer wish to give my power away and I no longer make another person my Higher Power.

Further Reflections...
"The regular practice of prayer and meditation rewards us with emotional balance, a sense of belonging and knowing that God watches lovingly over us."

S-Anon Twelve Steps, p. 129

Finding Humor

A few years ago, I was reading a book that I knew my mother was going to read after me. In it I found passages I thought she needed to hear—things I believed would make her a better person (by my definition, of course). These were things I didn't have the courage to say to her myself.

I didn't want her to miss any of these gems, so I highlighted them and passed the book on to her. I was anticipating hearing her response, but when weeks went by, I asked her casually about it. "Oh," she said, "I didn't have time to read it so I gave it to my friend as a gift. I'll get another copy for myself later." I'm still wondering what my mom's friend thought when she saw that the book had been pre-highlighted for her...

One of the gifts of the S-Anon program for me is laughter. I am able to laugh at my behavior, not with shame, but with love. I have done many things that were absurd if I look at them objectively—things that didn't seem funny at the time. I was desperate to control something that was beyond my control— usually another person. Later, when I described my behavior to my S-Anon group, I suddenly saw the humor and absurdity in it, and soon we were all laughing.

This is a major transformation for me, since I grew up in an environment where being laughed at meant being humiliated and disdained. Today, I can be both humorous and lovable at the same time, which was something I never knew.

Further Reflections...
"Every day I ask God to help me stop taking myself too seriously."

[A.A] Daily Reflections, p. 59

❖   ❖   ❖

New Messages

Unhealthy messages like *Men are no good, so you had better make sure you get a good education* plagued my self-esteem and fueled my fears about men and relationships. I became afraid of intimacy, fearing I would be abandoned. I believed I had to use my body to manipulate men, and use them before they used me. My mother also told me: *don't ever depend on a man for anything.* As I entered adulthood, I continually found myself in unhealthy relationships that reinforced those old "tapes" from my mother.

S-Anon has given me new "tapes" from healthy people. I have made tremendous progress in replacing the old negative messages with new messages about the real me – the person I was born to be. Now I believe I have the courage and wisdom to make good choices for myself today. I am learning to embrace my real self like a cherished friend, and I am able to be in relationships and share my truth with others.

Further Reflections...
"As we placed our spiritual growth first, we discovered a better way of living for ourselves and those around us."
S-Anon Twelve Steps, p. 144

From Horrified to Hope — Humiliated to Help

I was horrified and humiliated when I found a receipt in my husband's briefcase revealing that he had rented an apartment to "act out" sexually and to store his pornography. I am so grateful for the awareness that my Higher Power was taking care of me at that time.

Just moments before picking up the briefcase, my eyes fell on a magazine that a friend had sent us. It was a prison ministries magazine with an article about pornography and sex addiction. On the back of the magazine were phone numbers of groups that could be called for help if you thought there was a problem with sex addiction — The magazine "just so happened" to be in view with the back page showing.

When I found the receipt, I felt shock and grief at the same time. I woke up to the seriousness of this illness and the effects of living with my husband's behavior. Looking at the article, I felt a twinge of encouragement and hope that I wasn't alone in this problem. My Higher Power gave me the solution by placing S-Anon's phone number right there in front of me. By making that call to S-Anon, I got the support I needed to help me through this crisis. I am grateful that my Higher Power is working in my life. I don't always see it so clearly as I did in this experience, but I am trusting that God is there for me.

Further Reflections...
"Today, when I say, "keep coming back!" to newcomers, I wish for them the help and hope I have found in S-Anon."
Working The S-Anon Program, p. 4

Seeing God's Handy Work

For the longest time I struggled with seeing how God was working in my life and my marriage. I not only felt God owed me something (a godly husband, a healthy marriage, and children), I thought the life I was "entitled to" was being withheld from me. I continually asked God why my husband's problems were determining the outcome of my life — it just didn't seem fair.

I am now finding that I am able to see God's handy work more clearly. As my knowledge of the principles of the S-Anon program grows, I am able to learn more from those whose experiences are similar to mine. Instead of thinking God is withholding something from me as a punishment; I am learning to accept that life has difficult challenges, and my life is not exempt. When I feel I am missing out on something, I stop to consider God's timing and purposes for me. What I have, or don't have may be for my protection, education, or development — or that of others. I'm learning I can trust God's care for me.

Further Reflections...
"We can ask for the grace and the patience to seek God's will for just one day at a time. Circumstances will always change tomorrow. We can be comforted by the fact that even hardships in life have a way of working toward the good for those who honor God."

S-Anon Twelve Steps, p. 128

I Don't Get to Decide If Another Person Recovers

When I first came to S-Anon, I wasn't sure if sexaholism was a problem in my marriage, but the longer I stayed, the harder it became to deny it. In the name of "sharing my feelings," I spent the next couple of years trying to convince my husband that his affairs and use of pornography were hurting me and destroying our marriage. I finally began to work the Steps with my sponsor. I came to realize that I was not only powerless over sexaholism, but also over all the choices my husband was continuing to make. Clearly, he was choosing the addiction over our marriage, and I needed to allow him the dignity of making his own choices – to live his life as he chose, even if he didn't choose me. I had to Let Go and Let God.

I have such gratitude for my S-Anon program. I have learned to accept that I don't have the power to decide if another person chooses recovery. I can only make decisions for myself, such as setting boundaries to ensure my well-being and safety from my husband's active sexaholism. I am sad to say that my marriage is ending, yet I am so grateful to have happiness, health, and wholeness in my life today.

Further Reflections...
"...only through utter defeat are we able to take our first steps toward liberation and strength. Our admissions of personal powerlessness finally turn out to be firm bedrock upon which happy and purposeful lives may be built."
                              [AA] Twelve Steps and Twelve Traditions, p. 21

The Beauty of How My Higher Power Works

I recently had the experience of watching a sponsee go through a divorce. It was sad, yet inspiring to see how she worked her program, remained sane, and grew through the process.

About a year before her decision to divorce, it became clear to me that her marriage probably would not survive (an opinion I kept to myself because she did not ask for that feedback). I watched her continue to work her program and pray for the best possible outcome – and I held my tongue. One day she believed God finally showed her that she had done all she could and that it was time to let go of the marriage. With a certainty and conviction that could only come from God, she went through the divorce process.

It was a privilege to be with her through that process— to be a sympathetic ear, to be a sounding board when asked. I reminded her of program principles like applying the Traditions to her divorce and I could be a patient friend. At times it was not easy to keep my opinions to myself because I saw her in so much pain. I am grateful that God gave me the opportunity to be her sponsor through that process because I learned and grew so much in my own program. Of course, my growth had nothing to do with her divorce, but that's the beauty of how my Higher Power works: if I remain open, God uses all experiences for good.

Further Reflections...
"We soon learn true humility, which shows us God's presence and wisdom is found in the S-Anon fellowship."
S-Anon Twelve Steps, p. 15

Becoming Whole

I acquired many unhealthy ideas about sexuality in my childhood. My mother often came home drunk, bringing strangers with her, and had sex with them. Whether she was drunk or not, my mother spoke in negative ways about sex, her body, and about men. As I grew older, I became disgusted by her behavior and disrespected her.

Despite recognizing how unhealthy it all was, I still was affected by it. In every significant adult relationship I had two consistent patterns: the significant other was abusive, and I never enjoyed sex. For years I didn't even want to have sex because I associated it with abuse and fear.

I finally found a wonderful man and married him. I was able to open up and enjoy sex for the first time. Then I discovered his pornography obsession. I felt sick, traumatized, and used. All the fear from my childhood flooded back.

As I work my S-Anon program, I am aware that I am in need of healing around my understanding of healthy sexuality. I want to be free of fear and enjoy a healthy sexually intimate relationship. My husband is still acting out; just for today he is not a safe person for me to explore this with. Until then, my Higher Power is giving me the time I need to find out who I am, and lay the groundwork for a healthier way for me to live. I'm grateful I have an S-Anon program to help guide me to that goal.

Further Reflections…
"…today I accept that in order for me to achieve 'healthy sexuality' I will have to continue to look at myself…"
Working the S-Anon Program, p. 65

Learning About Boundaries Through the Traditions

My second S-Anon meeting was a Tradition meeting. My first thought was "Who cares? I want to work on the problem!" The Traditions didn't seem very important then because I was in so much pain. I also didn't realize how many of my problems would be solved by learning and using the Traditions.

It took me a while to understand that the Steps are the path to my personal recovery and that the Traditions are the path to recovery and health in my relationships with others. This includes relationships in my group, workplace, and family. I discovered through studying the Traditions just how much I needed healthy boundaries in my life, as well as learned how to respect the boundaries of others without getting offended. The Traditions are the boundaries that show me how to respect others. They show me where I stop and others begin.

I am fortunate that the groups I attend have provided regular Traditions discussions by using the "Tradition of the month" as the topic of the first meeting of the month. Over the course of a year, I can study each of the Twelve Traditions. I have come to enjoy Tradition meetings, because the sharing often focuses on practical applications of the Traditions, especially at home and work.

Further Reflections...
"Learning and using the Traditions has been just as important to me as learning and using the Steps."

Anonymous

Happiness

This past week my husband and I attended a local event. A woman asked us if we had met at one of these events or if we had become interested in this type of event after we had become a couple. Perplexed, I asked her why she thought this was new to us and why she thought we were new to each other. She commented that we looked so much in love that she assumed we were new to an intimate relationship. I burst out laughing, as we have had 26 years of marriage, a divorce, and a re-marriage in our relationship. Prior to recovery, there was so much drama caused by sexaholism that we could provide the material for a soap opera.

A few days later, I sat in my home group meeting, marveling that the woman had seen the love we have for each other, even if we cannot see it or feel it all the time ourselves. It occurred to me that I have been so used to being unhappy and focusing on the negative, it has become a habit. Just then the person next to me passed me the evening's reading — Al-Anon's Just For Today bookmark. How fitting was my paragraph:

> Just for Today I will be happy. This assumes to be true what Abraham Lincoln said, that "Most folks are as happy as they make up their minds to be."

That night I made a decision to choose to be happy and to look for the good, rather than to hang onto the unhappiness and pain of my past.

Further Reflections...
"Today, through using the tools of the program, many of us are happier in our relationships than we ever imagined possible, achieving levels of intimacy we only hoped for previously."
Recovering Together: Issues Faced by Couples (Rev. Booklet 2007), p. 3

❖ ❖ ❖

Newcomers...Courage and Faith

Tradition Five defines our fellowship's primary purpose: to help families of sexaholics. I think this
Tradition implies just how important newcomers are to
our fellowship and to our groups.

When I was a newcomer, I remember the storm of emotions that swirled just beneath my cool outer exterior. The
S-Anons in the room spoke freely and hopefully. Their
hope filled me with hope, and I longed to have what they
had. Today, each time a newcomer enters our meeting
room, I am given a chance to see myself as I once was. I see
the newcomer's pain and despair. I remember, through
hearing their stories, where I started and how far I have
come. Their growth reminds me that this program works
and keeps working as I give back what I was given. This
keeps the cycle of recovery growing.

Newcomers are the miracles of S-Anon and are blessings to our meetings. To walk into an S-Anon meeting is an
act of real courage; to keep coming back is an act of faith.
Newcomers remind us of God's ability to heal.

Further Reflection...
"Whatever feelings you may be having as you begin your
recovery in S-Anon are completely acceptable and okay.
Many of us believe that our first experience of unconditional love and acceptance occurred in the S-Anon fellowship."

We're Glad You're Here [S-Anon's] Newcomers Booklet, p. 16

Gifts of Sharing

Before coming to S-Anon, I didn't really know what a boundary was. I tended to share my whole life story with people I would meet, not waiting to see if they were trustworthy or even interested. That characteristic was still with me when I came to S-Anon, so I just started sharing a "new chapter" with people.

Looking back I can see now how inappropriate much of my sharing was. I often broke my husband's anonymity and told graphic and completely unnecessary details about his behavior and mine. I told friends and family members indiscriminately because I thought the information could "help" them. I feel that sharing my story – however imperfectly – truly has helped me come a long way in recovery. In recovery I've come to understand what boundaries are and why it's important to have them. I've learned to tell my story selectively, and to only tell details as appropriate. In fact, now I usually speak in general terms because that is often enough. It has definitely been "progress, not perfection," though, as I've made plenty of mistakes along the way.

Further Reflections...
"We come to realize that we need to speak with complete honesty about our own conflicts to reach true kinship with God and others."

S-Anon Twelve Steps, p. 53

Today's Wishes

I find it best when I start my day coming to my Higher Power as I am. I say what I'm feeling, whether I'm happy, sad, angry, or whatever. Recently I said, "I feel awful about myself today, but I want to believe you love and care for me just as I am. Thank you for loving me. Help me to love me and accept your love more. Thank you for going with me into this new day, I don't have to face anything alone. Help me not worry about the future, nor replay the past, but to focus on this day. Give me willingness to seek your wisdom and to take steps that are good for me and my spiritual growth. Place before me those things you want me to do, and help me do them with dignity and grace. Also, please help me to remember to thank you for what you do."

I struggle sometimes with self-esteem, but when I bring it, lug it, or even only nudge it toward my Higher Power, I feel more lovable.

Further Reflections…
"Sobriety in S-Anon is about me and the way I treat myself and whether I can look at my mirrored image and love the person I see."

Working the S-Anon Program, p. 54

A Roadmap to Face Life

Step Twelve: Having had a spiritual awakening as a result of these steps, we tried to carry this message to others and practice these principles in all our affairs.

Step Twelve has truly become a way of life for me. When I become upset or disturbed, my sponsor directs me back to the Steps. I start with Step One and work as many Steps as needed, until I can see what has brought me to the place of discomfort. At some point I am able to see my part and what it is I need to do differently.

When I am connected to my Higher Power, I can be an extension of God's love and compassion toward myself and others. The love I feel flowing through me today has replaced my roller coaster days of impulsively reacting and feeling that sickening fear in the pit of my stomach.

Allowing God to work through me is a result of practicing the spiritual principles of S-Anon in my life every day. Today I try to remember that the Steps are the most valuable gift I have been given. They are the roadmap to guide me as I face and deal with whatever life brings. They lead me back to God, love, and acceptance every time.

Further Reflections...
"...for most of us a spiritual awakening has been a gradual process — through practicing the Twelve Steps we found ourselves experiencing a degree of honesty, tolerance, unselfishness, serenity and love which seemed impossible before recovery."

Working the S-Anon Program, p. 28

500-Pound Telephone Receiver

I was in the program a short time when the pain I was in became so unbearable I wanted to die. I had been to meetings and had taken a phone list of those willing to be called, but I still thought I had to work the program alone. I thought calling for help was admitting I was weak and could not handle my own life. I also thought that I would be bothering the other person. I was hurting so much, that I finally became willing to pick up that 500-pound telephone receiver. I went down the phone list, secretly hoping no one would answer, while praying they would.

My Higher Power answered my prayer. I reached a woman who worked as a receptionist at a dentist office. We did not know one another, yet she was willing to stay on the phone with me for nearly an hour (while answering business calls). That day I experienced such kindness and caring that I regained hope and I made it through another day. I no longer wanted to die.

Today, I do not remember that woman's name, what was said, or the tragedy that got me to my knees to make that call. I do know that I have followed her example. Since then I have been on the other end of that 500-pound telephone receiver, speaking to someone on their knees, looking for hope. Today I give away what I was so generously given.

Further Reflections...
"Hearing the experience, strength, and hope of others gives us a basis upon which to begin to apply those principles in our own lives."

S-Anon/S-Ateen Service Manual, p. 13

Recovery from Snooping

Before I got into recovery, I was a terrible snooper. I would go through the sexaholic's personal belongings, try to listen in on phone conversations, and read his e-mail. When I actually did find evidence of his acting out, I was too ashamed of my behavior to admit what I had been doing. I suffered through the pain of what I had seen, and I also stuffed my feelings of rage because I did not think I could confront him.

In recovery, I have learned that I do not have to hurt myself by searching for evidence of my spouse's acting out. Trying to catch the sexaholic keeps the focus on my spouse and is a way for me to avoid my own recovery. I do, however, have a right to know if I am in danger of getting a sexually transmitted disease. Rather than snooping, I can directly ask my spouse for the truth, trust my intuition and ask my sponsor's perspective. I have learned to ask for God's help to see things as they are. Then I can decide if there are boundaries I need to set and implement for myself, for instance a period of abstinence for my safety or for my S-Anon sobriety. Keeping the focus on myself has eased my pain and increased my serenity. I know that I can trust God to reveal whatever "evidence" I need to know.

Further Reflections...
"We became preoccupied, even obsessed, with the sexual behavior of another. We were suspicious and tried to catch the sexaholic practicing the addiction."

S-Anon Twelve Steps, p. 2

Daily Miracles In My Life

Quiet attention in life's moments brings me closer to God. I am not attending to the moment if I am worrying about the future or replaying the past over and over again. To experience the present and be grateful for whatever it holds is a hallmark of my recovery. Precious moments are turned into precious memories, both wonderful gifts from God. When I am gentle with others and myself, I am open to the splendor and richness that is common, yet unique to all – the way one smiles, breathes in air, caresses a hand – all touch my heart. I have a greater understanding and appreciation for the daily miracles in my life when I am emotionally and spiritually connected.

Further Reflections...
"Through our growing trust in this Higher Power [of our understanding], sanity is restored in our lives, and we move toward peace, serenity and useful lives."

S-Anon Twelve Steps, p. 24

Expectations and Needs

There was a time, not so long ago, when I had just plain given up on having any expectations for my relationship. I thought I had to accept whatever treatment I received from my partner. I had heard in meetings that "expectations are resentments waiting to happen," so I thought, "I better not have any of those expectations!"

As I continued to grow in S-Anon, I came to believe that I was worthy of respect and consideration. I found the answer for me in exploring the difference between expectations (looking forward into the future) and needs (which are mine to express today). I need to be treated with affectionate love and regard. I am not always right, but I need my ideas to be met with respectful consideration. My interests and hobbies are important, and I need time to pursue them. I need a partner to help carry out the routine tasks of maintaining a household. I need a satisfying sex life and most important, a partner willing to work with me in all these areas to improve the relationship.

If my most important needs are to be met, I must let go of the expectation that "somebody" will meet my needs "someday" and, instead, consider the alternatives available to me today. Just for today, I will acknowledge my needs, affirm their importance, and choose to take one positive action in the direction of seeing that those needs are met.

Further Reflections...
"I am finding serenity and happiness in my life and my marriage by learning to focus on myself and by allowing my Higher Power to help me."

S-Anon Twelve Steps, p. 67

Setting Boundaries

Before S-Anon I did not have boundaries. As I started to practice setting boundaries, the sexaholic in my life sometimes accused me of trying to control him. As I look back I realize that sometimes I was trying to control him. At other times I was just taking care of myself, and the sexaholic did not like my boundary. Here are some questions I ask myself to determine my motives in setting a boundary:

- Am I expecting a certain result from someone? Is that person free to choose what he or she needs to do?
- Am I setting a boundary out of fear?
- Have I checked in with my sponsor or another S-Anon member?
- Have I admitted my powerlessness? Do I trust that God will help me know what I need to do if I ask?

I remind myself that I need to choose my boundaries carefully. There may come a time when a boundary I have set no longer matches my spiritual needs. At that point I am free to change the boundary, with the help of my sponsor and prayerful consideration. Trusting myself and having faith in my Higher Power brings the serenity I seek as I work on my recovery program.

Further Reflections...
"...we take positive actions to make our lives more serene and fulfilling."

S-Anon Keys to Recovery

Letting Go of Perfectionism

Before recovery it was difficult for me to let go of anything. My life was dedicated to perfectionism and control. Everything about me, my family, my work, and my life had to be the absolute best that it could be. Living with sexaholism increased my perfectionism compulsion. I felt my life was so chaotic that I needed everything else I did to be perfect. This very powerful unconscious drive was at the core of my being for many years. Then my sexaholic spouse's acting out became public, and I hit a very painful bottom. My illusions about perfectionism and control crumbled.

I found my way to the doors of S-Anon. After spending my first few meetings crying, the fog began to clear. My first question was, "How can I get a sponsor?" I chose a deeply spiritual woman who had been in S-Anon for several years. We began working the Steps and practicing the principles. It was as though I'd been given a toolbox for letting go and I began filling it with slogans, literature, telephone calls, service and sponsorship.

As the days turned into years, I became able to let go of things without putting claw marks in them first. While I still struggle with letting go some days, I now know I have a Higher Power, a sponsor, and a fellowship who are always there for me when I struggle.

Further Reflections...
"Is there any area of my life where I still depend only on myself or believe that will power is the answer? If so, how can my Higher Power help?"

S-Anon Twelve Steps, p. 71

Single Again

I found myself single again in S-Anon. Prior to this, I knew how to be a spouse, but I didn't know how to be a single person. This was uncharted territory, and I felt uncomfortable and afraid. During this time, I felt a God-given gift of hope; that good would come about. I found I was profoundly grateful to be away from the daily chaos of active addiction. I slowly began to develop more meaningful relationships with co-workers, family, and friends in program. I became more involved with my faith community activities. I discovered that I was important to others and had my own identity, apart from my spouse. I decided to postpone dating until after a period of recovery had passed and my sponsor and others agreed that I was ready to date again. I discovered that being single is not just a time of uncertainty; it's a time to discover what purpose God has in store for me in the single life. I am excited thinking of all I am learning. I now face the journey with anticipation that God can use this time, not only for my benefit, but for others' as well. I believe God has put me where I am today for a reason.

Further Reflections…
"I was humbled, knowing I was not the Higher Power and that my perspective was limited. My mind was opened to a much bigger Higher Power that was working in my life and the lives of others."

Working the S-Anon Program, p. 51-52

Overcoming Bitterness

I grew up in a sexaholic household. I went on to date sex-aholics and to marry a sexaholic. My life was a cycle of pain, and I was fired from a job due to my obsession with a sexaholic. I began recovery in another Twelve Step program. Aware of my issues with my family of origin, I sensed that there was more work to be done. I didn't know what work it was, and I feared the pain of exploring these issues.

Ten years later, God led me to S-Anon. My first meetings were at an International Convention, and it was there that I got my first glimmer of hope. When the closing SA speaker got up to share, I looked at him and thought to myself, "I don't have to hate them anymore. I don't have to resent them. I don't need to get revenge, and I don't have to live in the bitterness." That was the beginning of hope for me. I have experienced so much healing in S-Anon. Yes, I grew up in a sexaholic family, but today I have the freedom to no longer expect more from my family members than they can give.

Further Reflections...
"Help can be found in S-Anon whether the sexaholic who affected our lives the most is a partner, or spouse, or someone else."

Working the S-Anon Program, p. 76

Steps Forward and Steps Back

Some time ago, my sponsor challenged me to think about the ways I disregarded or acknowledged spiritual growth in my life.

I felt anxious and fearful as I considered the challenge. It occurred to me that I can feel afraid and still be growing spiritually. For instance, earlier in my recovery, I would tell people about my faults and weaknesses when I was afraid, thinking that this was a way to be humble. Unfortunately, any humility I might have felt was overshadowed by feeling bad about myself. I was overwhelmed with my shame that I hadn't seen the spiritual benefit in simply sharing with others, rather than isolating. At that time, in the recovery dance of "one step forward, two steps back," I tended to only focus only on the "two steps back."

Working the Steps and regularly sharing with my sponsor has helped me acknowledge my spiritual growth. Spending quiet time with our literature and praying for my Higher Power's guidance about a situation or concern, often affirms that I am changing and growing. Today I am grateful that I can see my "steps forward," as well as my "steps back."

Further Reflections...
"The Steps offer me a road map for living that leads to a spiritual awakening and beyond. I can't skip ahead to the end of the journey – which can at times be a hard one – but I can put one foot in front of the other and follow the directions I've been given, knowing that others who have gone before me have received more along the way than they had ever dreamed."

[Al-Anon] *Courage to Change, p. 26*

Allowing Communication

Before recovery, I was driven by fear and rage, and my partner's sexual behavior seemed to push me into those reactions frequently. S-Anon has helped me notice my feelings and then choose what to do with them; I don't have to react, I can respond.

Part of responding is allowing for communication from the sexaholic rather than jumping to conclusions. My recovery has taught me that I'm not always right and that being right doesn't really even matter. What matters is that I can politely, briefly, and sanely state my feelings to my partner, and allow him the dignity to choose what he needs to do next. Then, I can choose what the next healthy action is for me. We can make choices about how we show up in our relationship with one another and how we respond to each other.

Through going to meetings and trying to apply the principles of the S-Anon program, I have changed my behavior in my relationship. My changed behavior has contributed to a peace we previously had never known into our relationship. This peace is a miracle to me. I am so grateful for everything S-Anon offers me to learn.

Further Reflections...
"In recovery I'm becoming an active listener to what she [he] says, at least some of the time....This has not been easy or natural for me. Rather, communication and listening are things I've cultivated."

Recovering Together: Issues Faced by Couples
(Revised Booklet 2007), p. 7

The Art of Listening

I learned about listening through our suggested meeting guideline of "no cross talk." At first it was hard to listen without giving advice or "tuning out" to plan my sharing. I decided to take notes to help focus and "tune in" to the sharing of others. An old-timer observed my note-taking and after the meeting asked if I would like a suggestion. Since she seemed so calm and serene, I said, "Sure!" She said that while S-Anon has no rules about note-taking, I might consider just listening at meetings, paying attention to what resonates instead of jotting everything down. She had noticed that when she just listens, God makes it clear what sharing is important for her to remember.

I tried her suggestion and my recovery started to grow. I began to see that God speaks to me through the sharing of others. I also learned that no cross talk provides each person the dignity and respect that comes from being listened to without judgment or advice. I realized that listening is freeing — I don't have to fix or change anyone else. I can trust that a Higher Power is at work in the life of each person in the meeting, including me.

One of the greatest gifts of S-Anon for me has been the art of listening. To truly listen to another person and to receive the gift of being listened to are rare and wonderful things.

Further Reflections...
"If you wish to share, please wait to be recognized by the leader, as there is no cross talk. That is, we share with the group as a whole, rather than addressing comments or questions to individual members."
Suggested Format for an S-Anon Meeting (Guidelines For Sharing)

New Tools

Walking through the doors of my first S-Anon meeting took more courage than I thought I had. When I heard about living with sexaholism, one day at a time, I knew it was more than I could handle.

I quickly learned to use the new recovery tools I had heard about in the group. The meetings, slogans, and literature were so helpful. My favorite phrase was one I heard at my first meeting: "Let go and Let God." It has helped me relax and make it through the rough days. My Higher Power and the phone list help me along, too.

While coming out of denial was not easy, the program taught me I was not as hopeless as I had thought. I learned my life could and would get better.

Coming to S-Anon and working my program have given me a new outlook on life and the world around me and have helped me see more clearly. I am able to accept myself and the things around me as they are and not as I would like to see them.

Further Reflections....
"Many of us found that before we could begin to use the tools of S-Anon, we had to let go of, or at least loosen our grip on the "old tools" that may have helped us survive, but simply did not work well anymore. The old tools may have included denial, obsession with the sexaholic, covering up the problem, isolation, rage, and manipulation. In letting go of the old tools, we were able to try new, more effective ways to aid us in recovery."

Working the S-Anon Program, p. 1

Detaching with Love and Compassion

After I ended my relationship with my partner, I received a call from him in which he described how much pain he was in. My previous response would have been to rescue, but now, while he was talking, I remembered that I am powerless to change or control him. I have learned in S-Anon that I cannot make him go to meetings or take responsibility for his sexaholic behavior. I do not have the power to alter his path. The gift S-Anon has given me is knowing I have choices in that phone call. I chose to listen with love and compassion — a skill I am learning in S-Anon.

Detaching with love has given me the freedom to take better care of myself. I was able to end the phone call knowing that in ending the relationship I made the right choice for me, while allowing him to experience his pain and do what he needs to do to take care of himself. Working the Steps has opened my life to accept others for who they are, good and bad. I can also accept myself for who I am — a very grateful recovering S-Anon.

Further Reflections...
"When I am sober in this program I take control of my own actions and change what I can about myself, not other people."

Working the S-Anon Program, p. 56

The Beginning of My Recovery Journey

My sexaholic husband and I went to see a spiritual advisor for some counseling. The counselor gave us the name of a person to contact about the SA and S-Anon meetings in our area.

I certainly knew I needed help, but I felt so uneasy and skeptical going to that first meeting. I wondered what kind of weird people I would meet there. In stark contrast to my fears, my actual experience was one of being warmly welcomed into the S-Anon group. The S-Anon members openly and honestly shared their experience, strength, and hope. They weren't strange people at all. They were just people who had gone through experiences similar to mine.

I knew after the first meeting that I would be coming back. I was able to see and feel the love and support of the members in that meeting. It took me about three months of going to meetings before I felt comfortable enough to ask someone to be my sponsor. That was the beginning of my recovery journey. Now I am well on my way to finding the serenity that was promised at that first meeting. I thank God for helping me find this program.

Further Reflections...
"We welcome you to the S-Anon Family Group and hope that in this fellowship you will find the help and friendship that we have been privileged to enjoy. We would like you to feel that we understand as perhaps few can. We too were lonely and frustrated; but here we have found that there is no situation too difficult to be bettered and no unhappiness too great to be lessened."

The S-Anon Welcome

Carrying the Message

I was a scared, shocked, and horrified wife who needed someone to talk with, and somewhere to go where I would hear that there was hope and help for me and my family. Thanks to Step Twelve, when I arrived at the door of the local S-Anon meeting, people were willing to share their experience, strength, and hope with me.

I love the way, in our fellowship, people are there for the newcomer. I am ever so grateful that someone, actually several people, were there for me when I arrived. The spiritual awakening I have had is a direct result from much work on my part, and the extraordinary kindness that people in S-Anon shared with me. This has instilled in me the willingness to carry on the spirit of Twelve Step work in my daily life, which asks me to try and carry the message of hope to others.

One of the ways I have been able to give back has been to listen and share with newcomers as they come through the door. I have also participated in the incredible experience of starting an S-Anon group where there was none. This meeting has become a beacon of light for so many people looking for help from the effects of another person's sexual behavior.

I am grateful that I do not have to complete all of the other Steps to begin working Step Twelve. We have such an incredible message of hope to share.

Further Reflections...
"Having had a spiritual awakening as the result to these Steps, we tried to carry this message to others, and to practice these principles in all our affairs."

S-Anon's Step Twelve

Using the Tools to Stay Sober

The problem of sexaholism in my home has been terribly painful. I have needed all the tools I can get to stay sober enough to make good choices for my children and myself. Writing is a wonderful tool that I use to help process my feelings. Sometimes when I sit down to write, I find I can best express my feelings in the form of a poem. This poem came to me after a particularly difficult experience.

Sitting alone in the kitchen, my anxiety starts to rise.
I realize this is the perfect opportunity to search for clues…
Thoughts chase round in my mind.
I jump up, pulled by fear of finding the truth.
I have searched often and found nothing,
And sometimes found something.
What does it all mean? Am I crazy or is he?

Taking the time to write that day helped me to not snoop through my husband's computer for pornography. After writing this poem, I used another important tool — the phone — to call an S-Anon friend. I still felt shame because I wanted to snoop, but my S-Anon friend helped shift my attitude to one of gratitude. I did not try to soothe my rising anxiety by snooping.

Using the tools that day helped me connect with my Higher Power. I find that when I use the tools, I am infinitely better off.

Further Reflections…
"Each of these tools helps me gain space and time to untangle the threads of intellect and emotion. Then I can act rather than react."

[Al-Anon] *Hope for Today, p. 227*

Not What I Can Do, But Who I Am

As I was taking my inventory while working on Step Four, I wrote that one of my positive qualities was being good at handling crises. I've probably developed that quality through having had to work through so many! After I wrote down those words, the thought occurred to me that I do not have to be handling a crisis in order for me to have worth. When confronted with a crisis – whether the fallout of the sexaholic's addictive behavior or one of the crises that occasionally come with the ups and downs of life – I realize now that I am just as worthwhile as when I am sitting quietly reading a book. My self-worth is no longer based on what I can do, but on who I am.

Further Reflections...
"As we begin to hold still, we feel a Higher Power begin to offer us guidance and peace in every situation. The strife and battle ceases. There is relaxation and peace, and we find serenity and dignity within ourselves."

S-Anon Twelve Steps, p. 3

Tuning Out the "S-Anon Chatter"

As I worked the First Step, I got a clear picture of just how many clues the sexaholic had left regarding his sexual acting out behavior. I was disappointed in myself, because I had completely disregarded and blocked out my awareness, denying the clues that had obviously been there. This was a bitter pill to swallow because I thought I was highly intuitive. Instead of paying attention to that still quiet voice deep inside of me, I listened, instead, to what I call my "S-Anon Chatter." I bought hook, line, and sinker into what I wanted to believe, instead of acknowledging the reality of my situation.

S-Anon has given me tools to change how I take care of myself when the destructive "S-Anon chatter" goes off in my head. These tools help me to distinguish truth from fiction. Now I can sit down and consciously ask my Higher Power to guide me to the truth. I ask myself, "What am I really feeling about this situation?" and "What do I think is really going on?" This intentional, conscious process helps me to accept my feelings about a situation, and not just rely on what the sexaholic or others are telling me. When I accept my feelings, I can begin to work my program around the information in front of me, to make decisions with more clarity.

Further Reflections...
"Our whole attitude and outlook upon life will change... We will intuitively know how to handle situations which used to baffle us. We will suddenly realize that God is doing for us what we could not do for ourselves."
                                        Alcoholics Anonymous, p. 84

I Had Secrets Too!

After hearing the stories of so many recovering S-Anon's over the years, it occurred to me that a common theme in their stories is the effects of the lies that go along with the disease of sexaholism. Living with and believing these lies became a way of life for us. My husband kept his sexaholism a secret for so long that I'm surprised he didn't buckle under the pressure sooner than he did. When the truth came out, he said he was so relieved not to carry around the lies anymore. Meanwhile, I was amazed at how much I didn't know and how "easy" it seemed for him to hide so much.

As I grew in my understanding of the disease of sexaholism and began working Step Four. I learned that I had taken on the guilt, shame, and fear that the sexaholic had. I, too, lied. By sharing my Fifth Step with my sponsor, I was able to finally be freed from the lies. It was painful to admit the truth about my behavior of minimizing and denying the sexaholic's behavior. Then later I picked up snooping and setting up tests to check up on the sexaholic. All of these I admitted to my sponsor, who received them with gentleness. After having these secrets out in the open, I began to develop healthier ways of taking care of myself.

Further Reflections...
"We were afraid of what we would find, afraid that shedding light on ourselves would uncover so many shortcomings that we could not bear the truth about ourselves."
S-Anon Twelve Steps, p. 47

Our Common Problem

When I contemplated going to S-Anon, I thought I might be too different to be accepted in the group. I knew I needed the S-Anon program, but my fears almost stopped me from seeking help.

As the only man in our group, I worried that I might put a damper on what the female S-Anons would otherwise share. I feared I would feel left out of most discussions, because I thought that my spouse's acting out was unusual. Instead, I found commonality. I saw that the focus of S-Anon sharing was not on the sexaholic, but on ourselves. I discovered quickly that I have more than enough in common with the other S-Anons in our group to feel a bond with them. I even was told by one woman that it helped her to have a man in the group. She said that it gave her a chance to develop a trusting, non-threatening relationship with a man, and eased her journey on the road to recovering trust with other men and with the sexaholic in her life.

At times I have lapsed into giving advice, rather than speaking from the S-Anon point of view. I've had a reminder or two from other S-Anons about our sharing guidelines, so I am learning to keep my focus in meetings on my own S-Anon recovery. Only when I focus on myself am I able to recover from the effects on me of another person's sexaholism. I find that this is "our common problem," and that is my purpose in attending S-Anon.

Further Reflections…
"The only requirement for membership is that there be a problem of sexaholism in a relative or friend."

S-Anon's Tradition Three

Practicing Humility

The word humble came to mind as the Tradition Two was read during a recent meeting. I thought that was interesting because the word humble is not in the Tradition itself. (Tradition Two: For our group purpose there is but one authority — a loving God as He may express Himself in our group conscience. Our leaders are but trusted servants — they do not govern.) I think the word humble came to mind because of that part about leaders being trusted servants rather than governors. Being a trusted servant takes humility, instead of ego, which can sometimes plague those who govern.

Thinking about humility always takes me back to when I first came to S-Anon. I was truly broken and could not continue to carry the burden of living with a sexaholic anymore. I was finally at the point of being humble enough to ask for the help of others. Being humble allowed me to share my story and become emotionally vulnerable. How wonderful it felt to receive compassion, acceptance, and understanding in return!

That profound experience of being loved, accepted, and validated by others was life-changing. I began to feel that there was a Higher Power who loved me. I gradually grew to do service and help others who came to S-Anon in desperate conditions. Humility helped me to give without expectations. I am a trusted servant, rather than a self-serving person who tries to stroke his ego through governing others.

Further Reflections…
"Our very first problem is to accept our present circumstances as they are, ourselves as we are, and the people about us as they are. This is to adopt a realistic humility without which no genuine advance can even begin."
[*Alcoholics Anonymous*] *As Bill Sees It, p. 44*

❖   ❖   ❖

A Home in S-Anon

The other day, while getting ready for work, I saw my copy of AA's Twelve Steps and Twelve Traditions lying on my bedroom floor amidst the clothes and shoes. As I picked up the "Twelve and Twelve," I remembered that I purchased it soon after coming to S-Anon. I remembered how much pain I was in at that time. Aware of how far I have come since then, I felt a flood of gratitude come over me for having found this way of life. Like many who have gone before me, pain and desperation helped me to find a home in S-Anon.

In S-Anon I have found a healthy way to think about myself and a way to approach my life in a way that brings me serenity. I feel I am growing and gaining awareness in many areas of my life, including spiritual, for which I am grateful. It has been a slow process of coming to trust the Steps, my sponsor, my Higher Power, and the program. Today, I am grateful that the principles of the program are becoming a part of me, sort of like my "Twelve and Twelve" book has become a part of the stuff on my floor.

Further Reflections...
"The literature reminds me that I'm not alone and that there are others like me who faced and overcame the same struggles, depression and pain, and who can offer me their experience, strength and hope."

Working the S-Anon Program, p. 16

I Thanked God and Got on with My Fourth Step

There was one thing that I didn't want to write about and share with my sponsor, so I found myself procrastinating finishing my Fourth Step. When I got honest with myself, I realized the truth was I didn't really want to give up this one thing up, and I was "using it" as an excuse not to finish my Fourth Step.

Sitting in a meeting, I heard my story told by someone who had been procrastinating finishing their Fourth Step because of something they were not willing to call a character flaw. Hearing this helped clarify what I already knew. My progress was halted because I didn't want to face the fact I was living a lie. I thought that working Step Four meant I was willing to face my flaws, but this wasn't true. I didn't want to acknowledge the issue in my inventory, I might have to let it go.

That night I started asking my Higher Power to help me to become willing, even if it meant I had to give it up. To my amazement, within days, circumstances happened where I found myself loosen my grip and finally willing to give up the flaw I had been hanging on to so tightly. I thanked God and was able to finish my Fourth Step. It was then that I understood what is meant by "exploring the wonders of serenity, dignity, and emotional growth." I am forever grateful.

Further Reflections...
"S-Anon helped me to find the clarity to ask myself, 'Is this defect really so useful — particularly when it also brings up hurt, humiliation and guilt of my past?' Even though my answer is usually 'No,' I sometimes still hesitate to ask God to remove my short comings."

S-Anon Twelve Steps, p. 77

God Can...

When I was first working through the Twelve Steps, my sponsor suggested I make a list of what I believed my Higher Power could and could not do. At first, this seemed like a waste of time. Now I do it often. Here's my original list:

God can... love me completely, save me from myself, guide me if I let Him, heal all my wounds, give me serenity, do for me what I can't do for myself, satisfy all my needs.

God can't... stop loving me, ignore me, betray me, disown me, humiliate me, hurt me, make me change, abandon me, give up on me.

Further Reflection...
"Like all Twelve-Step programs, S-Anon is spiritual, not religious. It is spiritual in the sense that we come to depend upon a Power greater than ourselves – a Power that we are free to define as we wish – to help us to solve our problems and achieve peace of mind."
S-Anon Newcomers Booklet, p 12

No Longer Stuffing My Feelings

As long as I can remember, I stuffed my feelings down to the point that I thought I had none. With support from S-Anon friends, I started allowing myself to have feelings, and actually express them. I learned how to share feelings with my husband, including when I don't feel comfortable being sexual with him. I learned to say things gently and kindly.

I learned I had to allow him to have his feelings, too – to hear them and respect them, even if I disagreed with them. If I simply reacted to his feelings, I only made things worse.

By honoring my feelings and expressing them I learned to trust myself more. At one point I asked for a time of abstinence. I was grateful that my husband respected and honored my request. I was even more grateful that I trusted my feelings enough to know when something wasn't right for me. Eventually I was able to willingly and lovingly be sexual with him again.

I still need to work to be consciously honest with myself and my husband, because my part in the family disease of sexaholism can make me want to be dishonest with myself about my feelings. As I maintain my honesty, my trust in my own recovery process continues to grow.

Further Reflections...
"I am very grateful that I did have the opportunity to learn that sex can be an extension of an intimate relationship and not the only basis for our marriage."

Working the S-Anon Program, p. 72

The Importance of Sponsorship

In one of those amazing program coincidences, I attended an S-Anon meeting on sponsorship only a few hours after my sponsor asked me to do a mini-inventory of our sponsor/sponsee relationship. The meeting chairperson passed around a box containing questions about sponsorship on individual pieces of paper. She asked each of us to answer the question we drew from the box and to make our comments pertinent to what we hoped to gain from having a sponsor. My question was Why is sponsorship important? Here is my answer:

The major way sexaholism affected me was how it eroded my ability to participate in healthy relationships. It increased my difficulty in trusting others, setting boundaries, keeping the focus on myself, being honest about my feelings and respecting others. What I hope to gain from my sponsor is what I am receiving. My sponsor grounds me in reality, gently showing me the ways I deceive myself. She loves me unconditionally, a real benefit when admitting my unbecoming behavior and true feelings. She helps me improve my ability to apply the Twelve Steps and create a better life for my family and me. She gives generously of her time, her energy, and her positive outlook. This is by far the most honest relationship I have ever had, and I am finding that learning how to be healthy in this relationship is spilling over and improving all the other relationships in my life.

Further Reflections...
"The most important thing is that the relationship between sponsor and sponsee is based on honesty and trust."
Working The S-Anon Program, p. 9

No Longer Helpless

Before finding out about the sexaholic's behavior, a large part of my life was spent feeling a little insane. I felt something was wrong and found myself taking my anxiety out on other people through getting angry with them. I would furiously spew venom on those around me, but on the inside I was feeling "less than" and increasingly insane. Unfortunately, this cycle only brought more shame to my already-diminished sense of self.

In S-Anon I discovered that I don't have to berate someone else to feel better about myself. S-Anon helped me accept the reality of what was going on around me and within me. I have learned that I am not helpless and that I have the tools to take positive actions for myself. As I employ the tools of S-Anon, I find God is restoring me to sanity.

Further Reflections...
"Step Two tells me there's a spiritual solution to my insanity. If at any particular time I don't believe I'm worthy of God's blessings, there are other program tools to which I can turn. I can go to a meeting, call my sponsor, and do the next right thing. When I do the things that are right for me to do, I feel better about myself. I begin to feel worthy. I begin to trust that God is still there for me once I again choose sanity, faith, and healing for my life."

[Al-Anon] Hope for Today, p. 124

Friendly Faces

I was so grateful for those friendly faces when I came to my first S-Anon meetings. It felt good to know I was welcome there and that these people knew what I was going through. So what can I do to be a friendly, welcoming face for newcomers today? I just need to think back to my own experience with those friendly faces and what made me feel welcomed to S-Anon.

My first contact was over the telephone. An S-Anon member, who, after listening to what was going on in my life, briefly shared with me some of her S-Anon story. That conversation was so helpful to me, especially just having someone listen to me at such a painful time in my life.

I was welcomed by friendly faces as a newcomer. People sought me out after meetings to talk, or to let me know they could relate to something I had shared. I also had a temporary sponsor who was compassionate and helpful. Those connections kept me coming back week after week.

Today I "keep what I have been given" by walking up to the newcomers and welcoming them. I also take my turn volunteering for our S-Anon hotline. When I hesitate, out of feeling that I have too much to do or nothing to share, I try to recall my own experience as a newcomer, and I remember the words of my sponsor: "Just never forget how important the newcomer is." I let those words guide my actions.

Further Reflections...
"Freely you have received, now freely give..."
S-Anon Twelve Steps, p. 143

Keeping an Open Mind

I am an S-Anon who has worked the program for years while living with an active sexaholic. With recovery, I have taken care of myself in a relationship that has been very uncomfortable.

About a year ago, I realized I no longer wanted to live with someone unwilling to help himself. I respectfully let my husband know I wanted him to get help, and, if he was unwilling to do that, I would have to end our relationship. He finally made efforts to recover, and, while this was hopeful, I was afraid he would not continue with it. To get through that period and keep the focus on myself, I worked the Steps diligently. Through the Step work, I honestly had to admit I had left God out of the process of setting the ultimatum the year before. I had just wanted the discomfort of the relationship to end, so I set the boundary. The Step work made it clear to me that God's will for my relationship was still uncertain in my mind.

Not long after I gained that insight, my husband left. God's will for the outcome of my marriage has not yet been revealed. Even though it looks bleak, I am keeping an open mind. While I am ready to end the relationship, God may have different plans. I am willing to accept whatever changes might occur. For today, I am open to whatever the future might hold.

Further Reflections...
"Now my commitment to our marriage means I can love my husband best by just totally letting go of trying to control the relationship."

Recovering Together: Issues Faced by Couples
(Rev. Booklet 2007), p. 16

Not Participating in Gossip

I used to get overly involved in the lives of my ex-husband's family. One sister would call and gossip about another sister, his mother would discuss the marriage of one daughter, his brother would badmouth their father. Even though I stopped participating in this gossip after a short time in the S-Anon program, it took longer before I actively stopped listening. Although I wasn't passing it along, I still wanted to hear the gossip, which was the "bad" part – or so I thought.

I gradually came to see that listening to gossip predisposes me to thinking negatively about people who may have done nothing to harm me. I am grateful to S-Anon for showing me how to set boundaries for myself. Recalling The Three Obstacles to Recovery helped me keep my side of the street clean. For example, I quit asking about my ex-husband's family members; I just shared about my own life.

Sometimes it meant I had to give up talking to certain people entirely, because I was powerless over them steering our conversations into "gab fests" about someone else's problems. Staying away from gossip helped simplify my life. I found new topics of conversation.

In order to keep my side of the street clean, I have to set boundaries for myself. This has saved me a lot of grief. I have a lot more peace in my life today.

Further Reflections…
"Is there anything on 'my side of the street' that I need to clean up?"

S-Anon Twelve Steps, p. 110

A Funny Thing Happened

One of the things I love best about getting together with other S-Anon members is how much we laugh. It was not that way, in the early days of the Fellowship in my community. Back then there was very little laughter. At that time, our group met in an empty church building at the same time as a Sexaholics Anonymous (SA) meeting. As people entered the door of the building, S-Anon's turned right, SA's turned left. We didn't have a sound-proofed meeting space, and the sounds of muffled voices carried from one room to another.

The SA group had a "birthday" celebration once a month – complete with cake and singing – to mark milestones in sobriety. Inevitably, we S-Anons would hear the SAs' singing and laughing. This made some of us angry. We would wonder "What right do they have to be so happy?"

On one of those birthday nights, one S-Anon member suggested we have our own S-Anon birthday party each month, perhaps ending the regular meeting a bit early and having time for fellowship to celebrate our own recovery milestones. So we practiced "changing the things we can," and started our own celebration. A miracle happened: we no longer heard the SAs' laughter because we were generating our own!

That experience not only helped me see that we don't have to be victims to other people's choices, but that we all benefit when we can lighten up and learn to laugh, despite our pain.

Further Reflections…

"…there are others like me who faced and overcame the same struggles, depression and pain, and who can offer me their experience, strength and hope."

Working the S-Anon Program, p. 16

Learning to Focus on Myself

It was easier for me to understand that someone with the disease of alcoholism or drug addiction is not choosing between the substances or his or her loved one. It was much harder to accept that the acting out of the sexaholic was not about me. I took it personally. I tried to be better, smarter, more capable, sexier, anything to make him "choose" me again. Nothing I did helped, and my self-esteem sank lower and lower.

Through working the program, I now realize that I am not responsible for the sexaholic's acting out, and that as a result of my living with sexaholism, I have a progressive disease that can take a great, even deadly, toll on me. I now understand that I do have choices when it comes to my own behavior. I can focus on myself and find my own serenity, whether or not my loved one ever gets help. I can support him in his attempts to get help, but I can learn to trust and love myself no matter what is going on around me.

I will not wait for my loved one to "get well." Today I will concentrate on my own recovery. If I stay with the sexaholic, I will be better able to take care of myself in the relationship. If I leave, I will be better able to stand on my own.

Further Reflections...
"As we begin to recover in S-Anon, we learn how to manage our lives in a way much better than ever before. We become willing to accept responsibility for our own lives, and we begin to achieve our goals."

S-Anon Twelve Steps, p. 3

Parenting in Recovery

I became a parent after several years in recovery. One thing quickly became clear: raising children is a round-the-clock job. I realized that the way I worked my program had to change. I used to spend as much time as I wanted making conscious contact with God. Now sometimes two minutes was all the time I had to connect with my Higher Power. It occurred to me that it was important to use those two minutes wisely, noticing them when they came.

Many of the program tools I had used to live sanely with a sexaholic now helped me with my expanded family. For example, I came to see that it wasn't good for my children or me to sacrifice myself "for the sake of others." I learned that when someone else was acting crazy and having a tantrum, I didn't have to join them, so I used S-Anon tools to maintain my sanity and serenity. A quick phone call, a personal "time out," applying the H.A.L.T. slogan (for instance, seeing I needed to rest instead of cleaning the kitchen during the children's nap)… all of these self-care tools freed me up so I could bring the best possible "me" to the care of my children.

With parenting, more than ever, I must practice the principles of S-Anon in all my affairs.

Further Reflections...
"…if I am working my program on a daily basis, they will see it, feel it, and I can share what I have learned in S-Anon with my children at their level."

Working the S-Anon Program, p. 89

Changing My Definition of Self-Care

Prior to S-Anon, my definition of self-care was taking care of everyone around me and ensuring everything was in its proper place. This was my way of feeling safe in the world. In early recovery, my definition of self-care changed to devoting time to my personal care, such as getting my nails and hair done regularly.

As I grew in recovery, I realized my idea of self-care was missing something, but I could not quite put my finger on what it was. I asked my sponsor to share her experience with self-care, particularly self-care that went beyond pampering. As she shared, I noticed many of her comments had to do with self-responsibility. I realized that I had grown to resent many things that have to do with self-responsibility. For example, I used to hate getting the oil changed in my car, because I resented my husband for not taking care of it for me. In my mind, that was a husband's responsibility. It did not work to try to make him do it. Yet it had to be done so that I would have safe, reliable transportation.

My conversation with my sponsor about self-care helped to shift my perspective so that I could begin dropping my expectations of what I thought my husband should be doing and begin focusing on my well-being and serenity. By taking care of myself in this way, I find I have more serenity and peace of mind and that I am better able to give to others, as I am taking better care of myself.

Further Reflections…
"We will find that we have the strength and insight to make good choices for ourselves."

Gifts of the S-Anon Program

We Do Not Give Advice...

I used to spend hours every day trying to decide whether or not I should divorce. I have heard other S-Anons express that they, too, have done this, so I know it's a common problem.

Our meeting reading, The S-Anon Welcome, says S-Anons "realize that by banding together they can better solve their common problems..." It doesn't say "fix our individual problems." I am grateful that no S-Anon ever suggested to me that they know what is best for me. S-Anon is not a place for getting or giving advice; it is a place to learn, as we choose, from the experience of others.

When I share in a meeting about my divorce decision, I share how difficult making the decision was, and that many times my decision seemed to rest on how my partner was treating me that day. I share how I came to see the importance of sitting still, working my Steps and going to meetings. This gave me time to slow down and learn how to live in a healthier way. When I finished Step Five, I no longer was focused on the sexaholic and his acting out, and I was spending less time thinking about whether or not I should leave him.

In S-Anon, we each are free to work through the problems that arise from living with sexaholism. We do this in our own way, one day at a time. For this I am grateful.

Further Reflections...
"We do not give advice or analyze the personal situation of others... We speak as people who have found hope and recovery by working the S-Anon program."
Working the S-Anon Program, p. 103

Breaking the Pattern

Communications with my sexaholic spouse were so volatile that we were no longer living together, and resorted to e-mail in order to be civil. I asked for guidance and enlightenment about the nature of this disease and the part I played in it. As I reviewed our e-mails, I began to see a pattern: When I had unrealistic expectations, I would make a cutting remark. My spouse would say something hurtful and I would become self-righteous, telling him how he was wrong. My spouse would withdraw and I would feel abandoned. I would re-connect with him and we would reconcile, Then the insane pattern would start all over again.

I knew I was powerless over breaking this unhealthy pattern on my own. Through asking my Higher Power and other S-Anon members for guidance, I was able to see my insane thinking and behavior pattern. I understood more clearly why Step Two was critical for my recovery. I became aware that I could benefit from working on those things I could change. I could cease my nasty, cutting remarks, stop feeling sorry for myself, and begin to have realistic expectations. I am learning the difference between reacting and responding. I know that God is restoring me to sanity.

Further Reflections...
"I've found that in recovery, only when I do the healthy things I have been reluctant to do, and let go of the unhealthy; things that I have really grasped tightly, do I find the things that I've been looking for all along."

Recovering Together: Issues Faced by Couples
(Rev. Booklet 2007), p. 18

T-H-I-N-K

Despite the professional counseling I have received, and the effort I have put into my S-Anon recovery, I can still become aggravated and impatient with my husband and with myself. When I perceive that things are not "right," my serenity flies out the window, and I go into my old knee-jerk reactions of criticizing and analyzing myself, other people, and situations. During these times I feel the need to tell others the best way to deal with a situation and sometimes I will resort, once again, to snooping through my husbands personal items.

The good news is I am learning that I have choices. Now I can take a couple of deep breaths, pray to my Higher Power for serenity and patience, be quiet, count to ten, and use the slogan T-H-I-N-K. This slogan reminds me to control my tongue and my actions. I ask myself "Is what I am about to say or do Thoughtful, Helpful, Intelligent, Necessary, and Kind?" The snap-judgment feelings still can come, but now I can choose to notice them and take a healthier action, rather than bury them or feed their flames. Remembering to T-H-I-N-K gives me a much better chance of keeping my serenity and responding in a respectful way to my husband, to others, and to myself.

Further Reflections...
"Slogans: Short sayings that remind us of important principles of the program...; Helpful ideas that can have a calming and relaxing effect in times of stress."

S-Anon Newcomers Booklet, p. 15

Live to See Another Day

Out of desperation, I moved my family many miles to be reunited with my sexaholic husband. I was depressed, lonely, and confused before the move, and those feelings intensified afterwards. My life became so unmanageable that I thought the only way out was to die. I attempted suicide.

As I began crawling out of that dark place toward sanity, I found the miracle of S-Anon. With the help of the program (and a lot of help from outside S-Anon, too), I came to realize that sexaholism is a disease, and I am starting to understand that living with this disease has contributed greatly to the unmanageability of my life. I try hard to have compassion for my husband, who is still an active sexaholic, but it is not easy, because I see how painfully the disease affects our family every day.

I have been in the program a short time, and I already have experienced joy. I have reached a point where I have hope for my own recovery, even if my husband does not choose sobriety. Most days I feel that I can only take baby steps toward recovery. I'm not sure where my life will be a year from now; but I am getting stronger each day with the help of my Higher Power and through working the program. Today, I want to live to see another day.

Further Reflections...
"When we accepted our inability to solve our problems on our own, we became open to the idea of a Higher Power. As we let our Higher Power work in our lives, we were amazed at the changes that became possible, and we found a new freedom."

Working the S-Anon Program, p. 38

Forgiveness and Surrender

The disease of sexaholism wounded me deeply and I have felt tremendous anger. I know that continuing to carry hurt and anger is like dragging a big iron ball and chain everywhere I go. Dragging around that ball and chain has slowed my spiritual growth, and could destroy me physically. I believe I will be a happier and healthier person when I am able to forgive.

In S-Anon, I'm learning that to let go, I need to ask my Higher Power for help. So each day I am asking God's help to surrender and let go one day at a time. I notice on days when I practice this surrender, my hurt and anger does not take over my day and I experience forgiveness toward the sexaholic and myself. I feel a huge weight taken off me.

Sometimes, by looking back, I am better able to see the progress in my spiritual growth and serenity in my life. I trust that through continuing to work the S-Anon program I will be happier and healthier – mentally, spiritually, and physically.

Further Reflections...
"This was our course: We realized that the people who wronged us were perhaps spiritually sick. Though we did not like their symptoms and the way these disturbed us, they, like ourselves, were sick too. We asked God to help us show them the same tolerance, pity, and patience that we would cheerfully grant a sick friend. When a person offended we said to ourselves, 'This is a sick man. How can I be helpful to him? God save me from being angry. Thy will be done.'"

Alcoholics Anonymous, p. 66-67

Changed Attitudes

Change frightens me. I am afraid to trust the sexaholic.
I am afraid to open my heart to him again. I am afraid
I cannot forgive him, even if he never acts out sexually
again.

Yet I have to also admit that the changes in me since I
came to S-Anon have been miraculous. I no longer allow
myself to observe if and how my husband is looking at
other women. I can leave the area or find something else to
look at. I no longer make "drive-bys" past the house of his
former mistress or his therapist or his SA meetings to see if
he is there. I no longer go through anything that belongs to
him; I respect his privacy. I no longer rage at him uncon-
trollably about his past sexual behavior. Most profoundly,
with my Higher Power's help, I no longer spend most of
my day obsessing about him, his activities, his acting out,
his living situation, his character defects, or anything else
about him. I have come to mind my own business.

I am so very grateful for the serenity these changes
have brought into my life. Changed attitudes can aid my
recovery.

Further Reflections...
"Sometimes fear made letting go of our rigid ideas especially difficult. Yet we found truth in the saying, 'nothing
changes if nothing changes.'"

Working the S-Anon Program, p. 50

The Process of Forgiving

Forgiveness is a process for me. At times I feel compassion for the sexaholic, but I still have a lot of anger and resentment. I believe my anger and resentment indicate I have not yet forgiven my spouse. I can intellectually understand that he is a sexaholic, and that was why he behaved as he did. Yet, I still feel wounded by his actions.

I recently had insight that I haven't forgiven myself, either. I have not forgiven myself for the fact that I have a history of attraction to people with addiction problems. Despite what I am learning in S-Anon, I find myself still sustaining relationships with them, wanting to fix their problems. It is as though I pick people with problems that resemble my mother's addiction problems. I set myself up as their caretaker and "fixer".

I wasn't successful with my mother's problems; and I understand I won't be with these addicts, either. My sponsor has said I am just as powerless over my caretaking, fixing, and attraction to addicts as the sexaholic is over lust. Accepting powerlessness may be the key to begin forgiving myself and the sexaholic. That must be why it is the First Step.

Further Reflections...
"It helped to learn that the sexaholic is suffering from a spiritual and emotional illness, and it helped to learn that we can lovingly detach from that illness. Most of all, it helped to learn that we, too, are suffering from an illness, one that can drive us to unconsciously seek out rejection, victimization, and heartache."

S-Anon Twelve Steps, p. 2

Practicing Honesty

While she helped me work Step Nine, my sponsor pointed out that I needed to start to make amends to myself. One way I made amends to myself was to live honestly. During the time I was actively working this Step, by intentionally practicing honesty, my husband and I had an argument. As I was brushing my teeth, he asked if everything was all right. I angrily said, "I'm fine." Then, as I looked in the mirror, I knew I had just lied. I turned and said to him, "I just lied to you. Will you forgive me?"

That opened a door of communication and honesty in our relationship that we had never known before. It also gave me courage to be honest in other areas in my life. Practicing honesty has many rewards for me and for my relationships with others.

Further Reflections...
"I have spent most of my life honing my skills at figuring out what other people are thinking and feeling, in order to avoid conflict. True honestly for me only comes when I concentrate on myself."

Recovering Together: Issues Faced by Couples
(Rev. Booklet 2007), p. 10

Sponsorship Is for My Recovery

With much prayerful consideration, I knew it was time to end my sponsorship of one of my sponsees. A job change had left our schedules extremely different and finding regular time to talk and to do Step work had proven nearly impossible.

It was understandably a very difficult conversation as we had worked together for over a year. After the conversation, I noticed I was angry because she had not expressed appreciation to me for my help in the hard times she had experienced. Had I been used? This was a familiar thought. I often had experienced this same reaction with the sexaholic.

To sort it out, I called my own sponsor. She reminded me that the program tells us we give away what we have been given in order to keep it. Sponsorship ultimately is for my recovery, not just the sponsee's. It really did not matter why my sponsee did not express her appreciation; what was important was for me to look at my own motives and responses to the relationship.

After reaching out to my sponsor, I had a lot to think about; especially my motives in looking for appreciation. I was also aware of some feelings of sadness and loss, but I was grateful I had my sponsor's support to process my feelings in a healthy way.

Further Reflections...
"When working with sponsees, I have to actively practice the principles that develop the skills I need to live serenely: working the Steps and Traditions, setting boundaries, having compassion, and relying on God."

Working the S-Anon Program, p. 10

Learning Not to Abandon Myself

Before I came into S-Anon, I had been abandoned by my father at a young age and sexually abused. In my early adulthood I made poor choices for myself, and knowingly married a sexaholic.

In doing my Fourth and Fifth Steps, I recognized that I had no experience with nurturing or supportive relationships. I also realized that I have continually abandoned myself emotionally, by not acknowledging my feelings, wants or needs. I also recognized that by trying to control others, I actually cut myself off from them and made it difficult to have an intimate relationship with anyone. Through working Steps Six and Seven, I am experiencing many of these character defects being removed by my Higher Power.

With the support of my sponsor, by listening and sharing at meetings and through working the Steps, I have begun to feel God's love and the love of other S-Anon members in a way I did not think possible.

Today I am learning to love the real me – the way my Higher Power does. I do this by being true to myself. Today my life counts and I am worth it.

Further Reflections...
"We accept ourselves, as we travel at our own pace towards spiritual growth."

S-Anon Twelve Steps, p. 64

A Helpful Perspective

While my partner has been sober for over two years, I have to admit I still can become anxious. When I get anxious I tend to react, not to what she is doing, but to triggered memories of what she used to do, fearing she will do it again. In my anxiety I watch her closely for signs of impending trouble. A voice in my head says, "I will never let this happen to me again. She may have fooled me before, but now I am on the lookout for her sexaholic behavior."

I am learning that when I am anxious, it is important to reach out to other S-Anons. My program friends help me get perspective on what is really going on with me. They help me understand that I sometimes lapse into anxiety because I have not forgiven myself for my past mistakes. I still am angry with myself for all the denial and enabling behaviors I engaged in that were so hurtful to my marriage and to me. When I surrender my thoughts and past behaviors, I start to feel forgiveness for myself. Then I am able to relax and ease up on my partner and on myself.

I know that whatever the future brings I have the support of a loving Higher Power and my S-Anon group. Today I strive to let the past be the past and to put my future in the hands of my Higher Power.

Further Reflections...
"I am not immune to the surfacing of feelings from the past; no matter how many years I have been working this program."

S-Anews, December 1993, p. 4

A New Way of Life

I was told by two doctors that my husband's cross-dressing, as well as other sexual compulsive behaviors, was something I had to learn to live with. I began praying for a better answer. My prayers were answered after reading a response to someone in a syndicated newspaper column. As a result, I found S-Anon and my husband found SA.

I am now in recovery just over a year. My husband and I are working through the Steps in our respective fellowships. Through the grace of these programs, we are learning how to live a new way of life. I have learned there are no quick fixes to the family disease of sexaholism. Instead, I have found it to be a gradual positive solution. I am finding hope one day at a time, through the Twelve Steps and through applying the tools of recovery: writing, meetings, meditation, prayer, sponsorship, and more.

My relationship with my spouse has started to heal. By working the S-Anon program, I am getting out of the way of my Higher Power. I am devoting the same kind of energy and time to healthy living as I use to devote to obsessing about my husband's sexual behavior. I am starting to experience The Gifts of the S-Anon Program in my life today.

Further Reflections...
"If you persist, remarkable things will happen. When we look back, we realize that the things which came to us when we put ourselves in God's hands were better than anything we could have planned. Follow the dictates of a Higher Power and you will presently live in a new and wonderful world, no matter what your present circumstances!"

Alcoholics Anonymous, p. 100

❖ ❖ ❖

Allowing God in My Life

When I was growing up I learned to do what I was told, because dire consequences followed when I didn't. It was not O.K. for me to express my own needs and wants. As an adult, I made decisions based on fear of consequences from outside sources. When S-Anon introduced the idea that a Higher Power could restore me to sanity, I was confused — on one hand wanting to trust, but on the other fearing the consequences of my choices to take care of myself.

I am making progress. I am better able to know and say what I like and dislike. I have a loving family in S-Anon, and I feel sure that God loves me, no matter what choices I make. I am taking better care of my physical health and my emotional and financial well-being. I am taking better care of how I spend the money I earn and have been able to do some nice things for myself. I am clear about how I want to be treated in my relationships.

Today I don't spend as much time on emotional roller coasters or having emotional hangovers, so I can think more clearly about what may be the next thing for me to do. I am grateful that God guides my life today, through the spiritual principles of this program, and that my life is richer and fuller and more peaceful because of it.

Further Reflections...
"Going to meetings was the beginning of my recovery – and the beginning of trusting that a power greater than myself could help me."

Working the S-Anon Program, p. 4

Opening the Door to Recovery

Before coming to S-Anon, I reacted to situations presented by my sexaholic partner and then I'd feel crazy and
stripped of my dignity. If he was the one with the problem,
then why was I the one feeling guilty and afraid? My
thinking and behaviors became distorted during the many
years I lived with active sexaholism.

When my sexaholic partner would come home hours
past when he had promised, I would greet him at the door
with a phony hug. My motive was really to sniff his clothing to try to detect if another woman's perfume was on his
clothes. Often he would catch on to what I was doing and
react with anger and sarcasm. In my own anger and obsession, I would do this over and over, while he acted the role
of the victim, over and over. My behavior became a way to
distract both of us from the truth, as we continued to act in
unhealthy ways.

Through S-Anon, I learned to let go of my need to
"check-up" on his behavior, and started to gain a sense of
self-respect. I did this by not engaging in degrading behaviors, which in turn, gave the sexaholic the opportunity to
face his own behaviors. I opened the door to serenity and
dignity for myself, therefore, opening the door for dignity
and responsibility for my partner. It is in this way that
recovery entered our home and our lives.

Further Reflections...
"As our awareness grows about the truth of our situations
we have been involved in, we find strength and hope to
move forward, and eventually to seek healing in our relationships with the sexaholics in our lives."
Working the S-Anon Program, p. 59

Owning Responsibility

I received a telephone call from the wife of a man with whom I recently and briefly was involved. He had denied being married. As she talked, I realized I had chosen another sexaholic, despite being a member of S-Anon. I had my suspicions about him from the beginning, yet shoved those suspicions aside. The phone call was a wake-up call. This time, instead of becoming a victim and blaming the other person for my actions, I owned the responsibility for my choices. The conversation not only helped me see my own illness, but also helped me experience compassion as I grew to understand the illness of sexaholism on a new, deeper level. It helped me understand that I truly am powerless over my attraction to sexaholics.

I cried briefly, prayed, and read our S-Anon literature. I knew I would be calling my sponsor to discuss my slip, knowing there was no reason to hide my actions from her. I had come to know that "It works when you work it." My sponsor suggested that I consider working the first nine Steps around my attraction to unhealthy relationships, and I agreed to commit myself to work.

Further Reflections...
"...it helped to learn that we, too, are suffering from an illness, one that can drive us to unconsciously seek out rejection, victimization, and heartache."

S-Anon Twelve Steps, p. 2

Self Imposed Emotional Jail

One of the tools I have found helpful is journaling. In writing about my feelings I have been able to see patterns that I repeat. Lately I have seen how I am very judgmental of the sexaholic in my life. I continuously try to punish and belittle him. In not letting go of the past, I was trying to be ready for him to act out his sexaholism again. I saw that my reminding him directly and indirectly, how he has hurt me, was also trying to control our relationship. I began to see that by not letting go, I felt trapped in what seems like an emotional jail.

My sponsor helped me to focus on my own behavior and also to be open to seeing evidence of my husband's work in his recovery. I know that old patterns are difficult to change and I realized I needed extra help. I started going to more meetings, and focusing on the slogan "One Day At A Time." I began to feel hope that my Higher Power could restore me to sanity.

Slowly I am beginning to be released from my self imposed emotional jail.

Further Reflections...
"Many of us found that before we could begin to use the tools of S-Anon, we had to let go of... the 'old tools' that may have helped us survive, but simply did not work well any more. The old tools may have included denial, obsession with the sexaholic, covering up the problem, isolation, rage, and manipulation."

Working the S-Anon Program, p. 1

Secrets and Boundaries

Growing up, I was taught never to keep secrets, but to be as open and honest as I could. My parents impressed upon me that keeping secrets resulted in broken trust, pain, and hurt. As a result, I lived my life as if an open book, holding nothing back, even from acquaintances.

When I discovered that my husband was a sexaholic, and had kept a secret life from me, I was stunned. I felt terribly hurt and betrayed. Hoping to stop the pain, I nagged my husband, until he told me the truth. Under the banner of "no more secrets," I bullied him for every detail of his sexual "acting out" experiences. Unfortunately in my quest for "no more secrets," I only caused myself a lot more pain and hurt. Those details fueled the obsessive thoughts that plagued me about his sexual behavior.

In S-Anon, I am learning that it may not be productive for either my husband or me, to share all our thoughts, feelings, or details of every experience. I am starting to listen for the truth from my Higher Power and share what I am learning with my sponsor. I ask for guidance in discerning how much detail to share with my spouse, and how much detail to receive from him. I am confident that if I need to know something, my Higher Power will somehow reveal it to me.

In my recovery, I am working to distinguish between keeping secrets and having boundaries.

Further Reflections…
"Boundaries… aren't rules I can enforce on others. They are standards of conduct I set for my own benefit."
[Al-Anon] Hope for Today, p. 311

Being Restored to Sanity

Early in recovery, I was challenged by Step Two to understand sanity and insanity at a time when my life seemed to be turned upside down. I felt that I lived in a world where the attitude seemed to be "do as you please," with no accountability. Needless to say, there didn't seem to be much sanity in the world around me.

It was relatively easy for me to lie to myself and say that I had not behaved in an insane way. Yet when I reflected on my family of origin and my religion's doctrines and teachings as a part of my Step Two work, I came to understand that insane thinking was "normal" in my family. I had learned to think that way from early childhood. It was this insane thinking that enabled me to deny and tolerate the sexaholism that was active in my home, and eventually to participate in it as well.

Through S-Anon, I am breaking the chain of the "family disease." I am slowly being restored to sanity. The peace, serenity, and a connection to a Higher Power is greater than the insanity with which I grew up. I am grateful that I have made a commitment to the S-Anon Steps, so that I have the opportunity to know that there is a better way for me to live.

Further Reflections...
"Those of us who resisted the idea that we needed to be 'restored to sanity' were encouraged to return to our First Step writing and remind ourselves of the many ways in which our lives had become unmanageable."
S-Anon Twelve Steps, p. 24

A Dangerous Neighborhood

My head is a dangerous neighborhood to go into, and I shouldn't stay there alone. I often use this phrase to describe to newcomers why I find it so important to reach out and make telephone support calls between meetings. Even though I've been working the S-Anon program for a number of years, I can still slip back into obsessive thinking. Sometimes the solution is as simple as calling another S-Anon member and saying, "I'm having difficulty turning over this situation to my Higher Power." The person on the receiving end of my call might only be a listening ear or may offer a suggestion such as "Have you tried journaling about it?" The benefit for me is that once I've shared a problem with another S-Anon member, I am better able to turn it over to my Higher Power.

When I am spending too much time trying to solve a problem in my own head, I am reverting back to my old character defect of emotional isolation. Today I believe that I don't have to do this alone, and even if I could, why would I want to? My life is so much richer now with all the tools of the program, and the most important tool for me today is sharing with others who really understand.

Further Reflections...
"Many of us hesitated to call another member on the telephone because we felt we were a burden, but reaching out benefits both the caller and the person who receives the call."

Working the S-Anon Program, p. 6

Sponsorship Relationships

When I first came to S-Anon, I was in tremendous emotional pain. My spirit was broken and my self-esteem was non-existent. I believe my Higher Power led me to choose a sponsor almost immediately, before I understood very much about the S-Anon program.

Through the special relationship I developed with my sponsor, I learned that my feelings mattered. I learned to trust again. When I talked with my sponsor about a problem, she would help me work through it.

Eventually, I began to wonder if she ever had any struggles or difficulties herself. Then, one day she called me to talk over a problem that she was having. That phone call transformed our relationship and me. I realized that she also had struggles and crises. She was human and fallible. For the first time, I felt trustworthy and valuable. I thought I might possibly have something to offer others as well.

Now I use this experience when working with my own sponsees. I don't only call old-timers to process my difficulties. I have learned that we all have experience, strength, and hope to share. We encourage each other by sharing and listening. I feel this attitude has humbled me, and helped me value myself and others in a healthier way. I don't need to have it all together, nor does anyone else. My Higher Power speaks to me through others, no matter how long they have been working the program.

Further Reflections...
"The most important thing for me to remember in sponsoring another member is that I don't have to have all the answers... I just need to stick to sharing how the tools of the program have helped me to solve my own problems."
Working the S-Anon Program, p. 99

A Progressive Disease

As I worked the S-Anon program, I became more aware of the effects of sexaholism. One of the effects I had suffered for years was verbal abuse. As I grew in S-Anon I considered divorce, yet two things held me back. First, the needs of our children seemed to outweigh divorce, so I learned to take care of our children and myself when the sexaholic was abusive. The other was the struggle I had discerning God's will about whether or not to divorce. It wasn't clear what action to take, so I waited. Other S-Anon members shared they had intuitively known what to do when the time was right. Hearing this was hopeful, but the waiting was still very difficult.

I finally intuitively knew what to do the day we dropped off our son at camp. My husband became verbally abusive to people at the camp, including a police officer who then confronted my husband loudly through the window on my side of the car. Something about this confrontation brought to life what I had heard in many meetings: sexaholism is a progressive disease. I saw my husband's powerlessness and my own powerlessness over the disease of sexaholism. My husband had refused recovery, but with amazing clarity, I finally knew what I had to do for our children and me. It was time to let go of my marriage.

I am grateful now to be able to provide a life free of abuse for my children and myself, through the spiritual principles and support of the program.

Further Reflections...
"I didn't understand how my husband could choose to continue to act out and not seek recovery, but I had the courage and the strength to let the marriage go when it became time. Today, I am grateful to God for the gifts of that relationship..."

S-Anon Twelve Steps, p. 34

❖   ❖   ❖

From Resentment to Forgiveness and Gratitude

I once thought it was easier to harbor grudges and resentments rather than to deal with painful, tough issues. I found holding onto resentments made me sick with bitterness. I didn't want to become a sour old woman, so I made a decision to face the effects of sexaholism on my life.

By working with my sponsor, I started to find a different way to deal with resentments. First, I had to stop sweeping my pain under the rug. Then I learned to stop lying and saying I forgave my spouse, while still raging inside. My sponsor suggested that walking through the pain would eventually help me see what grace was really about. The healing I needed and wanted was a process directed by my Higher Power. I am making progress: not instantaneously, but miraculously.

Today, forgiveness means accepting the reality of what has happened, and then choosing to let go of the hurt and pain that the sexaholic's behavior caused. I also need to forgive myself for the unhealthy behavior I exhibited in reaction to living with sexaholism.

Worthy goals for me today are to get to a place where I am grateful for the events of the past that brought me to the present, and find true compassion for the sexaholic and me. While I'm not there yet, I am glad I am on the path of coming to terms with the effects of sexaholism on my life. I am grateful I am no longer harboring resentments.

Further Reflections...
"We may find resentment deep inside for the sexaholic and all we have been through; however, as we look at our own resentful behavior, we begin to see that resentment isn't any better than lusting. It is just a different defect of character."   *S-Anon Twelve Steps, p. 40*

Family Guidelines

My marriage and other relationships are much healthier after many years of working the S-Anon program. Yet as my spouse and I became healthier, our relationship with one of our sons became increasingly challenging. His unstable life had taken him into deeper and deeper trouble. He had become financially, emotionally, and spiritually bankrupt. Our son's inability to manage his life began to affect ours.

With the help of my sponsor and trusted S-Anon friends, I began to apply The Traditions to this situation. Tradition One states "Our common welfare should come first." I saw that my adult son's needs could not take precedence over my recovery, or my marriage. Turning to our Higher Power for wisdom and direction helped my husband and I apply Tradition Seven's principle of self-support. We stopped bailing out our son financially.

We tried to remain connected to our son by regular phone calls, emails, and occasional trips to his home out-of-state. We eventually found ourselves cut off from contact with him as he further isolated himself.

While this has been painful, I find comfort knowing that my son has a Higher Power, just as I do. Each day I visually and mentally place my son in his Higher Power's hands, and I place myself in God's hands as well. I trust that God is caring for my son better than I ever could.

Further Reflections…
"…A more compassionate way to respond to those I love might be to allow them to face the consequences of their actions, even when it will cause them pain."

[Al-Anon's] Courage to Change, p. 5

Incarceration

One of the worst days I've experienced in the disease of sexaholism was the day my partner phoned me from jail. I tried to control every situation, yet here I was with all control taken away. I so wanted to fix everything; but there was nothing I could do. My partner would remain in jail for the next 75 days. I was regularly attending S-Anon meetings. This allowed me an outlet to express the many emotions I was experiencing. I was very serious and tense about the whole experience.

Then one day a member said "Boy I sure could stand to have my partner in jail for a few weeks." I didn't know how to respond. Should I be angry? But then I saw this as a message from my Higher Power. I was being shown a different way to look at this situation. My partner was in a safe place where he and I had time to think. I didn't have to wonder where he was, I already knew. I learned a lot in the next 75 days. I'm grateful to my meeting, my friends, and my Higher Power for showing me a better way to live. I continue to be amazed by the courage, strength, and hope I find in S-Anon.

Further Reflections...
"Perhaps I can take a different view of my problems. If I accept them at face value without taking them personally, I may find that they are not problems at all, only things that have not gone as I would have liked. This change of attitude can help free me to evaluate the situation realistically and move forward constructively."

Courage to Change, p.171

The Power of Healthy Choices

Long before joining S-Anon, isolation was a way of life for me. Shutting me away from others perpetuated my magical thinking that maybe things would get better at home. Consequently, I did not face my fears and take responsibility for my choices. Isolation and ignoring the effects of living with sexaholism enabled me to hide from the reality of my life and the unproductive way I was parenting my daughter. Isolation had become an unhealthy habit.

S-Anon gave me back the power of healthy choices. Now I can choose to reach out by calling my sponsor regularly, and I encourage my sponsees to do the same. I volunteer for service at meetings, which gives me that extra nudge to show up and break my isolation. There are other options, too. I can have the World Service Office put me in contact with S-Anons in other communities. I can attend S-Anon Conventions, where I am reminded my local group and I are connected to a bigger fellowship. Writing a daily Tenth Step increases my awareness of what is happening inside me, and to help clear up little misunderstandings that motivate my isolation. I can use the slogans: This Too Shall Pass and How Important Is It?

Most important, I can ask my Higher Power for help when I wake up and remember to say thank you to God before I fall asleep. Isolating complicates my life. Choosing to stay out of isolation through working my program helps me Keep It Simple.

Further Reflections...
"Rarely have we seen a person who was not greatly benefited by working the S-Anon program."

Working the S-Anon Program, p. 112

❖   ❖   ❖

Higher Power Offers Opportunities

Ever since my first disastrous experience with writing a book report in school, I have resisted writing anything. Every time I've been asked to do some writing for the S-Anews or other S-Anon publications, I've cringed at the suggestion.

While at a recent S-Anon convention, I reconsidered my cringing response to writing when I heard someone there share a new (to me) spiritual concept. The concept: when asked to do service work, it might be Higher Power offering an opportunity for growth, and it may be a way to give back what freely has been given to me.

I realized this concept was similar to what I had heard throughout my time in S-Anon: we can no longer sit back and let someone else do for us what we can do for ourselves if we are to recover from our own fears, complacency, and feelings of inadequacy. After all, I knew from my own experience that when I tried to work the sexaholic's program for him, it was a total disaster.

So here I sit with pen in hand, and I see now that I do have something important to share!

Further Reflections...
"Although our own characters are still in need of much work, we have been greatly helped by encouraging others to find recovery, new purpose and meaning in life."
S-Anon Twelve Steps, p. 143

Cutting the Strings

After making great progress in focusing on myself, rather than my husband, I became aware of a recurring theme of difficulty in forgiving others. It seemed as though whenever I forgave someone, an even bigger offense would occur, leaving me thinking my forgiveness had been meaningless. This theme was so familiar that I began to recognize my understanding of forgiveness was lacking something.

I received a helpful insight listening to an older woman at a meeting. She related that she had been hurt not only by her sexaholic husbands' actions, but also by her adult children's lack of support for boundaries she had set with her husband. She said that after doing some very deep work, she realized that forgiveness was ultimately for her, and not for those who had hurt her. She said that forgiveness allowed her to cut the strings of anger and resentment that tied her to troubling events.

As I recalled the lightness in her step, the smile on her face, and the fact that she was almost twenty years my senior, I knew I didn't want to wait that long to embrace a more helpful concept of forgiveness – that forgiveness of someone was for me, not for the other person. I knew I had to shift my thinking and attitude, and I trusted that my emotions would follow.

Further Reflections...
"…I accepted that no one could change the past. I could let it continue to hurt me or I could choose to let it go. So while I still did not feel forgiving, I prayed for the ability to let go of the bitter feelings…"

S-Anon Twelve Steps, p. 90

I Like Being Me

It wasn't until I had about two years of recovery, that I understood just how much I had been struggling with issues that most S-Anons face; the effects of sexaholism in my own life. I was finally coming face to face with the realization of how I had been conducting much of my life, and that somewhere down the line; I had made the decision to push away the pain of living with sexaholism. My ticket in the door may have been my wife, but based on my experiences growing up; my seat in an S-Anon meeting had been reserved for me long ago.

I now see how my every action and reaction in my life was based on others, rather than on myself. It was as if I was a robot that only reacted to internal controls that I had no idea were there. I was trying to fill a giant hole where my heart was supposed to be. I was trying to prove I was lovable, by pleasing everyone else, by trying to be responsible for other people's mistakes, by lying about my accomplishments, by false pride and false humility. I tried to fill the hole with anything false…then I would deny that my pain even existed.

Today, thank God, this is not the way I live. Today, I strive to do the next right thing. I have integrity today. I am growing in my recovery. I like being me. Today is a better day.

Further Reflections…
"Sobriety is knowing and owning all my own behavior and choices. Sobriety is knowing that I am a grateful, recovering member of S-Anon because I have a problem that I am choosing to do something about."
Working the S-Anon Program, p. 54

Facing Fear

What a challenge it had been for me to face my fears. I used to act as if I had no part in the situation or that I was a victim of my circumstances. Refusing to face my fears had left me lonely and isolated. I was constantly angry with myself, for not taking control of my life, and towards my partner, for not fixing my feelings. I blamed everyone else for "making me feel this way." Underneath that anger was fear. I wanted to run far away, to hide from the pain and shame. I had no one to talk to, so I kept my fears inside for many years.

One day, I just couldn't handle it anymore. I went in search of someone to confide in and I found S-Anon. Now I have tools I can use to face my fears. For example, I can take pen to paper at the end of the day and write about my thoughts, feelings and actions. I can write down loving statements about myself. I can make a gratitude list. When I write things out, I can turn them over to my Higher Power and share them with my sponsor. I still experience fear at times, but I have tools today to face the fears.

Further Reflections...
"...I am learning to trust myself to rise to the occasion as a problem presents itself. I will have the resources when I need them. I don't have to control the outcome but can learn to trust the process. This allows me to be less afraid..."

Working the S-Anon Program, p. 42

Responding Instead of Reacting

I have allowed the sexaholic in my life to provoke me into knee-jerk reactions toward him. I notice this has been especially true when I am not feeling well or am stressed. At these times I am vulnerable to being manipulated and am tempted to take responsibility for the sexaholic's needs.

Sometimes when I have reacted angrily to the sexaholic, I have had inappropriate responses, such as slamming doors and making sarcastic remarks. Other times I have reacted by making myself listen and "be there" for him as caretaker and problem solver. I ignore my own needs, push down my anger, and interact with him in a way that feels unsafe and dishonest. Either way, I have directed the anger at myself. I really want to respond in a healthier way, such as taking some time out or calling my sponsor. The times when I have felt vulnerable – ill, tired, frustrated, hungry, are when it has been most difficult to control my reactions.

In S-Anon, I am learning that when I react rather than respond, I usually am doing the exact thing that I want to blame him for – not taking responsibility for personal needs. Today, I ask my Higher Power for the presence of mind to mentally step back when I am uncomfortable and ask myself, "How can I take care of myself in this situation?" If I act lovingly toward myself, I am better able to respond honestly and respectfully toward him and others.

Further Reflections…
"… we were not taught to think about our own needs and take positive action to meet them."

The S-Anon Problem

Drama of Addictive Relationships

It was always so easy for me to see the sexaholic's problems, and it was so hard to understand why he "didn't just fix them." I paid a lot of lip service to working on my own problems, but I devoted most of my energy to calculating how best to "save" him and our relationship. When the sexaholic left me, I panicked and was forced to see that I also have an addiction—I am addicted to the sexaholic and to the drama of addictive relationships. It was then that I understood why my partner had not been able to turn his life around "just like that" and I was flooded with compassion, not only for him, but also for myself. We both have problems we are powerless over, and we both need help.

Focusing on myself can be difficult and painful. Changing life-long habits seems impossible. In S-Anon I find courage to focus on the positive changes I can make in my own life. I accept spiritual progress rather than spiritual perfection.

Further Reflections...
"If I have come to believe that a Higher Power can restore me to sanity, I can trust that the same is true for my partner."

Working the S-Anon Program, p. 47

Adventures in Serenity

Learning to be content with who I am is a new adventure in serenity every day. Each day, I strive for one more piece of self-awareness. One choice at a time, I ask for guidance from my Higher Power. I have come to think of this guidance as a gentle, inner voice. I also ask myself questions. What will bring me the greatest peace? What will bring the greatest harmony of thought, mind, and action? How can I apply the principles of the Twelve Steps and Twelve Traditions to guide my decisions?

I need not ask these questions all at once or have the answers right away. When I take time to ask my Higher Power for guidance, and then get still through meditation and truly listen for my Higher Power's direction, the answers do come. Sometimes the answers come through personal insights that clarify my internal dialogues and motivations. Other times, the answers come in the form of kind words from a trusted friend. On other days, the answers come through another's experience expressed in our S-Anon literature. I am on a new path today, and I am grateful for the journey!

Further Reflections…
"Through Step Eleven we let go of relying on a strictly analytical approach to problem solving. We learn to include our intuition and the wisdom and direction of our Higher Power."

S-Anon Twelve Steps, p. 137

Why Do I Stay?

I discovered my husband's sexaholism shortly after we celebrated one of our wedding anniversaries. Life together was difficult, but I couldn't seem to leave.

I joined S-Anon and admired those who had left abusive situations. I felt unable to and I didn't understand why. In learning about sexaholism, I discovered that our marital boundaries could be broken without me knowing it, and my sponsor helped me take steps to build boundaries and protect myself from disease. That felt good, but it also added to my quandary, "Why do I stay?" I felt stupid and weak for not leaving.

I worked the program and began to trust that my Higher Power would let me know if and when I should leave the relationship. While inventorying my part in the relationship, I had several awarenesses. Despite my loneliness, there were joyful times in my marriage. Through the good times and bad times, we share a thirty-seven year history and six children. Most importantly, I still didn't perceive a message from my Higher Power to leave the relationship.

I let go of hating myself for staying in my marriage. I know I need to continue to take care of myself and set boundaries to keep myself safe. I feel peace with my decision and, for the first time in years, I don't feel self-hatred. I feel serenity.

Further Reflections...
"I am so sure of God's love that I can leave my concerns in His hands, knowing that I and those I love will be provided for 'one day at a time.' I believe that God will not leave me without a way out, even when I mistakenly interpret His will or my place in a situation."

Working the S-Anon Program, p. 75

❖   ❖   ❖

Grieved for the Relationship

When I first came to S-Anon, I grieved for the relationship I thought I had with the sexaholic. I felt the deep, painful emotions of loss. With the help of the S-Anon program, I came to see that my relationship with the sexaholic was different than I actually believed it was. I also grieved when I realized my relationships with family and friends had been affected by sexaholism, and that I had distorted the reality of those relationships, too. With help from my sponsor and through working the Steps, I grieved all those losses.

The process of grieving, working the program, and trusting my Higher Power gave me the opportunity to take an honest look at what I had been trying so hard to run away from—true intimacy with myself and others. I am now able to be honest, which in turn is helping to heal all my relationships.

Through devoting ourselves to Twelve Step recovery, we begin to practice true intimacy. When we let people know who we truly are and share the pain of our grief, we learn that we are not alone, that others love us for who we are. This is one of the miracles awaiting us in recovery.

Further Reflections...
"As we begin to devote ourselves to Twelve Step recovery, an amazing thing takes place. We let our hardships and problems become our teachers, and we become grateful for the lessons they teach us. We learn that we are not alone in facing the problem of sexaholism."

S-Anon Twelve Steps, p. 3

I Like What I See

Before coming to S-Anon, I couldn't understand how I ended up in a relationship where lies, deception, and betrayal were common. I could barely look at myself in the mirror without feeling shame and humiliation. I felt resentful toward my husband for putting my health and life at risk, and for spending a large portion of our earnings on prostitution and pornography. Yet I put up with it.

Why did I put up with it? Was I clinging to a fantasy of what the relationship could be through denying reality? Was I fearful of the unknown or of being alone? Was I afraid of change?

Coming to S-Anon and hearing the stories of others helped me acknowledge reality – I was powerless over how I was living and my life was truly unmanageable. Through sharing with others and listening, I found strength and faith in a Higher Power. I came to understand that I could not change the sexaholic, but I could learn to see reality, learn to detach, and learn to make healthy changes for me.

It wasn't easy. There were many times I thought my life would not get better. Yet The Gifts of the S-Anon Program are slowly coming true in my life. I can look at myself in the mirror today… and I like what I see.

Further Reflections...
"I'm even more grateful that in this program I have come to know a God who really cares for me, who has a better plan for my life than the one I have in mind."

S-Anon Twelve Steps, p. 22

Willing Adherence

I heard a wonderful discussion regarding Tradition Ten. These are some of the questions I heard: What would happen in an S-Anon business meeting if issues were never addressed, because each person believed their concern was more important than the other's? Wouldn't members have difficulty sharing, listening, and being heard? Could this lead to hurt feelings and frustrations? If a meeting chose not to practice Tradition Ten, could this cause loss of members, and possibly the disbanding of the group? Tradition Ten helps us focus on what is in front of us—issues that affect the group and S-Anon as a whole. Other concerns are outside issues.

I can also apply Tradition Ten at home. In the past, when the sexaholic would confront me with something about which he was uncomfortable, I would react by going into a tirade about his past behavior. I couldn't hear his issues when I had so many unresolved issues of my own. My spouse never felt heard, and thought I showed little regard for his feelings. I was left feeling fearful; consequently I went deeper into self-righteous indignation.

Applying the spiritual principles found in Tradition Ten helps me look at my responsibility in a new light. I have learned the value of listening, even when I do not agree. I am better able to share my feelings without causing controversy. Tradition Ten helps me to stay on my spiritual path and continue to improve my ability to be a part of an intimate relationship.

Further Reflections...
"The S-Anon Family Groups have no opinion on outside issues; hence our name ought never be drawn into public controversy."

S-Anon's Tradition Ten

Sexually Transmitted Disease (STD) and Responsibility

I thought I couldn't get a sexually transmitted disease (STD) because I was sexually conservative and had few partners. People who slept around were the ones who got STD's. Not only did I believe those myths, I also trusted the sexaholic. When he told me he had genital herpes, I assumed he would protect me from getting it. I was extremely angry and hurt when I was diagnosed with herpes. I blamed the sexaholic and felt angry, but I didn't trust myself to say anything for fear my rage would cause him to leave.

We broke up anyway, and I continued to experience my angry feelings. Thankfully, I was attending S-Anon by then and began a Fourth Step. Taking an inventory helped me work through my shame and anger. I finally saw my part: I had discounted, minimized, assumed, and trusted beyond common sense. I had surrendered my personal well-being to someone not well enough to take care of himself, much less me.

Over time I have accepted having herpes. It is part of me, not all of me. Believe it or not, today I have gratitude for contracting herpes. While it's not been pleasant, getting herpes helped me get off of a perilous path and actually helped me grow in recovery and self-responsibility.

Further Reflections...
"Everyone has the right to be safe from harm, no matter what the circumstances... It requires tremendous courage, but... consider taking some or all of the following actions: ask a doctor for tests for sexually transmitted diseases and follow the doctor's advice on self-protection..."

S-Anon Twelve Steps, pp. xix-xx

Connecting with Newcomers

S-Anon has given me hope that I can and will get better with the help of others and the tools of the program. I was not always so hopeful. I remember my first experience with S-Anon, talking on the telephone to a woman who briefly shared her story and then listened to me. She was very helpful and made it less threatening for me to attend my first meeting. I was blessed to be able to connect early with a sponsor who was compassionate and helpful. I truly feel indebted to her. Other S-Anon members sought me out after meetings to respond to something I had said and to offer encouragement. My connections with others helped me to keep coming back.

Today I try to give back what I was given by connecting with newcomers and welcoming them. It is very important to my recovery to pass on the message of hope that was given to me. Now I share the recovery I have found by working the S-Anon program to the best of my ability.

Further Reflections...
"We are seeing the lives of men and woman who share our message change from darkness to light and from despair to hope. We can help others who are suffering from the effects of sexaholism better than anyone else can."

S-Anon Twelve Steps, p. 143-144

Taking Positive Action

A line in The Keys to S-Anon Recovery reads "we take positive action to make our lives more serene and fulfilling." Even though I still struggle at times with believing in and trusting a Higher Power, I have chosen to take a positive action by beginning each day with meditation and prayer, using the first three Steps as a framework.

First, I remind myself that I am powerless over my continued insistence that other people, places, and situations are my only sources of love and indications of my worth. Next, I meditate on the new idea that a Higher Power loves me and wants me restored to sanity. After meditation, I turn over my will and life for that day to my Higher Power. I am finding that as I work Step Three, I am getting clearer about my true source of love.

I still struggle with my personal roadblocks, particularly rebellion, fear, and the illusion of power and control. Regularly reading the Keys to S-Anon Recovery and other Conference Approved Literature is helping to keep the door of healthy possibilities open for me. I am on an amazing journey.

Further Reflections...
"We realize we cannot find serenity for ourselves if we continue to focus on someone else's recovery, so we commit ourselves to our own recovery. With the loving help of other S-Anon members and the God our understanding, we take positive action to make our lives more serene and fulfilling."

The Keys to S-Anon Recovery

Finding Comfort for Today

The Serenity Prayer is such a comfort for me. When I say this prayer I like to add, "Higher Power, show me your will and give me the power to do it. Help me know that by helping myself, I help my family."

Working the S-Anon program and living the spiritual principles of the Steps have given me courage to change many things. I now accept my wife for who she is — a sex-aholic, and I can let go of the shame of being a victim. I am more aware when my trust has been violated, and I am better able to make healthy choices for myself and my children. The slogan "Live and Let Live" reminds me to accept my wife's efforts of showing love, instead of trying to get her to show me love the way I want her to. By working with my sponsor, I am better able to take care of myself, regardless of what my wife is doing or not doing.

Now I am able to find the courage to change the things I can. I can walk away from other's destructive behavior. I have the tools to detach with love and compassion, and I let God be in charge of whatever changes might be needed. Today, I allow others to follow the path they believe they need to take, and I find comfort for myself, regardless of the choices of others.

Further Reflections…
"God, grant me the serenity to accept the things I cannot change, courage to change the things I can, and the wisdom to know the difference."

The Serenity Prayer

Understanding Humility

In Step Seven, I struggled with humility. I used to think that I had to be the best or I was the absolute worst. In my relationship with my sexaholic partner, I always thought of myself as having authority because I believed I was, stronger, more capable, righteous, and the responsible one — I was at the top of the ladder so I didn't need to be humble. Humility was for my sexaholic partner — somewhere down toward the bottom of the ladder.

As I began to work the Steps, I was able to look at my own shortcomings, such as perfectionism, self-righteousness, pride and even arrogance. Over time I have learned to accept these shortcomings as part of my humanity, part of what makes me no better and no worse than anyone else.

Accepting the reality of my defects of character, as shown to me through my Forth and Fifth Steps, I have genuinely experienced humility. By accepting my strengths as well as my limitations, I have become a better companion, co-worker, and friend. I am a more compassionate person willing to help out and be a part of a greater whole. I understand now that all of us move around on the ladder, taking our turn on the various "rungs of life." In S-Anon, we give one another a hand as we move through wherever we are at the time. I am learning to practice the spiritual principles I am learning about humility in my relationship with my husband. Today I am a trusted servant.

Further Reflections...
"We frequently misunderstand the word humility. Often we think it implies weakness, lack of character, or helplessness."

S-Anon Twelve Steps, p. 73

So Many Miracles

I thank my Higher Power for the many miracles that have come into my life since I began to practice the S-Anon program. Here are just a few:
- I again know how to connect with a Higher Power.
- I now notice the mini-miracles and "coincidences" I see around me that confirm I'm on the right path.
- I now can open my eyes, ears, and heart to opportunities.
- I can feel gratitude, peace, and clarity as the treasures of recovery unfold.
- I feel lightness in my heart, as guilt and sadness give way to serenity and peace.
- I have people and places that remind me that a Higher Power is indeed here for me when I am burdened and in need of guidance.
- I am close with my Higher Power and can feel the joy and energy that comes from that connection. I no longer need to apply specific labels of what my Higher Power should be, or to understand who, what, or where my Higher Power is.

Today, I ask my Higher Power to give me the courage and the serenity to keep growing in our relationship, as I continue to surrender my will and my life. I now trust that my Higher Power wants the best for me, the best I can do in this world.

Further Reflections...
"We have been transformed through accepting the help of a Higher Power, a previously underused source of strength. We have experienced the freedom of knowing that God's help is always within reach. We have reached a new level of honesty, inner peace and love."

S-Anon Twelve Steps, p. 151

❖   ❖   ❖

Getting a Sponsor

Early in my S-Anon "career," I was a bit confused. I believed that without a sponsor, I couldn't officially start the program. This seemed like a great excuse for a quick journey to the end! When I learned I didn't need a sponsor to start working the program, I began working the Steps on my own. I can now see this thinking reflected my belief at the time that I was not worthy of others' attention. As I grew in my recovery, I finally asked someone to sponsor me. Much to my dismay, that person was unable to be my sponsor. She did take the time to encourage me to do a few things for myself, as I continued looking for someone else to sponsor me. She suggested going to lots of meetings, reading S-Anon literature, and calling other S-Anon members regularly.

Sponsorship really took flight for me at an S-Anon international convention. I found a temporary sponsor and went to meetings on sponsorship. I heard lots of ideas and experiences, even how members sometimes get new sponsors. By sharing my fears and concerns with others, I actually felt lighter. One of the ideas at the convention was to pray for a sponsor, so I did. I waited, listened, and took the next right action. While I waited, I felt clearer about what I was seeking in a sponsorship relationship. Eventually, I found a sponsor. It's just like that saying: "When the student is ready, the teacher comes."

Further Reflections...
"Sponsoring others in the program is one of the most vital and critical tools for growth in S-Anon. In the sponsor/sponsee relationship we find an opportunity to put into practice all the principles we learn in the program."

S-Anon pamphlet on Sponsorship

From Desperation to Gifts

Before S-Anon, I tried repeatedly to manipulate my spouse through sex, using it to keep him focused on me. Sometimes I withheld sex, feeling powerful and in control. All my sexual manipulations exhausted me and ultimately changed nothing, except to add more "baggage" to our sexual relationship. Exhaustion led to desperation and eventually to surrender – I became willing to give up my manipulative attempts and to finally start using the tools of recovery.

My sponsor helped me understand the tool of abstinence. I told my husband I needed a period of sexual abstinence to work my program and gain clarity about our relationship. We agreed on an abstinence of ninety days. I used that time to focus on my Step work and to build better relationships with my husband, friends, and my Higher Power. After ninety days, we mutually agreed to extend the time and ended up with six months of abstinence.

In ending the abstinence and resuming sexual relations, we focused on each other as human beings, on being honest, and on relying on the guidance of our Higher Power. What resulted was not the perfect romantic experience of the movies and romance novels, but a real experience of true intimacy. We were building a trusting and loving sexual relationship. Our marriage is still a work in process, and abstinence is still an occasional tool of recovery in our relationship.

Further Reflections…
"No matter how long we have been in recovery, a period of sexual abstinence can be a helpful way to gain insight into ourselves and our relationships by taking sex out of the equation."

Working the S-Anon Program, p. 68

Trusting My Higher Power

Like many of the S-Anon members in my group, I have
had serious problems in my marriage. When I came to
S-Anon I was on the verge of divorce. The stories of group
members challenged my thinking, inviting me to explore
every possible option. It was clear that I would have to
reach this difficult decision on my own.

Through counseling, meditation, talking with my sponsor, and attending meetings, the quiet voice my Higher
Power eventually whispered, "You are in charge of your
own happiness." S-Anon helped me gain the wisdom and
insight I needed to make the difficult decision about
whether to stay in or leave my marriage. I had come to
trust the voice of Higher Power and to trust myself. The
hardest decision I ever made was to divorce my husband.
I was sad, yet I felt amazing clarity. I centered myself by
using every S-Anon tool available: meetings, sponsor, telephone, literature, and intense application of the Steps and
Traditions every day. When self-doubt arose, I recalled the
quiet voice of my Higher Power and remembered that I
had explored every option and considered every possibil-
ity. My decision process had been slow, yet made from a
place of peace. Day by day, I moved through the divorce
and, eventually, serenity replaced my grief.

Further Reflections...
"We are now on a different basis: the basis of trusting and
relying upon God. We trust infinite God rather than our
finite selves. Just to the extent that we do as we think He
would have us do, and humbly rely on Him, does He
enable us to match calamity with serenity."
                              [*Alcoholics Anonymous*] *As Bill Sees It* p. 265

I No Longer Feel Sorry for Myself

I have struggled with feeling sorry for myself and this kept me from feeling gratitude. Instead of feeling grateful for my recovery, I would sit and feel sorry about everything negative that happened in my life, especially having to go to S-Anon. When I allowed the self-pity to creep in, I isolated from others and developed a bitter attitude toward my Higher Power, my husband, and others. I wanted someone to take the blame for my misery.

After some time in the program, I learned to accept the good with the bad, and I have actually experienced gratitude for both. By surrendering my will and life over to the care of my Higher Power, I made a deal with myself that I could feel sorry for myself for five minutes a day. Once my five minutes are up, I go through my gratitude list and I am reminded of all the miracles that have come my way since working the S-Anon program. Part of this deal is to have a change in attitude. Because of this I have moved forward and I can enjoy the day I've been given. If I need to cry, I allow the tears to come — something I never used to do. I know that healing will come with time through continued prayer and the loving support of my family, and my S-Anon group.

Today I no longer lament that I have to go to S-Anon, today I am grateful that I choose to go to S-Anon.

Further Reflections...
"Thanks to trust I am developing with my fellow S-Anon members, I am being more honest and finding warmth and loving acceptance. What a wonderful gift! I continue to be grateful for what I have been given."

Working the S-Anon Program, p. 50

Prayer and Forgiveness

Sexaholism has brought me to prayer like nothing else in my life. I pray to forgive the sexaholic. I pray to forgive myself for betraying myself. I pray to forgive my parents for initiating me into the family disease of sexaholism.

I find that some days I feel forgiving and other days I feel less forgiving. For example, today I feel forgiving. Today I have compassion for the sexaholic who is so clearly sick and lost in his addiction and denial. Today I feel forgiving of myself for making thousands of mistaken decisions that brought me to my bottom. Today I am faithful to prayer. Could there be a correlation?

Further Reflections...
"Those of us who have come to make regular use of prayer would no more do without it than we would refuse air, food, or sunshine. And for the same reason. When we refuse air, light, or food, the body suffers. And when we turn away from meditation and prayer, we likewise deprive our minds, our emotions, and our intuitions of vitally needed support. As the body can fail its purpose for lack of nourishment, so can the soul. We all need the light of God's reality, the nourishment of His strength, and the atmosphere of His grace. To an amazing extent the facts of A.A. life confirm this ageless truth."
[Alcoholics Anonymous] Twelve Steps and Twelve Traditions, p. 97-98

No Longer Focused on the Sexaholic

One of the most painful aspects of my husband's sexaholism was the loneliness I felt, not only when he was "acting out", but even when he was in the same room with me. I felt as if we were miles apart, and that I was invisible to him. The fact that I made him the center of my universe contributed to this a great deal. I was dependent on him, not only for companionship, but also for my self-esteem. He was the sole reason I woke up in the morning, and went to bed at night.

Through my recovery, I have grown to understand that though I was focused on wanting him to be focused on me 24/7; I was actually focused on him 24 hours a day. Through working on my Steps, I am learning to keep the focus on my own behavior. I am overcoming my dependency on my husband for my identity, and shifting that dependence on my Higher Power's will for me.

Our marriage is much different today, because I have learned to focus on myself and lovingly detach from my spouse. Even when he is busy with his own life, I am happier. I do not need him to entertain me 24 hours a day. I am no longer just a wife and mother. I am a person who has thoughts, feelings, interests, and goals. One day at a time, I am learning to live in the world, walk hand-in-hand with my Higher Power, and experience life in a healthier way.

Further Reflections…
"S-Anon has taught me to stop pointing fingers and to look at myself."

S-Anon Twelve Steps, p. 6

A Giant Refuge

One of my biggest defects has been people pleasing – attempting to keep everything and everyone around me on an even keel. I frequently responded in a passive-aggressive way when interacting with others. I would respond kindly initially, but later say or do unkind things.

My S-Anon program helps me focus on myself. I am working on being more in touch with my own needs, instead of meeting the needs of everyone else. I am learning to be more direct when communicating my needs. I see my program as a giant refuge – a safe place where I can take the risk to let go of my character defects and deal better with the outside world. I get so much support from the experience, strength, and hope of other members and my sponsor. That support also has helped me regain my sense of humor, something I had very little of when I first came to S-Anon.

I still have a tendency to want to hold on to my defects, but I am relying on my Higher Power's help and guidance. I slowly have acknowledged my defects and taken positive actions to replace those defects with positive behaviors. It is helpful to remember that it took a long time for me to develop my defects, and that they served well to protect me and help me in the past. Although I am a slow learner, I can trust the process. I know that my defects are being removed and God will continue to remove them in good time.

Further Reflections...
"Were entirely ready to have God remove all these defects of character."

S-Anon Step Six

Expectations Are Premeditated Resentments

I think I will always remember a phrase from an Al-Anon book: An expectation is a premeditated resentment.* Hearing those words read at my S-Anon group was an eye-opener for me, a defining moment. In the short time I have been coming to S-Anon, I have come to see that I am consumed with resentment. Now I understand why – my expectations fuel my resentments!

For example, I've always expected perfection from myself. When I make mistakes, however minor, I am filled with anxiety and fear. My self-worth plummets. The crazy thing is I know perfection is impossible, yet I still expect myself to achieve it.

Another example is how I expect my husband to fill the empty space I feel inside. I expect him to nurture me as my mother never did, to be my rescuer and my constant source of self-esteem, and to make me feel lovable. It is laughable when I think that I expect anyone to provide all of that! In reality, my husband has his own empty spaces, his own fears, and his own struggle with perfection. Expecting him to meet all my needs is insane.

I haven't been coming to S-Anon long, but I can already see that with the help of my Higher Power and the S-Anon program, I can learn healthier and saner ways to live.

Further Reflections…
"I have accepted myself and I'm beginning to accept other people the way they are each day. Now I have fewer resentments."

[Al-Anon] Courage to Change, p. 153

* *[Al-Anon] Courage to Change, p. 153*

Progressive Recovery

I knew my husband attended a Twelve Step program eight months prior to his revealing which one it was. One night he finally disclosed the truth. He said he wanted to put my mind at rest and assure me about what acting out he had not done.

Over time, he made more disclosures to me. I am grateful that as more of his story was revealed, I was establishing a deeper foundation in S-Anon. I learned that just as sexaholism is progressive, recovery is also progressive. I am learning to share honestly and to hear honesty from my spouse. With each revelation, I kept coming back to "The Three Cs:" I didn't Cause my husband's lust, I can't Cure it, and I can't Control it.

One afternoon the phone rang. By the grace of God and this program, I knew intuitively that it was a prostitute. Many things went through my mind before I responded: I did not want prostitutes calling my house, and I was not responsible for protecting my spouse from his disease. Two miracles happened that day. First, I gave her my husband's work number, wished her a pleasant day and called my sponsor. That evening my spouse asked me if I had known it was a prostitute that had called. Then he shared the second miracle of the day: he told her about his recovery program and gave her some numbers she could call for help.

Isn't it interesting how when I got out of God's way, everyone got what they needed?

Further Reflections...
"As we begin to hold still, we feel a Higher Power begin to offer us guidance and peace in every situation."

S-Anon Twelve Steps, p. 3

The State of My Self-Support

Over time, the percentage of household money the sex-aholic spent on pornography and prostitution put a strain on our ability to pay our monthly bills. Every month I found myself experiencing fear, anxiety, and knots in my stomach. I'd yell at family members and declare unrealistic "rules" to control how other family members spent money.

I am grateful the sexaholic's spending binges have ceased. I'm also grateful that, as a result of my unmanage-ability, I woke up to another area of my life where I must practice these principles in all my affairs – finances. I've seen the reality of my powerlessness over the financial cost of my husband's disease. I've seen how important it is for me to be clearer on specific boundaries I need, such as being more careful with my own spending habits and establishing a new household account that is protected from compulsive over-spending. Now bill-paying day is much less daunting, and I feel closer to my Higher Power as I practice the spiritual principles found in our program.

In a recent meeting, I shared about the fear and resentment I had had regarding finances and the healing I am experiencing as a result of applying the Steps to this situation. I was reminded, through the sharing of others, about the principle of being self-supporting in Tradition Seven. Intrigued by what I had heard, I felt my Higher Power was guiding me to continue on my path of self-examination regarding self-support, this time using the Traditions.

Further Reflections...
"Our ability to act positively on behalf of our health, families, jobs and bank accounts will amaze us."
                                    Gifts of the S-Anon Program

The Spiritual Basis of My Life

I used to pray with my own selfish agenda and wish list, not thinking about God's will for me. I spent my time and energy playing "god" for my family members. I thought I knew how my sexaholic husband should work his program and how he should parent our sons. I schemed and planned our sons' lives, trying to orchestrate the universe so that they would never have to deal with the life struggles my husband and I had faced, especially sexaholism.

Back then, I could not see that God has a much broader perspective than the one I have. I could not see that life's struggles and difficulties offer me an opportunity to draw closer to God. I could not see then that my Higher Power is trustworthy.

Now, through prayer and meditation, I humbly ask for God's will, rather than my idea of the perfect outcome. With the help of my sponsor and my S-Anon program, I no longer need to pray for my husband to do things my way. My husband and I work together to raise our sons, and I have learned to place my family members in the hands of their Higher Power. I may still have a wish list, but through practicing Step Eleven, I turn my wishes over to God and ask for God's will. Step Eleven is the spiritual basis of my life today.

Further Reflection...
"The combination of self-examination, meditation, and prayer gives us a foundation for living. The regular practice of prayer and meditation rewards us with emotional balance, a sense of belonging and knowing that God watches lovingly over us."

S-Anon Twelve Steps, p. 129

New Spiritual Depths

Before coming to S-Anon, I was already on a spiritual path. I acknowledged the presence of a Higher Power in my life. I prayed, with gratitude for God's will and for acceptance of however that might manifest itself, and I took the time to give thanks for the blessings I was given. Coming to S-Anon has taken me to a deeper spiritual experience. Total dependence on my Higher Power has been a new concept for me.

By working Steps One and Two, I saw the devastation I experienced by my reaction to living with the effects of a loved one's addiction to lust. I also became aware that I was missing a key ingredient of Step Three—completely turning my life over to the care of God. Instead, I had become completely swept up in the illusion that I could control the acting out behavior of a sexaholic.

Looking back I believe I was experiencing, as the Alcoholics put it, "incomprehensible demoralization." In the most powerless of moments in my life I needed to make "a decision to turn my will and my life over to the care of God as I understood Him". Until S-Anon, it had not occurred to me that this would be the healthiest action I could take.

The Twelve Steps of S-Anon help me put into daily practice the spiritual teachings I have learned over the years. The fellowship has become a safe place for me to practice what I am learning. and I am finding the courage to bring these principles into my daily life.

Further Reflections...
"Came to believe that a Power greater than ourselves could restore us to sanity."

S-Anon Step Two

❖   ❖   ❖

A Neat Way to Live

I was overwhelmed by all the new ideas I heard when I first started S-Anon. I knew my old way of doing things wasn't working, but I felt overwhelmed by the prospect of ever being able to follow this way of life. I wanted what they had, but did not think I could afford the luxury of time in order to get there. I wanted a quick fix to deal with my chaotic life. My fear of the future constantly drove me to take erratic actions just to get through the day. Working the S-Anon program felt as if I was being given a new garment to wear, one I thought couldn't possibly fit me. Fortunately, I did not know where to begin. I say this because I had to slow down long enough to ask for help. I could then see that this new garment fit so many of the S-Anon members I met.

I appreciate the wisdom of how the S-Anon program is broken down into many smaller parts such as: slogans, meetings, working the Steps, and sponsorship. All I need do is to pick one thing to help start my day over again. I am amazed at how most any meeting discussion can turn my thinking toward healthy spiritual principles over and over again — all fitting me. S-Anon always has my size garment, and it's always there for me anytime I need to see things from a different perspective.

Further Reflections...
"We urge you to give serious consideration to how you can use some of these tools to help your recovery...since these tools have been indispensable to our recovery."

Working The S-Anon Program, p. 2

Quiet Time

It's so hard for me to sit down for some quiet time with my Higher Power. I know an uncontrollable fear is at the root of this. I fear the challenges that I must face if I am honest with myself. So here I sit with all my fears. I feel a gentle tugging to stay in the quiet and let it do its work. My Higher Power has given me this precious time alone. I need to get in touch with what's going on with me (and only me) for today. It's time to leave any expectations at the door.

For now, it's time to let go of each little thing that crowds me, even if it means just letting go for one minute at a time. In this quiet, it is just me and my Higher Power. It is in this silence that I realize how little I really do know. Maybe that's the best place to start: humble beginnings. I pray I can be open to whatever comes my way in the quiet. I ask God to help me loosen my grip. I ask Him to help me open up to His will for me. I know I am not alone now.

[Excerpt from *Working the S-Anon Program*, p. 40]

Further Reflections…
"We grew in the faith that a loving and caring Higher Power would protect us. Then we were able to make a decision to trust in that care and seek to do God's will instead of our own."

Working the S-Anon Program, p. 24

Living In Reality

I recently had a huge insight: acceptance is not about ignoring the sexaholic's behavior or my feelings about it; acceptance is about fully acknowledging this reality and my feelings about it.

In the past, I had "accepted" the sexaholic's acting out, his apologies, and his pleas for forgiveness by swallowing my feelings. This allowed us to move on, because I glossed over my own grief. I finally saw that this kind of automatic forgiveness is artificial, delays my grieving and only cause's greater pain in the end. Acceptance has meant taking the time to grieve what I thought I had in my life.

I have found that I can safely deal with my feelings of grief by sharing them with S-Anon program members and my sponsor.

I am finding peace through accepting that sexaholism is a disease and that my reaction to sexaholism is part of that disease. I have hope that my husband and I can work through our problems and sort out decades of sexaholism with the help of S-Anon, SA, and qualified professionals. I also have hope that, with S-Anon's help, I even will be able to forgive my husband someday from a place of peace.

Today I pray for acceptance of the reality of what has happened and is happening, and I pray for God's guidance in dealing with that reality.

Further Reflections…
"As I had feared, it was painful to face the truth, but in doing so I began laying the foundation for the serenity I would come to find."

S-Anon Twelve Steps, p. 20

I Can Laugh at Myself Now

When I am out of balance in my life, I find myself obsessing over the same old situations and then carrying them around like an old bowling bag. At these times I not only lose my sense of humor and my connection with God, I also slip back into relying upon others to make me happy. (I wonder how I can expect others to be happy with me when I am not happy with myself).

Frequently, I do a Tenth Step to help me back off of others and myself. I drop the "bowling bag" (sometimes on my foot). Then I get to laugh at myself and how serious I can be. Someone suggested to me that the next time I notice my shoulders drooping from carrying around that heavy bowling bag, I take the ball out of the bag and roll it toward God so that God can take care of it.

Working the S-Anon program has helped me find laughter and the lighter side of my life. Laughter is healing and is one of the gifts of my recovery. I can actually be silly and have a good time today! I can laugh at myself now and not take things so seriously. S-Anon has given me the freedom to lighten up.

Further Reflections...
"I thought I had good reason to be angry for the rest of my life, but found that I am not hurting inside anymore. I have hope, and I can laugh again. It is a miracle."
Working the S-Anon Program, p. 38

I Started to See My Part

When I first came to S-Anon, I was so hurt and angry that I was unable to keep from exploding at my husband for just about anything. I thought everything was his fault; especially my horrible life.

My sponsor continually encouraged me to put the focus back on myself. She gently suggested that I was perhaps blaming my husband for situations in which I had willingly put myself.

While working Step Four, I started to see my part in creating an unsafe environment for myself, by not setting healthy boundaries. I finally saw that taking myself out of uncomfortable or even dangerous situations was my responsibility, not the sexaholic's.

I need guidance, support, meetings, and most of all, a connection with my Higher Power to keep me focused on a healthy path – The path of S-Anon recovery. The slogan "One Day At A Time" helps to keep me focused.

Today I am so grateful for my recovery and the positive changes in my life. I no longer blow up at my husband. Instead I make a phone call, go to a meeting, or take a walk to connect with my Higher Power. With those supports, I can lovingly look at the reasons for my misery and see some positive choices. "First Things First" reminds me to put the focus on myself and take care of me instead of automatically blaming my husband.

Further Reflections....
"Our human will cannot break the bond of compulsive behavior, but our admission of powerlessness lays a firm foundation upon which to build our lives."

S-Anon Twelve Steps, p. 3

Filling the Vacuum

In my first science class, years ago, I learned a fact that intrigued me: nature abhors a vacuum. I was reminded of that fact of nature recently at an S-Anon meeting when a member spoke words that could have come right from my own mouth — if I had been honest enough to say them.

She spoke of wanting to stop being so judgmental of the sexaholic and others in her family. She shared about surrendering her critical and judgmental attitude to her Higher Power, and how God was replacing that attitude with a spirit of compassion and cooperation. She said she was feeling so much better about herself and others.

I knew that was what I wanted. I didn't want to have to be so "right" all the time. So I prayed to be released from my own judgmental and critical spirit and to be given an attitude of compassion.

I find now I am learning to be more affirming and encouraging — not only to others, but to myself, as well. Since I was given the words from my S-Anon friend, I am beginning to walk alongside my sexaholic with a more understanding heart. A spirit of compassion and cooperation is replacing my judgmental and critical spirit; it is filling the vacuum.

Further Reflection…
"It takes a brave person to step unarmed into the arena of the unknown, desiring only to relate to God and others with honesty and intimacy for the first time."
S-Anon Twelve Steps, p. 64

Came to Believe...

Step Two: Came to believe that a Power greater than ourselves could restore us to sanity.

My understanding of Higher Power has changed numerous times in my twenty-two years of Twelve Step recovery. Initially my understanding of a Higher Power was a sort of gentle, hip, funny, easygoing version of the religious ideal of my youth. Nine years ago, when faced with an extreme challenge in my life, my understanding changed because I found I needed to depend on a Higher Power who was firm and trustworthy, in addition to being gentle and loving.

As I experimented with new understandings of God, I learned that when I searched for truth and love, my faith grew and my Higher Power came to mean much more to me. Over time, my growing faith in the God of my understanding helped me to see that the best direction in my life included sexual abstinence, service, and a sense of humor. When I strive for these things, I am at my best.

Further Reflections
"The wisdom of the ages seems to agree that it is not only all right, but necessary to develop and maintain a concept of God that meets our changing understanding of ourselves and our world, as long as it is a Power greater than ourselves."

S-Anon Twelve Steps, p. 24

Encouraging and Understanding

The dictionary defines "encourage" as to inspire with courage, spirit, or hope. In encouraging and understanding my sexaholic relative, it helps to think of him as another member of S-Anon.

To encourage newcomers in S-Anon, I first try to live by the principles set down in the S-Anon program. As I have gained more serenity and recovery by working the program, I have become more centered and more pleasant to be around. This way I encourage by example, not only in my meeting, but at home with the sexaholic as well.

With newcomers, I try to practice "live and let live." Likewise, I encourage the sexaholic's recovery by respecting his need to attend meetings and to spend time on the phone with sponsors and sponsees, even when I would rather have his attention for our family and myself.

I continue to learn what I can about sexaholism as a disease and its effect on individuals and families, so I can understand myself and help the newcomer. This also increases my understanding of my husband. My increased understanding and compassion for him replaces some of my anger, hurt, and disappointment. Tradition Five is a spiritual principle I am inspired to practice daily.

Further Reflections...
"Each S-Anon Family Group has but one purpose: to help families of sexaholics. We do this by practicing the Twelve Steps of AA ourselves, by encouraging and understanding our sexaholic relatives, and by welcoming and giving comfort to families of sexaholics."

S-Anon's Tradition Five

I Complicated Life with Busyness

I never thought of the slogans as a tool to help me in my recovery from the effects of sexaholism. That all changed for me when I heard another member share about "Keep It Simple," and how that slogan had been such a help to her. Hearing this helped me to stop and reflect on whether I was "Keeping It Simple" in my life. It prompted me to take an inventory of my daily activities, obsessive thinking and the decisions with which I was faced. A direct result of this inventory was discovering that I often stay incredibly busy to distract myself from uncomfortable feelings or to avoid decisions I do not want to make.

Today, I can still clutter my life with too many activities and too many thoughts, as well as looking for complicated answers. But I can now stop before I go overboard and hurt myself through busyness. Sexaholism is only one of the challenges in my life. The fact that I complicate my life by keeping too busy and extending myself beyond my personal limits is challenging whether or not I choose to live with a practicing sexaholic. "Keeping It Simple" is a way of taking care of me and letting God do the rest.

Further Reflections...
"Slogans help many of us focus our thoughts on positive attitudes especially during difficult and stressful times. Although at first they may seem trite or simplistic, they are a form of shorthand, easily remembered in times of need that bring to mind important principles of recovery."

Working the S-Anon Program, p. 12

Tools for the Journey of Growth

I am so grateful for the S-Anon program. It is a journey of growth, sometimes a bumpy and painful journey, yet one filled with wonderful moments of insight and happiness, as well. My growth lets me experience the full range of the emotional spectrum. Today, I am grateful that I have tools that I can depend on and that I am willing to use them.

For example, I can receive peace and a deep serenity through reading Conference Approved Literature each day. Usually the reading speaks right to the issue that has been in my heart and mind. When this happens, I feel so connected to God and the fellowship. I know that I do not take this journey alone, and reading another person's experience inspires me to go on growing.

Using another tool, the telephone, makes me grateful that there is an active and growing fellowship of S-Anons to journey with me. Program phone calls fill me with the spirit of gratitude and with loving feelings. How lucky I am to have S-Anon in my life.

Further Reflections...
"I found that the literature continued to speak to me as I grew in recovery. Many times I thought, 'Wait! That must be a new part to that reading!' No it wasn't, I just heard it with 'new ears!'"

Working the S-Anon Program, p. 16

Doing vs. Believing

For a long time, I struggled with re-living the trauma and pain from the sexaholic's early days of sobriety – the times when I was learning the details of his acting out. Images filled my head, my anxiety rose, and I frequently erupted in anger. It seemed like a vicious cycle: the more I tried to get the images out of my head, the angrier I got. The angrier I got, the faster the images came.

I didn't know how to break the obsessive cycle, so I went back to the basics, reviewing Steps One, Two, and Three. I discovered that while I believed in Step Three, I was having difficulty actually surrendering.

Then it hit me: when my anxiety rose, I became inconsolable — this was the time to surrender! So I put that awareness into action by keeping a God Jar on my desk. Now when I feel anxious, I write down what my anxiety is about, and I release it by putting the slip of paper into the jar and praying a prayer of surrender. If anxiety returns, I look at the jar and remind myself that God is taking care of my concern.

At the end of each month, I pull the slips of paper out of the jar and review them. Then I burn them, knowing I have surrendered. Some months there are enough slips to toast a marshmallow! Still I know that I am taking the actions that have brought serenity into my life.

Further Reflections...
"I now know on a deeper level that the God of my understanding will always be there to strengthen me if I surrender my will and my life."

S-Anon Twelve Steps, p. 32

Truth Spoken Aloud

After many years in another program, I finally started looking at my S-Anon issues. A friend suggested that I call someone she knew in S-Anon. I did not want to make that call, but because I was in so much pain, I finally took the plunge. That night, after thinking about what was said, I was inspired to write the following poem:

Beginning

*I listened with painful tears streaming down my face
She read aloud the story of my life: The S-Anon Problem.
I identified with every word, hated it all,
And was so relieved to hear my truth spoken aloud.
True words, read with love, set me free.*

That was over two years ago, and every time I hear The S-Anon Problem read at our meeting I remember that call and how someone passed the S-Anon program on to me. I continue to be inspired by the love and support of this program and I am grateful for the opportunity to pass it on to others.

Further Reflections…
"Whether or not we were exposed to sexaholism as children, most of us think that we acquired some unhealthy beliefs about ourselves very early in our lives—that we were not worthwhile and lovable, that we were able to control other people's behavior, and that sex was the most important sign of love."

The S-Anon Problem (long version)

I Will Choose to Be Happy and Grateful

Before finding S-Anon, I wasted a lot of time and energy trying to figure out how to manage my problems. I was obsessed with fixing everything that I perceived to be wrong in my life and in the lives of my loved ones. It seemed to me that fixing problems was my role and responsibility in life. Yet because I spent so much time focusing on problems, I was not able to enjoy the many blessings and good things that happen every day.

Recovery has helped me see that I have choices. I can choose to enjoy the day and look for the goodness in my life or I can choose to dwell on what may or may not become a problem. When I choose to look for things for which to be grateful, I am able to find them: my daughter's smile, a joke shared, kind words from a friend or stranger. I experience the love of my Higher Power through the actions of many people.

I am glad that recovery has shown me that I have choices. Today, I will choose to be happy and grateful. When negative thoughts come, I will surrender them to my Higher Power. Thank you, S-Anon, for showing me my choices.

Further Reflections...
"We will become able to surrender our self-defeating behavior. We will find we have the strength and insight to make good choices for ourselves."

Gifts of the S-Anon Program

Changing My Negative Thinking

Wedding anniversaries are often a painful reminder of the turbulent relationship I have with my spouse. We were re-married in a beautiful ceremony in the Caribbean Islands. Two days later we separated, after a fight over his sexual behavior.

At the present time we are separated. My husband was out of town this past anniversary, but he left me a beautiful card. At first, I felt loved and grateful after receiving the card, but when I spoke to him that night, I found he was traveling with a female co-worker. In anger, I burned the card and stuffed the ashes into an envelope, along with an angry note. As I walked to mail it to him, my thoughts were racing. I imagined trying to explain to police that the white ashes were from an anniversary card! I didn't mail it.

I recognized that my feelings of anger and hurt were coming from inside me. Once I took responsibility for my negative thinking, I felt a sense of relief. I realized I couldn't always control an unhealthy thought from entering my mind, but I do have choices about how to respond to that thought. I can use the tools of my program, by connecting with my Higher Power, and sharing the thought with my sponsor or another S-Anon member. I can take action to change my thinking. Taking action will lead me to find the serenity I long for in my life.

Further Reflections…
"If I just stick with the program and stick with the tools, I know that I can get beyond whatever the difficulty is."
Recovering Together: Issues Faced by Couples
(Rev. Booklet 2007) p. 10

Recovery with Family Members

Very early in recovery, before I really connected with other members of S-Anon, I tried to deal with my pain by talking with family members. I shared my feelings and what I was learning in my new S-Anon program. My secret hope was that these conversations would convey recovery principles that would somehow make my family more understanding of my dilemma. Not surprisingly, my plan did not work. I was placing unrealistic demands upon my family, as well as unstated expectations. These conversations only set me up for further resentment and pain.

As I finally began connecting with members of my S-Anon group, it occurred to me that God was providing me with new people with whom I could share my pain, concerns, revelations, and questions. I found that my fellow S-Anons usually were much better equipped than my family members to support me in ways that were healthy and affirming. Connecting with group members has helped me let go of the expectations I had of my loved ones. By surrendering my expectations, I have become free to relate to my family just as they are. Today, I actually have begun to enjoy being with my family. Amazingly, by letting go I have found a deeper connection with them – just what I wanted all along.

Further Reflections...
"It was important to find someone other than a relative to confide in and to be as honest with that person as possible, both about our situation and about our own feelings."
S-Anon Newcomers Booklet, p. 15

Honesty

I am noticing that the word "honesty" is surfacing over and over again in my readings, conversations, and meditations. I know that when I pay attention to coincidences such as these, there can be lessons for me to learn.

As I wait for that lesson to be fully revealed, I recall that the Fourth Step gave me a way to discover just how dishonest I could be with myself and others in order to avoid painful situations. I frequently held onto my own opinions silently, rather than share them with others, just so I could avoid potential disagreement. Sharing my inventory with my sponsor in the Fifth Step gave me the opportunity to admit my faults and allow another person to see me as I really am. That was the beginning of my journey toward honesty. Working the rest of the Steps revealed more insights. For instance, the Eleventh Step helped me see that when I am not honest, I am not in conscious contact with my Higher Power and I am not allowing God or others to know who I truly am.

As I am reminded about honesty today, I recommit myself to listening to my Higher Power and to practicing the attitude of honesty.

Further Reflections...
"As I connect at deeper levels with my Higher Power's love for me, I feel a greater ability to be honest... ."
Working the S-Anon Program, p. 49

More Serene and Fulfilling

The longer I attended S-Anon meetings, the more I realized that the tools of the program would work in all areas of my life and in all of my relationships, not just in my relationship with the sexaholic.

Detaching with love, for example, helped me not to be drawn into arguments with my family of origin. Certain family members were angry when I would no longer join in the arguments, but working my S-Anon program strengthened my ability to remove myself from unhealthy conflict situations.

In my workplace, using the slogan "Keep It Simple" was a gift for two reasons. One, it guided me not to concern myself with office issues that did not involve me. Two, it helped me undo the damage I'd done to myself over the years as a result of exhaustively trying to please people by anticipating their wishes instead of simply asking their preferences.

With the sexaholic, my family, my co-workers, and others, I have learned that the tools of the program indeed make my life "more serene and fulfilling."

Further Reflections.....
"Each member uses the tools that work best for him or her, and we have even found that some things that did not work for us in early recovery become mainstays of our program later on. We use what helps us today and leave the rest for later."

Working the S-Anon Program, p. 2

Not Focusing on Her Disease

When I found out that my wife was a sexaholic, I was hurt and angry, but also relieved, because it confirmed there was a real basis for my suspicions. I determined that I would study the problem and come up with a logical strategy to resolve these issues. The problem was my feelings were not logical and sexaholism does not follow my rules; soon I felt defeated. Then I found S-Anon and discovered that by "studying" her disease, I was distracting myself from taking care of me.

Through working the Steps I have come to understand the choices I have made in my life, as well as my part in this relationship. I am learning how to trust God and live Step Eleven. I have found that by working the Steps and checking in with my sponsor, I am more aware when something is wrong, even though the sexaholic might be telling me everything is all right.

Through the help of S-Anon, I am learning to value myself rather than define myself by the relationship. I am learning to stop focusing on her behavior and to start focusing on the next right thing for me to do. I have begun to trust my instincts and believe that, with the help of my Higher Power, I will be okay, no matter what.

Further Reflections...
"Just as we did not cause the sexaholic's acting out, we cannot 'cure' it — the sexual sobriety of the sexaholic is not our responsibility."

S-Anon Newcomers Booklet, p. 4

A Good Start

I remember being eager to do my first Fourth Step inventory. In looking back, I think that was because I wrote everyone else's inventory rather than my own. That was as searching and fearless as I could get at the time. I recall anticipating my Fifth Step with more trepidation because I was sure I would be judged. Early in life I had learned "don't air your dirty laundry in public." So giving my Fourth Step to a "stranger" seemed wrong. I feared I would be shedding a "bad light" on family. In truth, I had been doing that anyway every time I called a friend or relative to complain and gossip about someone else.

I gained courage from hearing about the Fifth Step experiences of other S-Anons. I was motivated by how so many of them felt remarkably relieved afterward. I prayed for willingness to do the Fifth Step. Months after completing my inventory, I met with my sponsor and finally did my Fifth Step. As I read my Fourth Step to her, we laughed and talked for almost three hours. She was a great listener. When I finished, she said, "That was a good start". So here I am, a few Fifth Steps and sponsors later, and I am writing yet another Fourth Step — this time keeping the focus on myself. I love the process of the S-Anon program. I have the Steps to help guide me on my recovery path.

Further Reflections…
"Finally it seems that genuine humility cannot be reached without our admitting our character defects to another human being."

S-Anon Twelve Steps, p. 52

Taking Responsibility

Before finding out that sexaholism existed in my home, a large part of my life was spent feeling a little insane. Even though I couldn't put my finger on it, I felt something was wrong. I found myself behaving in ways that only brought more shame to my already diminished sense of self. On the outside I was furious at whatever was happening in my home and I raged at everyone; but on the inside, I felt "less-than", and could do nothing to stop the insanity.

S-Anon helped me name the disease of sexaholism, and accept that it was active in my home. S-Anon also helped me see that I am powerless over sexaholism, but I am not helpless. I can take responsibility for my own actions. I do not have to berate someone else to feel better about myself. It took time and help from my Higher Power for me to remember not to react, but to respond in my interactions with others. As I gained control over my own actions and attitudes, I also gained dignity and serenity. I can have serenity and feel good about myself, whether or not someone else chooses sobriety.

Further Reflections...
"Our serenity depends upon changing our attitudes and eliminating our self-defeating behaviors, so we commit ourselves to our own recovery. We take full responsibility for our actions and reactions."

Keys to S-Anon Recovery (long version)

Praying Individually

Recently I found myself in several relationship struggles: needing to make an apology at work, having to be uncomfortably honest with a friend about her having hurt my feelings, and desperately trying to stay out of a conflict between my sister and my mother. On top of all that, I had to talk with two sponsees who were not working their program to our mutually agreed upon expectations. It felt like a snowball rolling downhill about to become an avalanche.

I called another S-Anon member. Her words of wisdom: Have you tried praying about these situations and praying for the people individually? While I had prayed about it all in general, I had not yet prayed for each individual. I started to feel some relief right away. I didn't have to do a thing at this point but pray and wait. It was the right thing to do; the answers became clear one by one.

Whenever I want to have the answer right away or feel I need to make things happen, it is a clue that I'm trying to control outcomes and I'm active in my own role in the disease of sexaholism. I've learned that this is the time to stop and let go through prayer.

Further Reflections...
"For we are now on a different basis; the basis of trusting and relying upon God. We trust infinite God rather than our finite selves. We are in the world to play the role He assigns. Just to the extent that we do as we think He would have us, and humbly rely on Him, does he enable us to match calamity with serenity."

Alcoholics Anonymous, p. 68

Stay or Leave?

After being in recovery for awhile I became aware of how much living with active sexaholism was hurting me. I knew I needed help and felt fortunate to have a wise S-Anon sponsor who helped me stay focused on the spiritual principles of the program. I needed to set boundaries for myself. I wanted to stop being angry, sarcastic, and spiteful. I worried how my behavior was also affecting our young daughter. My behavior improved as I worked my program, but my husband continued his active sexaholism. I eventually came to the place where I separated myself physically from him.

Our divorce, though painful, seemed to be my best option. I continue to work an S-Anon program because I am still greatly affected by the disease of sexaholism. We have a very important bond, our daughter. As she grows up, I am sure there will be lots of challenges to be faced in cooperating with her dad. With the help of my S-Anon program, I will be a good mom to her, and I am ever so grateful for that.

Further Reflections...
"As we now ask God to remove our shortcomings, even more tranquility will come to us. We can enjoy peace for longer periods of time."

S-Anon Twelve Steps, p. 74

Came to Save My Marriage

I first came to S-Anon to save my marriage, and I was willing to do anything to accomplish this. By working the Steps of the program, I learned to let go of the outcome completely. S-Anon provided me with a safe place to share my feelings. I learned about the tools of the program from listening to other members and reading the literature. Real serenity came when I started working Step Three. I turned my husband and marriage over to the care of my Higher Power, and a huge load was taken off my shoulders. Only then, was I able to focus on myself in a healthier way.

"One Day at a Time" seems like such a trite and overused expression, but it is one of the mainstays of my program. Today I can refrain from taking my husband's (kids, boss's, friend's, parents') inventory. I can admit my powerlessness and I can let go of my fears of the future. Today I can be grateful for what I have. I can work my program, call my sponsor, pray, and meditate. I get confused and frightened when I try to handle the rest of my life. One Day at a Time is a simple slogan that reminds me to deal with today and turn over everything else to God.

Further Reflections...
"I had been sure if I were just good enough, smart enough, or had tried long enough and hard enough, things would turn out O.K.—or the way I wanted."
Working the S-Anon Program, p. 39

The Courage to Change Myself

One S-Anon tool is the Serenity Prayer. Another version of that prayer is "God, grant me the serenity to accept the people I cannot change, the courage to change myself and the wisdom to know I can." This tells me that I CAN change myself and that God can give me the courage to do so.

I put these principles into practice when my husband directed me to tell our son to mow the grass. In the past I accepted the messenger role between my husband and my son. I was caught between my angry son, who did not want to do the chore, and my husband, who became angry when the chore was not completed. This time I changed the things I could by telling my husband that he needed to tell our son what he wanted done. I was not going to relay that message. This initially created conflict, but it took me out of the middle. I had the courage to change my behavior, to say no.

I've learned that courage does not mean the absence of fear. Courage is the ability to walk through changes that would have overwhelmed me previously. As I enlist God's help, my shortcomings have changed into more positive ways of acting. I consciously think of the way I want to act, and then implement new behaviors. It hasn't been easy, but the results have been worth it.

Further Reflections...
"I am learning to trust myself to rise to the occasion as a problem presents itself. I will have the resources when I need them. I don't have to control the outcome but can learn to trust the process. This allows me to be less afraid of the future."

Working the S-Anon Program, p. 42

Sexaholism — A Family Disease

Over time, I have grown to understand that there are many similarities among S-Anon members. Although I arrived thinking I was unique, my experience in meetings has taught me otherwise. I remember the first time I shared a well kept secret with my S-Anon group. Although I was sure I would be thought of poorly, I gathered the courage. I shared that after my husband's disclosure of the details of his acting out, I daydreamed that his life would take the ultimate geographic cure—that he would die on a business trip. The reaction of group members astounded me. Heads around the table began to nod in recognition and there was even some laughter.

Later my sponsor shared that she had a similar experience. She reminded me, that the nodding heads and laughter were recognizing in one another the insane thinking of those affected by the disease of sexaholism. She said that sexaholism is a family disease because entire families as well as extended family can be affected. She said that she considers those of us sharing in a group a family, because we can share and be supported in similar experiences.

When left untreated, the disease can take us down very dismal roads. When we have the courage to share a secret, we all gain healthy understanding about our common problem and the healthy growth we can achieve in S-Anon.

Further Reflections...
"No matter how we tried to struggle against it, deny it or minimize its effects, the failure of our efforts to cope with sexaholism brought us to the point of despair. This is what we mean when we say in the First Step, 'our lives had become unmanageable.'"

The S-Anon Problem (Short Version)

Carrying the Message – Sharing Hope

I like sharing the hope I have experienced from my S-Anon meetings. I feel hope that life can be better by practicing the spiritual principles of the program. Over time, I have learned that discernment about when, and with whom, I share my experiences has become a healthy boundary for me.

For a long time I found it difficult to understand that a cry for help does not mean it is a time for me to meddle in other people's lives. First I ask for God's will for me, and how I can be of service. By learning the importance of listening from my meetings, I listen better and don't interrupt with my "answers". I might ask if the person is O.K. or if he or she needs to talk. I can offer a hug, a listening ear or, perhaps, just have an attitude of quiet support. Sometimes, just being available to a person in turmoil is carrying the message. If I pay attention, I am usually guided as to what might be the most respectful way for me to carry the message.

By regularly attending S-Anon meetings, I have been reaching out to many newcomers. I feel joy in being able to give away what I have been freely given. I give by being there, listening, sharing my experiences when appropriate, and sharing how the Twelve Steps and the S-Anon tools have helped me. When I reach my hand out to others in a healthy way, my life keeps getting better.

Further Reflections...
"We find that careful listening with our hearts and our heads can help us to share with newcomers in a loving way."

Working the S-Anon Program, p. 102

I Chose to Respond

One day, my spouse seemed especially irritable. I asked if he was O.K., and he responded by handing me a stack of papers. I immediately read the papers and discovered they were a new disclosure about his sexaholism. Today I know that when faced with a sweeping disclosure from the sexaholic, I can say, "that's too much information for me today" I now know that hearing too many details about his story damages my serenity. Yet I didn't see that choice on that particular day – I read the papers even after realizing what they were.

Before recovery, this would have triggered a downward spiral. I would have obsessed about the disclosure, allowing my mind to create even more details. I would have questioned him and demanded answers, taking up the familiar victim role. I would have considered forcing some immediate action about the relationship.

That day I chose to respond, rather than react to the upsetting news. I chose to be gentle with myself and stayed with my feelings, not carrying around shame about his behavior. I surrendered the information to my Higher Power. I chose to live in that day only, not making major decisions about my marriage until I was in a clear frame of mind. I chose to focus on doing the next right thing: I took a walk, I went to a meeting, I talked with my sponsor. I trusted God to guide me when the time was right. I still had serenity that day because I chose to respond, rather than react.

Further Reflections...
"I know honesty is a tool of my program, but hopefully it is a gentle tool and not a tool with which I abuse my partner."

Working the S-Anon Program, p. 63

A Serenity Boost

I came to S-Anon a very short time before moving to a new city with my partner. It was a well-timed gift.

When I first started attending meetings, my goal was to learn how to live with a sexaholic on a daily basis. Learning to live life in the present and "doing the next right thing" with the help of my Higher Power were a real help to me. Coming to see my own level of denial about many aspects of my life was painful, but it was helpful to understand that I am a work in progress. Meeting such wonderful friends in this program really helped me become acclimated to my new hometown and to my new "eyes open" way of life.

A few months after beginning the program, I attended my first local S-Anon convention. It was a wonderful event and I returned home with a serene recovery boost. I found I needed it, because the next week I discovered my partner had relapsed. I was shocked and disappointed.

Thankfully, I had my convention "booster shot." I was prepared with recovery tools and the reinforced knowledge that his relapse was not my fault and I could not work his program for him. While it was not an easy time for me, I was so grateful I had this program and my wonderful fellow S-Anon members to help me through it with new-found serenity.

Further Reflections...
"A new life has been given us or, if you prefer, 'a design for living' that really works."

Alcoholics Anonymous (3rd ed.), p. 28

Giving in Service

When thinking about service I think of a line in a prayer: "For it is in giving that we receive…" quoted in the Al-Anon piece of literature "Just For Today". When I practice service in a healthy way, I "get out of myself" and I find that I'm less controlling. There are many ways for me to serve. I can start with the smallest and simplest things, such as setting up chairs or making coffee. I can work my way to other opportunities as they arise, like leading a meeting or volunteering to be our group's treasurer.

For sometime I didn't feel worthy or ready to perform service. I was afraid of making mistakes, but was reminded that I wasn't alone. There were others who would help me and guidelines that I could follow. Making myself available for service provided me with opportunities to develop talents I didn't know I had. It affirmed my work in my program and gave me much more than I could give.

Further Reflections...
"God doesn't call the qualified. God qualifies those who are called. Am I listening?"

[Al-Anon] Hope For Today, p.101

Acting Lovingly Toward Myself

At times I still have difficulty detaching with love and compassion from the sexaholic's behavior. When I react to my husband's behavior I end up feeling angry at myself and resentful toward my spouse. I have found that I sometimes act out of my own neediness in my marriage. I am doing the exact thing that I want to blame my spouse for: not taking care of myself.

I have heard the wisdom that I don't have to go to every fight that I am invited to. I often have difficulty remembering this bit of wisdom when I want something different to happen, or when I am triggered back to painful memories from my childhood.

Some of the tools I now use to help me stay focused on what the next right thing for me to do include using the slogans "How Important Is It?" and "First Things First." An important action I try to remember to take is doing at least one loving thing for me today.

If I act lovingly toward myself and am honest about how I am feeling, I find I am much more emotionally available to give to others. This helps me to know when I need to pull back and detach with love and compassion, for myself, as well as for the sexaholic.

Further Reflections...
"A slogan I'm using a lot lately is 'First Things First.' I am reminded that 'First Things' might include participating in something I enjoy or taking time to relax, praying and meditating, or working a Step."

Working the S-Anon Program, p. 13

Distorted Perceptions of Self

I was physically battered by my alcoholic father in the name of "discipline." He would tell me that I was bad and deserved a beating. It made an indelible impression on me as I was very young. As an adult, I continued to believe what my father had said. I brought my low self-esteem into my adult relationships. I chose to marry a man who was an alcoholic and a sexaholic, from whom I received similar messages. I allowed myself to take on the blame and shame of his lusting and infidelities. I believed many of his blaming accusations and reproaches. These experiences added to my old belief, that I was bad and deserved to be maltreated.

Thank God for my S-Anon friends and my therapist who all helped me challenge these misperceptions. They helped me see the need to recover my self and to see myself accurately – with mercy and compassion. I am now beginning to recover from the trauma of being sexually betrayed and emotionally abused. I am no longer taking on blame or responsibility for other people's choices. I no longer have to be so hard on myself. My recovery includes spending time with people who love me and accept me just as I am. I now know I have a Higher Power who is not my husband or my father.

Further Reflections...
"I learned that although I was definitely a participant in unhealthy relationships, the shortcomings of others are not my fault. It has been painful at times, but I have learned how to find serenity, healing, and love in my life."

Working the S-Anon Program, p. 80

Changing Perceptions

Living by the slogan "One Day at a Time" changes how I perceive myself. In recovery, I live in the present. My self-perception is now much more dependent on my relationship with my Higher Power and much less situational and dependent on what I receive from others.

As I grow in faith that my Higher Power loves me unconditionally, I am becoming less judgmental about myself. My goal in recovery is no longer to allow my self-perception to be molded by those around me, especially by the sexaholic or by my mother's distorted view of who I am. I pray to accept the love and care of my Higher Power today, and to reflect that love for me by striving to love and accept myself.

Further Reflections…
"With every hardship we face, our Higher Power also provides an outlet. One of those ways out is to change our own attitudes with the help of our Higher Power and the S-Anon program."

S-Anon Twelve Steps, p. 16

Room To Grow

My first few years of recovering from the effects of sexaholism were very difficult. Often I did not feel safe around my recovering sexaholic spouse. I was grateful for S-Anon service opportunities for which my sponsor encouraged me to volunteer. Service gave me space from the uncomfortable things that were going on in our home — space I needed to work my program.

Volunteering to do service also gave me a chance to learn how to work with others by using the spiritual principles of the Twelve Traditions. Adhering to the Traditions was not always easy. My ego was constantly challenged, and I got to look closer at my defects of character through my Step work.

My sponsor instilled in me the spiritual significance of giving away what I have been given. God has certainly used the service opportunities I've had in S-Anon to change my life. My ability to cooperate with others – in the program, at home, at work and in my family – has greatly improved. I have developed a deepened sense of compassion and patience for others and myself. I have learned how important it is to be fully informed before making a decision. I have been increasingly aware that things happen in God's time. I am grateful for so much. S-Anon has given me room to grow.

Further Reflections…
"Any activity that makes it possible for the meeting to take place and to be a source of hope and recovery for the newcomer is Twelfth Step work."

Working the S-Anon Program, p. 98

Discovering the Real Me

As I strive to recover from the effects of living with and loving a sexaholic, I am uncovering a new self-awareness. I am learning many positive things about myself that I used to attribute only to my spouse. For instance, I often think of my husband as a strong, emotionally aware person, who is sensitive, kind, and loving. I never attributed those positive characteristics to myself. I did not feel worthwhile and lovable most of my life.

Through working the Steps and talking to others in S-Anon, I saw that a lot of my negative perceptions go back to childhood. Being in a relationship with a sexually-addicted person, helped those misperceptions grow and flourish.

Holding onto my distorted beliefs influenced my behavior and helped prolong the active sexaholism in our home. I believed I was neither lovable nor capable. I thought I needed the sexaholic for my stability and security and to feel lovable – the very things I later came to understand that active sexaholism was destroying.

With the help of S-Anon, I am starting to believe that I am lovable and capable. My perception that someone has to provide for me is just another distortion.

Further Reflections...
"One day while watching small children play, I realized they were the healthiest, most sane people I knew... They definitely had lives of their own and had no false shame. They liked and enjoyed being themselves... I can strive to bring the healthy attitudes expressed by those children into my adult life."

S-Anon Twelve Steps, p. 19-20

Hope in the Form of a Smile

I have been recovering from a serious medical condition. Friends have been wonderful about helping me, despite my feelings of unworthiness. Recently, a friend and I headed to the mall. As she helped me step up from the car to the curb, I fell.

Somehow I was pulled back into a standing position. This is when those old feelings of failure and inadequacy, coupled with the thoughts of how the other person must feel, started creeping in —I haven't been working hard enough in physical therapy. And, my friend must feel guilty for "allowing" me to fall. My foot began to swell. I felt embarrassed and I thought I would be more of burden if I asked her to help ice my ankle. I ignored taking care of myself.

I started making program calls. I was able to see how self destructive I had been, and just how important it was that I be gentle with myself. I saw my medical specialist, who diagnosed my problem. The difficulty with balance was a result of the steroids I needed to take. My Higher Power made it even clearer — it was not my fault that I fell, and I am not the failure I thought I was. A streak of hope came across my face in the form of a smile.

S-Anon continues to help me understand that whenever I accept myself as worthy of love, I am open to joy, happiness, and laughter in my life. I am learning to accept myself as I am, sometimes clumsy, not perfect, and loved just as I am.

Further Reflections...
"Today I can take myself and my circumstances more lightly. I can even allow joy and laughter to be part of a difficult experience."

[Al-Anon] *Courage to Change, p. 205*

Good Enough

After working the S-Anon program for some time, I realized my fear of abandonment had influenced my attitudes and actions my entire life. My father died when I was very young. This was clearly was the root of why I continued to expect to be abandoned in relationships. All the changes, challenges, and wounds after my father's death reinforced my fear that I wasn't good enough.

This affected my life in a number of ways. The men I chose for serious relationships turned out to be either incapable of commitment or emotionally unavailable. It was as though I unconsciously set myself up for repeated abandonment. Another example was my faith. While I believed that God loved me and would always be with me, there was a disconnection between what my head knew and what my heart felt. It wasn't until I had the very down-to-earth, practical experience of working this program that I came fully to trust God – for the past, the present, and the future.

Working the S-Anon program has taught me a new lesson: I will never be abandoned by God – the one who loves me the most and considers me definitely good enough.

Further Reflections...
"We are now on a different basis: the basis of trusting and relying upon God. We trust infinite God rather than our finite selves."

[AA] As Bill Sees It, p. 265

Detachment

Detaching from sexaholism has been one of the most difficult feats I have ever attempted. I had been so hurt and wounded by the effects of sexaholism that I was reactive and triggered by every aspect of the disease. After decades of living in my own denial and fantasy to cope with the lies and betrayals by my partner, the idea of detachment was a foreign one. So when I came to S-Anon and first tried to detach from active sexaholism, it wasn't surprising that I could not. I was powerless over my own reactions. When I was triggered, I ended up screaming and shaming the sexaholic, leaving myself emotionally exhausted.

Through regular S-Anon meetings, phone calls, Step work, prayer, and meditation, I was given a reprieve by my Higher Power from my unmanageability. I was able to begin detaching from the sexaholic. Now, some years later, I have developed compassion for my partner, even though he continues to act out sexually. I have also gained compassion for myself, realizing my previous actions came from living in the family disease of sexaholism. Now I find that when I detach, I can do so with love.

Further Reflections...
"While I'm still committed to my spouse, my commitment to him has changed because I see him as such a different person now. I used to be so committed to other people. But I've had a strong dose of reality and I've come out of denial. I'm a lot more committed to myself today because I'm learning who I am and what I need."

Recovering Together: Issues Faced by Couples
(Rev. Booklet 2007) p. 16

Awakened to a New Concept

Years ago, I started picking up lost coins on the ground. One time, I noticed a coin's date was the birth year of one of my children. I had been looking for ways to increase prayer in my life, so I decided each time I found a coin with a birth year of one of my children, I would pray for that child. Even after I began my recovery in S-Anon, I continued the habit.

One day, while my son was on a trip, I found three coins with his birth year. I panicked, thinking that finding these coins must mean he was in trouble and needed prayers. I left an urgent message for him to call. He did call; he was fine. Then my youngest daughter left for a three-month trip. The day after she left, I found a coin with her birth year and, again, began to panic, thinking that something was terribly wrong. Immediately, a strong real-ization came to me. Finding a coin didn't necessarily mean a prayer was needed. I could choose to let the coins simply remind me that I had turned over the care of my children to my Higher Power.

After a while, it occurred to me I hadn't found a coin in quite some time. My sponsor suggested, "Maybe your Higher Power believes you don't need the coins any more." I realized then I had learned to trust my children to the care of my Higher Power.

Further Reflections...
"We have awakened to a concept of a loving God in our lives. We truly have been changed."
Working the S-Anon Program, p. 28

We Are All Winners

I never thought I belonged in a Twelve Step program. I thought people who attended those programs were inferior and I did not want to spend my time with "losers." I thought I would never fit in and yet I did. At my very first meeting, not only did I hear my own feelings voiced through the words of the other S-Anons, the nodding heads told me they identified with my story, too. Halfway through my first meeting I realized that the other "losers" in the room were people I would be proud to know and with whom I would actually choose to spend time. I sensed that I could rely on them for help.

At every S-Anon meeting I attend, I meet people whose thoughts and ideas touch me. By attending meetings regularly, I practice ways to develop and maintain healthy, loving relationships. I now have friends in this program, people I trust and with whom I enjoy spending time. I have learned to listen to those who have differing points of view and accept other S-Anons just as they are. None of us are alone. We are all "winners" just by making the effort to attend meetings and work together toward a better life.

Further Reflections...
"Meetings give us a place where we can be ourselves and be unconditionally accepted."

Working the S-Anon Program, p. 3

Words and Action

I n the past I found it is easy to say "I'm sorry," because I anticipated forgiveness. My apology would flow easily, and I often believed that all was forgiven. I could just go on as if I had fixed everything. My attitude was "There, I said it. Now, I'm done."

S-Anon taught me that words and actions must match. That means that when I apologize, I must take a risk and apologize with my behavior, as well. I've heard it called making a "living amends" for the harm I have done. I try to follow the guidance of my Higher Power and my sponsor or an S-Anon friend in deciding which of my behaviors needs changing and how best to initiate my amends. I couple my amends with prayer.

Today, I turn my will over to God and ask God that the words and actions of my amends be heard and felt in the hearts of those I have harmed.

Further Reflections...
"The readiness to take the full consequences of our past acts, and to take responsibility for the well-being of others at the same time, is the very spirit of Step Nine."

Alcoholics Anonymous, p. 87

A Precious Child

I am grateful that I no longer shame and berate myself with cutting criticisms over past failures and shortcomings. Today, I encourage myself, like a loving mother encouraging her child as she goes down the playground slide for the first time: Come on! You can do it! That's it! You're doing it! I'm so proud of you!

Through working the S-Anon program, I've come to believe that I really am a precious child of a loving Higher Power, deserving of being treated with loving acceptance by myself. I do this today by listening to myself, and, when I harshly put myself down, I tell myself that those thoughts are part of my past behavior. I replace those cruel words with gentle encouragement and loving self-approval.

Living with the effects of sexaholism can be challenging. There are days when I think I've forgotten all the lessons I've learned in S-Anon, but when I stop to connect with my Higher Power, I lovingly am reminded that I am doing the very best that I can. I strive to give myself the love and acceptance to which I've always been entitled as a very worthwhile child of God.

Further Reflections...
"Today I'm grateful that I can trust that I will always be in the care of my Higher Power whose perspective is so much wider than my own, and that with each decision I face, I can choose His will for my life with confidence."

S-Anon Twelve Steps, p. 33

Tolerance and Acceptance

As I looked around the room in my S-Anon meeting one evening, I was struck by the amount of love and tenderness I felt for each person there. We were all doing the very best that we could to overcome the effects of sexaholism in our lives. I saw a Higher Power at work in the lives of others and I felt tremendous hope. Tolerance and acceptance had begun to blossom for me in S-Anon and I even found my new attitude spilling over into all aspects of my life.

I am more accepting of my spouse's choices. I am more tolerant of my daughter's differences. I find I am beginning to love and embrace their humanness. Gentle, tender acceptance of myself has followed my acceptance of others. By loving and trusting others, I am learning to love and trust myself. I am learning to embrace the humanness in all of us and to trust my Higher Power's hand in my life.

Further Reflections...
"The love and support we got when we shared with and learned from other people who had similar experiences and feelings became a basis upon which to build a new life."

S-Anon Newcomers Booklet, p. 1

I Will Not Abandon Myself

I n living with sexaholism, I found myself sacrificing what I wanted out of life and feeling resentful about it. I would recommit myself to the relationship, accepting it as a challenge to hang in there and try harder. Nothing changed, and each time I felt a sense of loss, sadness, and abandonment.

After I came to S-Anon, I accepted that I was powerless over sexaholism and that the only choices I really had were about myself. With the help of others in the S-Anon program, I learned that boundaries don't mean "no, you can't," but rather "no, I won't." I worked to set boundaries for myself that included no longer participating in behaviors that felt uncomfortable to me. I finally began to take care of me.

As I became more connected with myself and my Higher Power, my connection with the sexaholic grew less enmeshed. I gave myself lots of room to grow and heal. My long-time fear of being abandoned actually started to be remedied as I no longer abandoned myself.

With the help I found in S-Anon, I now am committed to making choices that are healthy for me. With the help of my Higher Power, I will not abandon myself again.

Further Reflections...
"We remind ourselves that we are powerless over the behavior caused by sexaholism. We ask a Higher Power to help us to stop blaming and trying to control the sexaholic; the sobriety of the sexaholic is not our responsibility. We realize we cannot find serenity for ourselves if we continue to focus on someone else's recovery, so we commit ourselves to our own recovery."

The Keys to S-Anon Recovery

The Peace Acceptance Brings

When it came to accepting that my partner was addicted to lust, I felt I went through the stages of grief – like accepting a death. I went from "That can't be!" to "How did this happen?" to "Why me?" to "How could he love me, yet stab me in the heart?"

There were so many feelings to work through – disbelief, humiliation, anger, betrayal, and more. I needed to acknowledge my feelings and be patient while I worked through them. After some time of talking about my feelings in meetings and with my sponsor and working Step Three, I started to feel some relief. Acceptance came when I realized I had no control over anything except me and my attitude toward my situation.

At first it was scary to surrender my attempts to control the sexaholic and my circumstances, but once I did, peace followed. While I can still struggle with acceptance, I find staying in the moment and letting go of worry about the future enables me to maintain the peace acceptance brings.

Further Reflections....
" need to concentrate not so much on what needs to be changed in the world as on what needs to be changed in me and in my attitudes."

Alcoholics Anonymous (4th ed), p. 417

I Can Only Change Myself

Recently, my sponsor and I were discussing an invitation I had received to reapply for a professional position. There were several people advocating for me to interview for the job. I had been daydreaming about how I would impress my supporters and how everyone enthusiastically would recognize my unique qualifications.

My sponsor's response brought me down to earth: "Just do your footwork, trust God and believe that no matter what happens, the outcome will be exactly the way it is supposed to be. Nothing will be a loss."

With that, I realized that I, once again, was imagining that somehow I could change other people. I thought if I was just "good enough," everything would work out my way. I had fallen back into the same unhealthy thinking pattern that had caused so much unmanageability in my life with the sexaholic.

I took my cue from the Serenity Prayer, asking my Higher Power to help me find the courage to change the things I could. I took contrary action by doing something different from my usual way of doing things: I reapplied for the position, and I kept my feet on the ground by using the tools of the S-Anon program and placing the outcome in my Higher Power's hands.

Further Reflections...
"The serenity prayer... involves taking control of myself and letting go of my control of others' actions and opinions. It is unrealistic to expect everyone to like me. With such an expectation, I set myself up to fail and give myself an excuse to blame that failure on others. I can't change other people, but I can change my own attitudes."

Working the S-Anon Program, p. 42

I Am Enough

I had felt unloved and unlovable in the relationship with my sexaholic husband. Each time he acted out, my self-esteem sank a little lower; so I tried to change myself to please him. I thought if I were somehow "more" he wouldn't feel the need to act out. The pain of believing that I was responsible for the sexaholic being drawn elsewhere was heartbreaking.

Through S-Anon, I came to see that regardless of anything I tried to do to control my husband's behavior, he was still an active sexaholic. I came to realize that the shame and self-hate that I inflicted upon myself is a characteristic of my disease, and that was what I needed to change — not my looks, but how I thought about myself and how I took care of myself.

Today I understand that my husband's behavior was never about my not being enough. I am recovering my self-esteem, and I am respecting myself enough to step out of the way of this devastating disease. With the support of my group and my Higher Power, I am learning not to take my husband's behavior personally. Without S-Anon, I would never have discovered this, and I never would have found the love and level of self-care I now have for myself.

Further Reflections...
"...we are loved and accepted just as we are. Feelings of failure and inadequacy will be replaced by self-confidence and independence of spirit. We will no longer expect other people to provide us with an identity or a sense of self-worth. We will find the courage to be true to ourselves."
Gifts of the S-Anon Program

Sex – One Expression of Intimacy and Love

Prior to working the S-Anon program, my definition of intimacy was having sex. If my partner had sex with me, that meant we were in love. The first time I heard The S-Anon Problem read out loud was my first clue that something might be wrong with my definition.

Changing life-long beliefs can be as hard as changing life-long habits. Yet like most changes, it can be done. I started changing my beliefs about sex and intimacy with baby steps. I did this through prayer, meditation, writing, and spending time listening to others share ideas and experiences about sex and intimacy.

After I started that process of change, it occurred to me that my first true experience with intimacy was in S-Anon meetings where I shared my feelings honestly, even if that meant crying. By the time I completed my Fourth and Fifth Steps, my definition of intimacy had changed quite a bit. Now I define intimacy as being emotionally vulnerable – sharing my true self with another person. I have come to understand that sex is just one expression out of many possible expressions of love. For me, the choice to be intimate is the most important sign of love.

Further Reflections...
"We acquired some unhealthy beliefs about ourselves very early in our lives—that we were not worthwhile and lovable, that we were able to control other peoples behavior, and that sex was the most important sign of love."

The S-Anon Problem (Short Version)

Spiritual Awakenings

When I was new in the program, I thought that S-Anon was either about getting the sexaholic sober or leaving the relationship. It wasn't long before I was "awakened" to the knowledge that it was not a mistake that I was in a relationship with a sexaholic – I had been attracted to them my whole life. A key spiritual awakening came soon after: S-Anon was about healing for me, regardless of whether or not I was in a relationship with a sexaholic.

I had a different kind of spiritual awakening when I grasped the true meaning of the Third Step and finally felt safe to turn my will and my life over to the care of a Power greater than myself. In that shift, I knew that the God of my understanding loved me, and that feelings of fear or doubt were irrelevant. My Higher Power would always take care of me. With that spiritual awakening, I experienced an incredible change in my outlook. Suddenly the sky was bluer and the sun was brighter and warmer. It was as if I had never experienced a spring day before!

As I read Step Twelve, I know that my desire to pass on what I have been given is also indicative of spiritual awakening. It is clear that all of the spiritual awakenings I have experienced – large and small – make me want to be a better person, and they have brought me closer to God.

Further Reflections...
"Working the Steps has given each of us spiritual awakenings, some dramatic and some so gradual they can only be seen through hindsight, yet our experiences have much in common."

S-Anon Twelve Steps, p. 151

Service Helps Me Grow

There is an Al-Anon booklet entitled "When I Got Busy, I Got Better." I smile when I think of the title of that booklet, because I know how true that statement has been for me. I got busy with service work, my pain and fear eased, and my distorted thinking started to clear. Doing service in S-Anon allows me to share with others and learn from others. I grew in connection with them, as well. Getting out of myself and doing for others in healthy ways helps me grow the recovery S-Anon planted within me.

I found that service is an opportunity to express the experience, strength, and hope that are at the heart of my S-Anon program. Talking on the phone and welcoming a newcomer allows me to share my experience. As I use my skills through helping my group function, I share my strength. When I am in the moment doing Twelfth Step work and bringing the message of recovery to others, I am demonstrating my hope. Service work helps ensure that I keep what I have been given. Service helps me grow.

Further Reflections...
"When we speak the truth, the truth sets us free. That is a spiritual principle that always works. And carrying that message of truth to someone else sets them free, because it's like turning the light on in a room. The darkness just goes. We can help others to see that there is a clearer path that they can walk. I love to carry this message of hope and recovery."

Working the S-Anon Program, p. 104

Tolerance and Individual Freedom

When I came into the program I was opposed to any mention of God. I sat by the door and left just before the end to avoid the closing prayer and holding hands. I was grateful that I could do that, taking what I wanted and leaving the rest. I had a desire to squelch the God talk — I was intolerant of views other than mine. I was afraid that someone was going to try to push their brand of religion on me; I'd had enough of that for a lifetime.

What intrigued me was the tolerance and individual freedom. Each member expressed his or her own spiritual views, using the universal terms "God" or a "Higher Power" and with the understanding that they don't represent the views of the group as a whole.

I remember at one meeting someone talking about God in flowery speech, the next person used swear words during their share. I was stunned when no religious argument or debate broke out. The meeting seemed to carry on as if nothing outrageous had happened. That experience helped me to "Keep Coming Back" partly out of need, and partly out of curiosity.

Over time I got a sponsor and worked through the Steps. I had tremendous growth and freedom from that work. To my surprise I developed a spiritual life and had a spiritual path of my own.

Further Reflections...
"We were relieved to discover that Step Two suggested only that we admit that we were not the greatest power in the universe. That recognition laid a foundation for 'coming to believe'—a process of becoming aware of the presence of a Higher Power in our lives."

S-Anon Twelve Steps, p. 23

The Rewards of Letting Go

A recent awareness prompted me to see that by not letting go of my sexaholic husband's past behavior, I am remaining a victim. By constantly reviewing his behaviors in my mind, I continued to feel betrayed. I asked myself, "Why am I holding on for so long? And at what cost to me?" When I refuse to let go of the past, I lose many hours of potential serenity. I felt stuck in fear, anger, resentment, and bitterness.

In working the Twelve Steps of S-Anon, I gradually began to open up to new ideas: How could I be of service to the relationship today? What positive behaviors and actions of my husband could I acknowledge, just as he is, in our relationship today? In changing my attitude, I am making room for compassion and intimacy. I am letting go of the illusion that I have control over his choices and that I have the right to punish him for past choices. In choosing to live one day at a time and by letting go and letting God take care of my pain, fear, and anxieties; I am becoming a stronger, healthier human being. I have a chance of having an intimate relationship with my husband, and am moving closer to loving myself and experiencing serenity.

Further Reflections...
"We have to surrender our will and lives over and over again. Now, in all times of emotional disturbance and indecision we can pause, get quiet and in that stillness let go of our problems and worries. We can have the confidence that we have an ever-present help in times of need."
S-Anon Twelve Steps, p. 29

Replacing Obsessive Thinking

I once shared with my sponsor that I struggled with obsessive thinking about the sexaholic's acting out, often with vivid detailed pictures coming to my mind. She remarked that allowing those thoughts and images to stay in my head was like pouring salt on an open wound. She encouraged me to let go of these thoughts by acknowledging my hurt, anger, and feelings of betrayal, and then turning these feelings over to my Higher Power.

Now when I start to obsess, I pray to my Higher Power asking for help and guidance. Then I write down my feelings and then share them with another program member as soon as possible. I ask God to remove the images and replace them with thoughts and ideas that are more useful. While I am powerless over my tendency to obsess, I now have the tools necessary to help me move away from my obsessive and sometimes morbid thinking and lean into God's will for me.

Further Reflections…
"I will exercise the power of choice by refusing the invitation of obsessive thoughts. If I don't pick them up, I won't have to let them go."

[Al-Anon] Courage to Change, p. 141

A Safe Place

For years I had become more and more depressed, wondering what was going on in my relationship. I didn't know what was wrong, but I knew something was definitely wrong. My suspicions were confirmed when I went in for my annual checkup and was told I had a sexually transmitted disease (STD). It was one of the worst days of my life – I discovered that my partner had been lying to me for years.

A week after this horrible revelation, I went to my first S-Anon meeting. I knew I was home. The group members welcomed me, and I felt like it was the only place I could talk openly about what I had experienced. I was able to work through the shame, anger, and betrayal I felt, by working through the steps with my sponsor. I learned how to keep the focus on myself and how to keep myself safe.

My partner also chose recovery, and for that I am very grateful. Yet regardless of his path in life, I know I will have a safe place to share, a sponsor to guide me, and a Higher Power who keeps me going on a positive road.

Further Reflections.....
"We emerge from isolation, and when we risk sharing our stories with supportive people, our guilt is relieved and we come to a place of greater peace…"

S-Anon Twelve Steps, p. 53

I Went, I Went, I Went, I Was Home

My husband is an admitted sexaholic. He was able to get a precious amount of sobriety, then slip back into his old acting out behavior, over and over again. Each time he went back out, the "acting out" got worse. Along with each of those times, my heart would race and I would panic. I would become hysterical in front of my children and I felt I was being stupid when I was around the few friends I had left. I wanted to die. This went on for close to 22 years of marriage.

It was out of desperation, after an "acting out" episode, that I made a call to the local S-Anon hot line. I discovered that the only meeting offered locally was starting in a few hours. Not knowing what to expect, I knew I had to be there. At the end of the meeting they would say, "Keep coming back." I took them up on it. Here is how I express those first many meetings; "I went, I went, I went, and I was home."

There was a room full of wonderful people who had gone through similar experiences, who didn't think I was stupid or ugly — who understood. These S-Anons are now a very important part of my family. I can share things with them that even my biological family members don't know. They love me just as I am.

Further Reflections...
"Keep Coming Back! It works if you work it!"
S-Anon suggested meeting format.

What Is Going on with Me?

The day after I formally worked Step Seven with my sponsor, I had a coworker stop by my desk and share some gossip about an old boss of ours. I listened to the gossip and felt a strong urge to pass it on, but I stopped. Gossip was one of the shortcomings I'd just asked God to remove from me the day before. In that instant, I realized I had a choice. While I had still participated in gossip by listening to my co-worker, I changed what I could in that moment by not passing on the gossip.

Thinking about how strong my urge to gossip had been, I asked myself what was going on with me that I wanted to gossip in the first place. Then it hit me: I was feeling insecure about a project that I had turned in the day before. I had wanted to gossip to distract me from those uncomfortable insecure feelings. Thinking about why I was insecure in the first place, I saw that I still didn't believe that I was good enough.

I thanked God for the gift of that revelation and asked that my belief about my inadequacy be removed. I went on about my day feeling victorious and aware that the program works when I work it.

Further Reflections...
"Today, if I'm tempted to gossip or to create a drama around someone else's life, I will ask myself, 'What is going on with me?'"

[Al-Anon] *Courage to Change*, p. 25

Every Worker Should Be Autonomous...

I am applying the Traditions to all my relationships, not just my S-Anon group. At work I recently practiced Tradition Four "Each group should be autonomous except in matters affecting S-Anon or SA as a whole."

I resented and envied a coworker because she worked from home – something I wanted, but never had pursued. When business calls came to our office for this person, I felt I had to take care of them since she wasn't there. My resentment and jealousy grew, and my work suffered. I finally realized something had to give; I had no control over whether or not she worked from home.

Then I remembered Tradition Four. Two principles applied. The first principle was self-responsibility – I needed to make sure I was doing my own job before I challenged the autonomy of others in doing theirs. Second, Tradition Four suggested that where my co-worker did her job didn't matter – unless it affected me or our department as a whole.

In doing the work of those calls for my co-worker, I clearly had not been self-responsible. I began to set boundaries. I simply forwarded calls for the home-based employee instead of taking care of them. Letting go of her job eased my jealousy and resentment. Ironically, I noticed when I let go of doing her job; the work of the department flowed more smoothly.

Further Reflections...
"Learning to act autonomously while keeping an eye out for harmony with others is a vital skill... We learn the importance of being our individual selves, but don't need to impose our perceptions on everyone else in order for those perceptions to be valid."
Paths to Recovery: Al-Anon's Steps, Traditions and Concepts, p. 166

Loving Connections

Growing up, I never felt very close to my father. I think I compensated for my hunger for love by trying desperately to please the men I dated, hoping to gain their love. It seemed to me that sex was the core of experiencing intimacy with a man – the most important sign of love. I thought if I were sexually active and did what these men wanted, I would in turn have my emotional needs met. Eventually I married a sexaholic, and thankfully entered the doors of S-Anon.

My recovering husband relapsed about a year and a half ago. My husband and I decided to completely abstain from sex for a while. Our abstinence revealed so much about our connection with each other – or lack of connection with each other. We began to learn ways of being intimate – through sharing, listening, giving or receiving a touch, a glance, a smile, or a tear. I also started to love myself and accept the love of a Higher Power.

As I look back at my husband's relapse, I can see how a "bad" thing became a wonderful opportunity for me and for us and for our marriage. Through abstinence, I have had so many insights into myself and my history of relationships. I now know sex is not the most important sign of love.

Further Reflections...
"One gift that I've felt we've received as a couple is learning about other ways to connect—to experience intimacy outside of the bedroom. I've started to learn how to express my feelings more, and become intimate by being honest."

Recovering Together: Issues Faced by Couples
(Rev. Booklet 2007) p. 13

New Hope

When I first came to S-Anon, I was seeking a safe haven in the midst of my isolated, fear-driven existence. Ironically, that S-Anon group was named New Hope – words that turned out to be prophetic. For months I just listened. I knew I needed to listen and learn from the members who were solving their own problems through S-Anon. I was highly resistant to the idea that I was powerless. I had spent years going to various seminars on empowerment, reading self-help books and going to counseling. Finally, at age 67, I thought I had become very powerful. Now I was to admit I was powerless? No way!

Yet my desperation kept me coming back, and I gradually realized there was unmanageability in my life. I was still feeling angry, bitter, self-righteous, and troubled about my marriage. Those feelings affected almost every part of my life. An awareness emerged that since my life was unmanageable because of how poorly I was handling those feelings, perhaps there were things over which I was powerless, too!

With this powerful realization, I felt a hope that I, too, could experience recovery like others in the group. It was as though my S-Anon friends had thrown me a lifeline. Propelled by that new sense of hope, I risked admitting that my life was unmanageable and that I was powerless over everything but me and my attitudes. Taking that risk to admit my powerlessness was freeing, and it brought me the safe haven for which I had been searching.

Further Reflections...
"We accept the help of the group and the help of our Higher Power. We allow that Power, far greater than ourselves, to come to our aid, and we find hope."
S-Anon Twelve Steps, p. 3

❖   ❖   ❖

Learning to Respond in Healthy Ways

My anger has served me well over the years. Anger served as a driving force to move me from my childhood abuse and trauma, to accomplish, achieve, and excel. I was comfortable with anger. It worked for me, kept me from depression, sadness and sorrow. Anger was my universal emotion.

Sexaholism gave me plenty of kindling to feed the angry fire. I raged, the children hid, and the furniture flew. It all seemed perfectly normal; after all, anger and chaos were my childhood norms.

Now the time has come to change my response to my angry feelings. I see my life with new eyes, and I do not like what I see. I see the eyes of my husband and children following me – worried, and waiting to see me react out of my anger. I see my co-worker's looks of apprehension, dread, and avoidance after I voiced hurtful words that I wish I had never said. I see myself as much addicted to anger as my husband has described his addiction to lust.

I now know anger is an important emotion for me. It serves as a signal of another emotion, such as fear or hurt. I realize now for my dignity and that of others, I can no longer give anger free rein. Instead, I must pay attention to my feelings and then choose how I will respond.

Further Reflections…
"With time it has gotten easier to recognize these feelings for what they are, without having to act on them."

Working the S-Anon Program, p. 55

My Journey to Reality

My journey to reality started with a dream that left me suspecting my husband was being dishonest with me. I told him about my dream, and I asked if there was anything he was keeping from me. He didn't answer – instead he got drunk. That event shifted something in my awareness regarding the life I had been living. It was as if my eyes were now open, ready to learn the truth.

Through a set of events, I learned for the first time about my husband's secret life as a sexaholic. The revelations were difficult, but thankfully I found the loving and useful support of the S-Anon fellowship.

Learning the truth about my relationship, though painful, started me on the journey of recovery from the effects of my husband's addiction to lust. I've learned I can't recover alone; I depend on the help of a loving God and the support of my S-Anon sponsor and friends in the fellowship. Today I live one day at a time with my eyes open. I am a much stronger person since I started living in reality.

Further Reflections...
"I can see now that before recovery I was committed to fantasies of what I wanted things to be like, particularly in my relationship with my husband. Today when we have difficulty in our relationship, inevitably what's going on is me bumping up against my old ideas of how things 'should' be."

Working the S-Anon Program, p. 73

H.A.L.T.

My state of serenity goes downhill when I allow myself to become over-tired, when I bring drama into my life, or when I do not take care of my basic needs. It sometimes takes a little while for me to realize that this is what is actually going on. S-Anon introduced me to the slogan H.A.L.T.: Don't get too Hungry, Angry, Lonely or Tired. This slogan helps me identify what is really going on with me. It could be any one of these conditions or all of them.

Depending upon which conditions I've allowed to develop, my first step is pretty clear cut: remedy the condition. If I'm hungry, I eat something nutritious. If I'm angry, I examine the circumstances of my anger. If I have harmed someone through the expression of that anger, I own up to it and ask for forgiveness. Perhaps setting a boundary is needed. Reading, meditating, or a change in my scenery might give me some perspective if I am not clear on what my part is. If I am lonely, I can pick up the phone and call an S-Anon friend. If I'm tired, I can take a break to address my needs.

Often the loss of serenity happens because I underestimate my capacity in some way. I expect too much of myself or I have unrealistic expectations of others.

Further Reflections...
"Recognizing when I am Hungry, Angry, Lonely or Tired has been valuable to me as a quick assessment. When I feel old thinking and frustration creeping in, I am most grateful that this slogan directs me to self-care and responsiveness rather than reactivity."

Working the S-Anon Program, p. 13

From Darkness to Light

Before program, living with active sexaholism caused tremendous feelings of shame. With each occasion of acting out, I spiraled into depression and social isolation. I vividly remember a bright sunny May morning. Instead of feeling happy, I just wanted to die. I had just discovered that my husband had spent part of our mortgage payment at a strip bar. Although the sun was shining, I had a dark, morbid feeling as if I were drowning in my fear and shame. I managed to take my children to school, but I could barely talk or look them in the eyes. The pain and shame I felt were overwhelming.

After finding S-Anon and working the program, I feel remarkably different. I realize that I was taking on my husband's shame from his sexual acting out, as if it were mine. My husband has a progressive illness; however, the choices he makes no longer spiral me into the depression and despair that once engulfed me. I share my experiences with S-Anon friends, my sponsor, or at meetings. I find that life does go on, that I'm not crazy, and that my value as a person is not linked to another person's actions. The clouds of darkness that once permeated my life and led to isolation, have been replaced by the light of the S-Anon program, that continues to nourish my path of recovery.

Further Reflections...
"With the loving help of other S-Anon members and the God of our understanding, we take positive action to make our lives more serene and fulfilling."

Keys to S-Anon Recovery (short version)

An Opportunity to Grow

Sponsoring other members is one of my favorite parts about working the S-Anon program. I find that the insights I share with a sponsee about his or her situation are often the same ones I need to be applying to my own life.

For example, last night I told a sponsee, "When I distract myself with outside concerns, I am taking my attention away from the inside work I need to do. The only thing I have power to change is me, with God's help." On reflection, I knew that my Higher Power was telling me what I need to be doing. I have been spending a lot of time lately distracting myself with a family issue over which I have no control. I now have the awareness I need to get busy minding my own business and to take the time to get in touch with my feelings.

I am so grateful for the opportunities that arise for me in recovery by being a sponsor. It is a privilege to listen and speak with a sponsee and to give away what I have been given. It is an opportunity to grow.

Further Reflections...
"Many members who have sponsored others have expressed a lot of gratitude for the experience and feel that they have received far more than they have been given."
Working the S-Anon Program, p. 99

Delighted with the Person I Am Becoming

Working the Steps uncovered many of my self-defeating thoughts and behaviors. I had thought "I am less than my spouse" and "I am not good enough or he would not compulsively masturbate." I felt his problem fell on my shoulders, so I tried to be all things to him and be sexy enough to keep his interest. I resorted to a fantasy life, twisting my perceptions of the way I was living. Eventually my Step work helped me realize that I was taking on more responsibility for others than was mine to take.

I found the courage to detach from unhealthy thinking and to take actions to live a spiritual way of life. By walking out of the room and calling my sponsor when I was tempted to say something manipulative, I stopped trying to control my spouse's compulsive masturbation. I ceased eavesdropping at closed doors, and I refused to do things that sexually repulsed me. When emotionally painful situations arose, I didn't mentally exit to my fantasy life; I stood still in the present and allowed myself time to feel and work through the pain.

Life is much less complicated now. I have long wonderful days filled with peace of mind. While I do not have control over my spouse's sexaholism or sobriety, I do have the ability to take care of myself. I feel delighted with the person I am becoming.

Further Reflections...
"Some of us minimized the importance of the sexaholic behavior or denied it until we felt emotionally numb. Others focused on the sexaholic to the point of obsession and tried every known method to control it."

The S-Anon Problem (Short Version)

A Daily Way of Life

Working the S-Anon program is a daily way of life for me and an act of faith. Through S-Anon, I have developed a sustaining link to my Higher Power, acknowledging that God is with me in every facet of my life.

Going to meetings, working with others, reading Conference Approved Literature, writing and praying to the God of my understanding, are actions I choose every day, to the best of my ability. These actions provide me with a solid foundation. This foundation allows me to live in balance and to be of use to God as I go about my daily business. For example, I may find that applying my program today includes helping a coworker or taking an extra minute to listen to a friend in pain.

Learning to do this – to "practice these principles in all my affairs" – has come as a result of working the Steps and making my S-Anon program my priority, my way of life. Living life within the framework of these principles has given me a peace and a joy I didn't think were possible. I am so grateful for the S-Anon program!

Further Reflections...
"We... obey spiritual principles, at first because we must, then because we ought to, and ultimately because we love the kind of life such obedience brings."

[AA] *As Bill Sees It, p. 27*

The Only Person I Can Change Is Me

I tried everything to change the sexaholic. I was silent. I was angry. I begged, pleaded and manipulated. Nothing worked. I just brought myself more frustration, hurt, resentment, and misery.

S-Anon is helping me learn I need to let go of trying to change someone else, because the only one I can change is me. I don't like change; it is uncomfortable and scary to me. Sometimes I try to stay safe by taking no risks, but I am seeing that change happens anyway because change is a part of life.

I am taking little baby steps, working to change myself with God's help. While I still want to change over night, these baby steps are adding up to a significant difference in my life, despite sometimes going one step forward and two steps backward. When I'm off balance, I can slip back into trying to change others. I need to bring the focus back to me and remind myself that progress, not perfection, is what counts.

I am doing the best I can today, and when I let go and let God guide me, I remember that God will take care of changing what or whoever needs to be changed.

Further Reflections...

"I recognized my powerlessness over sexaholism and my own crazy thinking. I saw I was not helpless to take positive action to face my pain. With this admission, I really started to work the First Step and my own program."

S-Anon Twelve Steps, p. 10

The Truth about Me

When my sexaholic husband criticized my appearance, saying how disappointed he was with my body, I wanted to shrivel up and die. I tried all kinds of things to make myself look different, even seriously considering plastic surgery. I spent countless days, weeks, and months focusing on how to change my appearance, so I could stop his cruel words to me.

Listening to others in meetings and concentrating on Step One has given me the courage to stop focusing on my husband's opinions. Several times each day I repeat the First Step, changing the words slightly: I am powerless over my husband's opinion of my body, and my life has become unmanageable. S-Anon has helped me understand that sexaholism is a disease, and rather than taking personally the distorted view my husband has of me, I have the choice to affirm my worth by turning my will and my life over to a Power greater than myself.

Today I choose to believe the truth about me – I am beautiful, inside and out. My body is unique and I am special and lovable as I am. With this in mind, I have begun to let go of my all-consuming obsession with how I appear to others, especially to the sexaholic. I place myself in my Higher Power's loving care and realize that today I have a choice about what I believe about myself.

Further Reflections...
"When I risked going through my fear and once again surrendered my life to my Higher Power, I found the serenity, peace, and acceptance I so badly wanted to regain."
S-Anon Twelve Steps, p. 32

A Step Toward Freedom

Forgiveness was a topic I heard almost immediately when I got into recovery. I knew I wanted to forgive the sexaholic because I had invested 20 years in our marriage and I just was not going to throw in the towel. I imagined I could forgive the sexaholic if he would make up for the pain he had caused me. I thought he could do this by changing immediately into the person I had always thought he was.

As I began to listen and learn from other S-Anons, I realized that he could never make up for the pain caused by his acting out. I also saw I would be setting myself up for more hurt and resentment if I based my forgiveness on the chance that he would change the way I thought he should. It was not up to me to decide how he should change. I learned that the only one I could change was myself. I had to change into the kind of person that had the willingness to forgive and free myself from the pain. This was only possible with the help of God and the S-Anon program. Accepting this was an important step toward freedom.

Further Reflections...
"We also see how self-defeating it is to continue to be hurt by people who, just like us, are trying to grow, even if their efforts are not obvious to us."

S-Anon Twelve Steps, p. 114

Living Life Imperfectly and Humanly

I used to think trying to gauge my husband's mood for the "perfect" time to address an issue was just being a good wife. I thought my job as a wife was to manage the house and family, so my husband could have a stress-free experience at home. I felt important and irreplaceable, having the sole responsibility of planning and managing everything. While household management is a worthy vocation, I took it to an extreme. I also felt resentful and better than my husband. In truth, I was a self-righteous martyr.

Then I came to S-Anon and surrendered my husband and his sexaholism to God. I learned I am not responsible for my husband's disease, his mood, or his choices, or how much stress either of us are under. Now when I wonder if I should talk to him about a family issue while he is not in a great mood, I ask myself if I am trying to control his disease or his mood.

I often make mistakes in trying to work my program, but I feel a great relief now that I can live my life fully and imperfectly, one day at a time. It is liberating and humbling to look at those people and situations over which I am powerless and remember there is a Power greater than myself. I understand now that I am not responsible for another's behavior – thank you, God.

Further Reflections...
"...in S-Anon I am not asked to achieve perfection; I am just asked to make progress in becoming the person my Higher Power made me to be."
Working the S-Anon Program, p. 15

Focused on Changing and Growing

I had been attending S-Anon for about six months when I became aware of emotions and needs I had ignored for years. I started to learn new ways to express those emotions and fulfill those needs. I took action on what I had learned. Healthy internal changes began to take place, and I knew I was doing what was right for me.

My family members weren't happy about my new assertiveness, and I felt pressure to return to my old ways of thinking and behaving. I noticed some old fears cropping up. Would I lose my family if I didn't conform to their wishes? I wanted so desperately to be loved and accepted by them.

I talked things over with my sponsor, and I began to understand more about my family patterns and my need for recovery. My sponsor suggested that I immerse myself in my program, and practice loving detachment from my family members. She suggested that I attend more meetings each week, read conference-approved literature daily, make program phone calls, and do service in my home group. I'm so glad I followed her suggestions, because doing these simple things kept me focused on changing and growing, and kept me out of my fear.

I practice Steps One, Two, and Three each day, surrendering the pressure I occasionally feel to return to old behaviors. Even though I still sometimes feel that pressure, through working the S-Anon program, I have found the courage to make miraculous changes in my life.

Further Reflections...
"We find our faith deepening as we surrender the parts of ourselves we have always held back from God."
S-Anon Twelve Steps, p. 15-16

❖ ❖ ❖

Trusting with Eyes Wide Open

I came into S-Anon with broken trust. My sexaholic husband had betrayed me and I no longer trusted anything he said or did. I see now that I didn't even trust myself or know how to trust a Higher Power. It frightened me that I had not been aware of my husband's sexual acting out for many years. How could I trust I would not be fooled if he should act out again?

Through the S-Anon fellowship my ability to trust slowly grew. First I began learning to trust members of my group and I took a risk to share some of my secrets and struggles. I experienced acceptance, love, and understanding. This process started to heal my damaged trust and empowered me to experience my Higher Power's love and acceptance. I began to see God guiding me through this difficult process of my recovery, one step at a time. Amazingly, I started to trust myself again and began to believe that I would be OK, no matter what my husband was doing in his life.

My perception of trusting my spouse is different now. Trust is not blind or absolute. Trusting my Higher Power and myself has to be part of trusting my spouse and others. Trust is loving with eyes wide open. Learning to trust in a healthy way is a gift of the S-Anon program.

Further Reflections...
"Remaining silent is always our option, but eventually we found that sharing with other members and with a sponsor helped us to grow."

Working the S-Anon Program, p. 6

I Need to Consciously Work My Program

I was out of town on a business trip that involved more than the usual number of flight delays and rental car mix-ups. I checked into my hotel room well after midnight and decided to listen to my telephone messages before going to bed. One of the messages let me know that I had broken the anonymity of some S-Anon members while doing program service work. Even though my error had been unintentional, the impact on others was real. I immediately turned to my Higher Power for comfort and guidance.

It was obvious to me that I needed to work the Tenth Step and that I owed amends to each of the affected parties. As I reflected on the situation, it was clear to me how and why the error occurred. I realized that I had allowed myself to become too busy and overwhelmed. I had lost sight of my initial purpose, to be useful to God and others. The result was a breech of one of the most fundamental principles of the program: anonymity.

I am continually amazed by how cunning my old thinking and behavior are, and how quickly my life can become unmanageable if I am not consciously working my program. I am very grateful that the Tenth Step and my Higher Power give me the tools to deal with and learn from painful situations as they arise.

[Excerpt from *S-Anon Twelve Steps*, p. 116-117]

Further Reflections...
"Through Step Ten we observe the daily nitty-gritty of our lives, making ongoing midcourse corrections and letting our lapses be lessons for growth."

S-Anon Twelve Steps, p. 122

It Works When I Work It

O nce again I gave my sexaholic husband an ultimatum; I would stay in the relationship only if each of us was working a recovery program. He agreed, and over time, the crisis passed.

I continued to go to S-Anon meetings, yet I felt uncomfortable around my husband and thought he was not working his program as I thought he should. After all, wasn't it my job with an ultimatum to keep an eye on him to see that he was following through? With each succeeding ultimatum, I had become even more focused on him, rather than on myself and my own S-Anon program.

As time went on, my husband's sobriety eluded my best efforts. I had to accept that I could not enforce his recovery or how he worked his program. It also became clear that as long as I remained focused on my husband's recovery and complacent about my own, I wouldn't have any true peace. I attended an S-Anon International Convention and got a real boost for my own recovery work. I began to work the Steps in earnest, including making amends to my spouse for my angry, aggressive, and controlling behaviors towards him. This opened the door for frank and honest discussions about our interactions in our marriage.

At times I am frustrated with myself, as if I should have had this all figured out by now. With help from my sponsor, I am seeing there is always more to learn.

Further Reflections...
"Willingness moves us toward the promised gifts of the S-Anon program, which includes serenity, dignity, and emotional growth."

Working the S-Anon Program, p. 52

Sponsees Are Mirrors

M any years ago I discovered a pattern among the women who asked me to sponsor them. It appeared that I attracted people (like myself) who did not think about doing the basic essentials for themselves, like buying oneself new underwear when it was needed. For me, this characteristic was about being a martyr, especially when there was active sexaholism in the home. We all made sure our families' needs were taken care of, often to our own detriment.

After I recognized the pattern, I began asking new sponsees, "When was the last time you bought yourself a new pair of underwear?" The look on their faces said it all. The usual response was "How did you know?" By working with these wonderful sponsees, my Higher Power helped me learn that I need to take better care of myself and my personal needs.

Now I am noticing a shift in this pattern among the women asking for my sponsorship. Their underwear drawer is in fine shape, but they are constantly trying to get their homes, paper work, and finances perfectly organized. Not surprisingly, I am caught in that same never-ending perfectionist cycle. I have come to believe that my sponsees are mirrors my Higher Power is holding up for me

So now my question to a new sponsee is "When was the last time you took a break from trying to get your life perfectly organized?" More important, my question to my Higher Power is "What can this new sponsee teach me about caring for myself?"

Further Reflections...
"Being a mirror for one's sponsees: This means reflecting as accurately and honestly as we can the reality of a sponsee's life back to him or her."

Sponsorship in S-Anon Pamphlet

❖   ❖   ❖

Finding Meaning in Tradition Four

I used to inwardly groan when my local S-Anon meeting held our monthly Traditions meeting. These meetings were often boring to me and didn't seem very relevant to my life.

One day when my group was discussing Tradition Four, a light bulb suddenly went on. I realized that I could apply this Tradition to my relationship with my husband and adult children. It was so clear! Each family member should be autonomous in his or her actions and discussions, except when it affects another family member, our family or society as a whole. In other words, instead of attempting to direct the lives of my family members, I can allow each of them the space to make decisions about there own actions.

With this spiritual awakening, came another: all the Traditions could apply to my relationships with others, not just the relationships within my S-Anon group. Now I look forward to those Traditions meetings, and with each Tradition discussed, I try to find new insights to help me improve all my relationships.

Further Reflections…
"S-Anon's Twelve Traditions are principles that guide the conduct and unity of our groups. The Traditions guide the growth and health of our groups and our world wide fellowship, just as the Twelve Steps guide our growth and our lives as individual members….. As we grow in our understanding of the Traditions, we also find that applying these principles to other areas of our lives can guide us toward healthier relationships with family, friends, co-workers and others."

Working the S-Anon Program, p. 29

I Had Been My Own Worst Critic

My sponsor helped me understand why I needed to be on my amends list, too. She pointed out that I had been my own worst critic. I often accepted blame and said, "I'm sorry," whether I was responsible for a situation or not. She reminded me how I had put my interests and priorities, such as finishing my college degree, on the back burner time after time. I indeed had harmed myself and I wrote my name down, too.

God brought to mind the many others who rounded out my amends list: extended family, co-workers, people I had known socially and in my faith community, even some who had died. Today, even though I've moved on in my Step work, I still make it a practice to review my Eighth Step list periodically. I prayerfully consider if there are more things I need to be willing to do in each case. With my mind and heart in a willing place, it's amazing how my Higher Power leads me.

Further Reflections...
"Most of us had to make amends for being too hard on ourselves, especially in the beginning of recovery. We saw how often the "shoulds" and "oughts" entered our vocabulary. We began to forgive ourselves, too."
S-Anon Twelve Steps, p. 86

Not Just Surviving...Thriving through Service

I was just surviving day-to-day when I was living with active sexaholism. I was still in survival mode in my early S-Anon days, so I did not understand the importance of service work. I was confused as to what service had to do with the problems that brought me to S-Anon or how service would help me get the sexaholic sober.

As I progressed in recovery, I began to see how other members greatly benefited by the service work they were doing. Over time I followed the example of my sponsor and other group members and began doing some service. That is when I began to see what is meant by "to keep what we have been given, we have to give it away."

Today, I serve by sponsoring other members, welcoming newcomers, periodically chairing meetings and even putting chairs away after meetings. Every time I reach out my hand in service, I am giving myself a healthy alternative to focusing on what the sexaholic is doing or not doing. Through service, I am improving myself. For example, by practicing patience and tolerance with my fellow S-Anon members, I am better able to bring kindness and respect into my home.

Each time I reach out in some way, whether large or small, noticed or unnoticed, I become connected with something greater than myself. Service helps me put my problems in their true perspective — I am no longer alone. Today I am not just surviving; I am thriving through service.

Further Reflections...
"Our reward is the satisfaction of seeing lives change. We know that our experience, though painful, has been transformed and can benefit others."

S-Anon Twelve Steps, p. 152

A Safe and Healthy Place

Unfortunately, the S-Anon group I first attended folded after only six months. Six months later, with no meeting to attend, one other S-Anon member and I started a new S-Anon meeting.

Learning from our previous meeting experience, the other S-Anon person and myself, agreed that our new group might benefit from a more structured format such as the one suggested in the S-Anon Handbook. We developed a schedule for topics that would keep us focused on the solution. We now alternate meeting topics. Week one is a Step, week two a Tradition, week three a Step and remaining weeks are open topics. The structure is especially helpful because we don't have to try to decide at the last minute what we want or need. It also makes it possible to cover all of the Steps and Traditions over time, which supports a good balance.

In a small group, we have found it difficult not to crosstalk, so after we have all shared, we sometimes decide to close early, after which we stay after and chat. In this way we are able to support each other while still respecting our "no crosstalk" boundary during our meeting time.

Even though the meeting is small, I have found it to be a safe and healthy place for me to come to and share my recovery with other S-Anons.

Further Reflections...
"Our group has had a tradition of going out for coffee after the meeting. This fellowship time is not required, but it has certainly helped me break out of isolation and take time for myself. It also gives newcomers an opportunity for fellowship and a relaxed setting in which to ask questions about how the program works."

Working the S-Anon Program, p. 7-8

Awareness and Understanding of Anonymity

Anonymity was a concern for our group, since one of our members also attended a local SA meeting. This person was concerned that what she shared as an S-Anon member would be transmitted, through spouses repeating her share, to members of the SA meeting, which her partner also attended. When this issue was raised in our meeting, it was suggested that we have some specific guidelines about anonymity. This led to the creation of a study group on anonymity, which met before our regular S-Anon meeting for several weeks.

Everyone brought different Conference-Approved Literature to read and share with the study group regarding the topic of anonymity. I had expected the definition of anonymity to be set out in black and white, but it wasn't that straightforward. It brought up hard issues for me to look at, such as my own tendency to gossip. Becoming aware of the fundamental principles of anonymity enabled me to not want to gossip or say who I saw or not at the meeting. For me, anonymity means being respectful of other people's privacy and not taking their inventory.

We learned there are many gray areas in defining anonymity. We agreed to set hard and fast rules were not appropriate. Making our group welcoming and safe for all members to share, is how we practice anonymity to the best of our ability. While anonymity cannot be totally guaranteed, the group discussion raised our awareness to new levels.

Further Reflections...
"I have also had to continue to work a strong recovery program despite my trust issues. The importance of respecting everyone's anonymity regarding what is shared in meetings cannot be overstated, from my point of view."
Working the S-Anon Program, p. 44

I Am Not a Victim

My young son and I were attending the celebration of my mom's 70th birthday. It began with breakfast at Mom's very small home, with a lot of family members. Shortly after we arrived, my son needed a nap. The house was bursting at the seams with family running around, preparing breakfast. I was ready to scream.

I put my son in the stroller, grabbed my cell phone, and went for a walk around the neighborhood. I made a long-distance phone call to another S-Anon member and after I shared all my frustrations with her, she reminded me that I had choices – and that I had already made two healthy choices by getting out of the house and making a call. I realized that my first thought had been to stay in that small house with all those people and go crazy. Because of my recovery, I went to plan "B," which was clearly the better option.

When we hung up I felt more clarity and considered different choices. After a while I decided to take a drive. My son could sleep and I could be alone to regroup. I knew my family would not like my missing the start of the breakfast, and I feel uncomfortable when they disapprove. S-Anon has shown me that even in the craziest of times, I am NOT a victim. I have choices and with these choices come the freedom to take better care of myself.

Further Reflections…
"…our attitude is an important key to recovery"
Working the S-Anon Program, p. 12

Balance

I am learning in recovery that if I want to experience peace and happiness, I need to do some basic, but necessary foot work. I have found I need to consciously work on four areas of my life to find balance.

The first is my conscious contact with my Higher Power. Practicing Step Eleven each day reminds me that I am not alone and not in charge. With this, most all other aspects of finding balance seem to flow much easier. Without this, things just don't flow well at all. The second area is the rest of my program: getting to meetings regularly, and intentionally practicing the Steps and Traditions. This helps me continue to grow and feel healthier and happier with who I am.

A commitment to prayer and meditation, and working the S-Anon program, help to support me in the third and fourth areas of my life: relationships with family and friends and responsibilities at work and outside activities, respectively. With recovery providing the solid foundation for my life, I am guided to do the next right thing. With recovery, I have a solid foundation to keep my life in balance and to be the best that I can be.

Further Reflections...
"We have seen the importance of 'walking the walk,' not just 'talking the talk.'"

S-Anon Twelve Steps, p. 144

From Anger and Hurt to Healing

In my marriage to a sexaholic, I felt so much anger, hurt, and resentment that I didn't think I would ever get over it. After all, I still carried resentment about a previous unhealthy relationship. Coming to S-Anon meetings, and finding a sponsor was a tremendous help.

My sponsor encouraged me, offering hope from her own experience. She assured me that I would be able to work through my feelings of anger, hurt, and resentment if I was willing. She said repeating the slogans had helped her put things in perspective. She told me "This Too Shall Pass" and "Easy Does It" so many times that it must have rubbed off — I began to see that my situation wasn't the end of the world.

At her suggestion, I have spent much time on my knees in prayer, talking to my Higher Power. I have asked God to give me the strength to walk through these hard times. I try to have an attitude of gratitude for the many blessings in my life. I seek guidance for healing from the effects of the disease of sexaholism and ask for the next healthy action to take.

I am amazed that my anger is subsiding and my trust and courage have been renewed. For this I am so grateful.

Further Reflections...
"We see that we do have a way out; we have options and choices we can make for our own lives. With every hardship we face, our Higher Power also provides an outlet. One of those ways out is to change our own attitudes with the help of our Higher Power and the S-Anon program."

S-Anon Twelve Steps, p. 16

Powerless...Not an Admission of Failure

I always thought that if I read a book or took a class on a subject, I could learn enough to tackle any task or solve any problem. I lived under this illusion for 43 years until I discovered my wife's sexaholism. I read every book, went to seminars, and talked to experts, yet I only felt more and more crazy. When I tried the S-Anon program, I finally started to feel calm and sane. I learned that admitting I was powerless over sexaholism was not an admission of failure, but the beginning of recovery. S-Anon taught me that I do not need to analyze what she does. It is hard enough for me to learn why I do the things I do. When I spend so much time trying to understand her illness, I see that I really am avoiding looking at my own S-Anon problem.

Today I can let go of the need to understand the inner workings of the sexaholic, and I can ask my Higher Power to reveal the truth about myself. I try to remember that as I come to know myself, I am better able to let go of others.

Further Reflections...
"Our primary purpose is to recover from the effects upon us of another person's sexaholism, and to help families and friends of sexaholics."

S-Anon Preamble to the Twelve Steps

Expectations and Boundaries

I believe it is reasonable that a healthy, intimate, sexual relationship should include fidelity, honesty, flexibility, companionship, sexual satisfaction, compatibility, and commitment. For me to expect those things from an active sexaholic – now that was unreasonable!

By attending S-Anon, I am learning to set reasonable personal boundaries that work for me. For example, I am not willing to stay in my marriage unless my husband is in recovery from sexaholism. I consider this to be a reasonable boundary for me. However, my husband is choosing to recover from his sexaholism through a recovery program other than SA. I discussed this matter with my sponsor and others in S-Anon. The message I received helped me to have a broader picture of what an unreasonable expectation is. The consistent answer: "You have a right to expect fidelity and honesty, but how he achieves that is between him and his Higher Power."

Today, I know I cannot dictate how my spouse works his program. I can reasonably expect my Higher Power to be there for me, and, by working the Steps, I will be clear about whether or not I need to leave my marriage. I do not have sex when I am not feeling safe. I speak about my feelings when it is appropriate. I trust God is taking care of me, despite the occasional fear to the contrary. These are reasonable expectations and boundaries on which to rely.

Further Reflections…
"For me this is the critical first step: before I can be honest with my spouse, I need to be honest with myself."
Recovering Together: Issues Faced by Couples
(Rev. Booklet 2007), p. 7

Shaking Off Negative Thinking

Since joining S-Anon two years ago, finding serenity has been my most important goal. Why? When I am in a state of serenity, I know that I'm caring for myself in a balanced and loving way. When I am serene, I feel as though I am living my life, according to the way God intended – it just feels right.

I thought I had made a lot of progress in regaining serenity, but over the past month, I have regressed. I had gone through some significant changes and noticed the re-emergence of a lot of fear, grief, anxiety, and panic. I also noticed old attitudes: not feeling good enough, not feeling worthy of love, and not feeling joy. No matter how much I noticed these feelings, I wasn't able to shake this negativity.

After struggling on my own, I finally remembered to call my sponsor. She reminded me that regaining serenity comes from my relationship with my Higher Power. She asked me if I had taken my problem to my Higher Power. I was embarrassed that my answer was "No." I had been trying to handle it all on my own, just like before recovery.

Not surprisingly, when I started re-focusing on connecting with God, serenity came back. I again felt balanced, and my problems became more manageable.

Further Reflections...
"What are the things I can do to become willing to trust my Higher Power? What situations in my life could I trust to my Higher Power right now?"

S-Anon Twelve Steps, p. 37

Learning about the Traditions

I learned about the Twelve Traditions through a formal Traditions study, answering questions on each Tradition in Al-Anon's *Paths to Recovery*. I didn't necessarily like doing it, but I gained more peace through better incorporation of the Traditions into my life.

I also learned about the Traditions through experience. For example, one time I served as chair of an S-Anon event and was given a service sponsor as a guide. At the beginning of planning, the sponsor mapped out my tasks over a phone call, but because of a chronic medical condition I have, I didn't pay close attention or write the plan down.

I had told her about my condition, but she also had professional knowledge of that condition. Later when I failed to do a part of the plan, she suggested to me it was because my medical condition had gotten in the way.

In our next conversation, she apologized, saying she had violated Tradition Eight (that S-Anon shall remain non-professional). She admitted she had been wearing her professional hat rather than her S-Anon hat, and she regretted not focusing on program principles in the conversation. Her self-honesty and application of the Traditions were really instructive.

The Traditions are boundaries for getting along with others. How pleasant it is to know that in the S-Anon fellowship or at home, "our common welfare should come first" instead of the needs and desires of any one person.

Further Reflections...
"As we grow in our understanding of the Traditions, we also find that applying these principles to other areas of our lives can guide us toward healthier relationships with family, friends, co-workers, and others."

Working the S-Anon Program, p. 29

Just the Right Step

The couple leading our S-Anon couples meeting brought up the Twelve Steps as a topic. They used a pair of dice to pass around and each person threw the dice to find out which Step to share on

We all got a kick out of how the number came out to the Step we needed to share about. As a side note, there was no way for me to "prepare" as it got around to my turn, because I wouldn't know, until I threw the dice, which Step I would share on. This was a good thing for me, because I could listen better and not plan what I would say.

My throw landed on Step Six. I came away from that meeting wanting to look further into my understanding of becoming "...entirely ready to have God remove all these defects of character." Meetings help me to see both where my faulty thinking is and the progress I have made.

Further Reflections...
"Meetings have been a safe learning environment for me."
Working the S-Anon Program, p. 4

Defects to Assets

When life hands you lemons, make lemonade. I've heard that saying a million times, yet I could never seem to make the lemonade in my life "sweet enough." As I worked my Fourth Step, I began to think of my defects as being like lemons – often useful even without adding sugar. I thought of all of the unique uses of lemons in their natural state: removing bad smells, flavoring fish and chicken, and smoothing out the bitterness in tea.

My thought on the nature of lemons, led me to realize that many of my character defects were actually character assets that were taken to an extreme. The difference seemed to be that sometimes I took an asset such as persistence and applied it without restraint until it became a defect such as stubbornness. My Fourth Step process helped me to see my assets and liabilities and to realize that sometimes returning a defect to an asset is just a matter of achieving a little more balance in my emotional life.

In S-Anon I am learning to recognize my character defects as misdirected human instincts, and I am learning to "make lemonade" by finding the assets those defects may be masking.

Further Reflections...
"As we work our program we will see that our shortcomings can become assets, and we will find serenity."

S-Anon Twelve Steps, p. 41

The Secret Ingredient

I was terrified at the thought of going to my first S-Anon meeting. I was so isolated at that time, I feared being swallowed up like "Alice in Wonderland." When I think back to that first night, I don't remember anything that was said, but I do recall being greeted by a friendly person when I entered the S-Anon meeting room. I felt more comfortable blending into the woodwork, so I was shocked when an S-Anon member paid attention to me, and asked me how I was doing. I left not only amazed I had made it through the meeting, but also grateful for that kind, gentle and unassuming attention.

I now have attended S-Anon for over two years, and I've become one of the kind, welcoming persons at the door. I have seen many newcomers return and many who did not, yet it never ceases to amaze me how much I can learn when the newcomer shares his or her experience. Their countenance and spirit are ever-humbling. How joyful it is to see those who come back, work the program, and recognize the value of self-care and the care from their Higher Power! The newcomer reminds me of that fearful, isolated place from where I have come – and just how far I have come in recovery. I personally believe the success of the S-Anon program is due to a secret ingredient: the newcomers. They are a gift of this program.

Further Reflections...
"When I heard 'keep coming back' at the end of meetings, I felt the tug to come back even though I was discouraged with my situation. I came back (trudged back) and found help and friendship."

Working the S-Anon Program, p. 3

Love, Love, Love

I thought love would solve all my problems and make life beautiful. This fairy tale thinking clouded my perceptions of reality during dating relationships. I worked at the college bookstore. A young man approached me one day and asked me out. We ended up getting along well; we had great conversations, and eventually fell in love and married.

After we were married, his sexaholism became evident. I thought God must have made a terrible mistake. This wasn't supposed to be part of my love story. I felt hurt, angry, and in shock. We sought counseling together and that is when he disclosed his sexual addiction.

I started going to S-Anon, and I decided, one day at a time, to stay with him. I began to accept that this is a love story. I believe we love each other and that our love was severely tested. I slowly began learning the principles in the S-Anon program, including "Sexaholic's are sick people, not bad people."

I recently had a debilitating illness and required over two months of hospitalization. During this time, I saw my husband take the actions of love and I witnessed his commitment to our relationship. I feel more confident of his love today. I am also more confident of my love for him and my commitment to our marriage.

Further Reflections...

"Today I know that human beings have diseases and that they fail, but God does not fail. So as I keep trusting my Higher Power with my life, I believe that I will be OK..."

Recovering Together: Issues Faced by Couples
(Rev. Booklet 2007), p. 6

Trusting a Higher Power of My Understanding

I once thought my marriage was a failure, and that I could never again trust my husband to remain faithful to me. For years, I had believed my husband's primary goal should be to please me. Now, with some years of S-Anon recovery behind me, I pray that my husband works to please his Higher Power.

While my husband is sexually sober today, the reality is he is still a sexaholic and he could choose his sexaholism over recovery. That used to cause me a lot of fear, but S-Anon has shown me that I don't have to be fearful as long as I place my trust in my Higher Power, rather than my husband. My experience has shown me that I can trust God to give me what I need to face each day with serenity, courage, and wisdom.

God stands at the door and waits for me. If I am willing to ask for help, He will give it perfectly. I don't need to check up on God or evaluate His plan. I simply trust in God's wisdom, and I experience the serenity that comes from His love.

Further Reflections…
"We can trust God to do what we cannot do for ourselves. Trust is an ingredient of believing, and to believe is to actively pursue the thing hoped for."

S-Anon Twelve Steps, p. 16

Surrendering with the Serenity Prayer

I am constantly amazed at how much importance I place on what others think of me. I remember times when my partner, a friend, or a parent was angry with me and criticized me harshly. Their judgments and low opinions hurt my feelings, and I actually believed what they were saying. This occurred despite thinking I was someone "who could take it."

The Serenity Prayer has been valuable in surrendering others' judgments of me. I am able to stop, take a deep breath, say the Serenity Prayer, check in with my sponsor to see if there is some action I need to take, and then let it go. The more I practice the Serenity Prayer in my daily life, the better I am getting to know myself and the will of my Higher Power. I am spending more time in a state of gratitude. When I have the wisdom to know the difference between what I can change and what I can't, then what other people think of me becomes none of my business. The added bonus often has been the better I take care of myself, the more often others treat me respectfully.

Further Reflections...
"I am learning to distinguish between what I can do and what's not my responsibility. I can take responsibility for myself and stop my own negative behaviors."
Working the S-Anon Program, p. 42

Just for Today I Can Enjoy Our Life Together

When I began my S-Anon program, I felt confused about whether to leave a 37 year marriage or stay and try to work things out. I criticized myself for thinking that a "better person" would have the courage to leave a spouse who would not admit to his sexaholism. I thought other S-Anon members would judge and ostracize me for staying.

Somewhere along my path of recovery, I realized the spiritual principles of the S-Anon program gave me the tools I needed to regain my life, whether or not my sexaholic husband recovered. I practiced using these life saving tools. I stopped searching for evidence that my heart told me existed. Every time my mind strayed to "What is he doing now?" I refocused my thoughts to "What is my Higher Power's will for me today?" I learned to walk away from insane arguments and give myself space to work my program. I came to trust my Higher Power would show me what I needed to know when I needed to know it. I learned to trust my feelings about my sexuality. I discovered I don't need to feel shame about staying in this marriage one day at time.

My husband and I love to travel, enjoy the same music, attend concerts and the theater, and have many values in common. I am no longer terrified of leaving my marriage and I do not know what tomorrow will bring. Today I can enjoy our life together, as long as I honor my boundaries and work my program.

Further Reflections...
"...it is our job to manage our own lives, whether or not the sexaholic chooses sobriety."

S-Anon Twelve Steps, p. 2

Dressing to Reflect All of Me

When I was growing up, I was encouraged by my mother to dress very provocatively, and I continued doing so in my adult life. I liked the way I felt when men turned their heads to look at me. Dressing to emphasize my sexuality gave me a lot of attention.

After attending S-Anon for some time, I realized I no longer wanted or needed the kind of attention that was based solely on my sexuality. I became uncomfortable with my wardrobe. I talked to my sponsor about it, and she shared that some members gave articles of clothing they were no longer comfortable with to second hand stores. After much deliberation, I decided that most of my clothes were so revealing and provocative that I did not even feel comfortable passing them on. I decided to throw away those clothes. I kept a few things I was comfortable wearing and gradually started replacing my wardrobe with clothing that better reflected all of me, not just my sexuality.

Today, when I shop for clothes, I am careful to check my motives before making a purchase: Am I buying this for me or for the attention it will get me?

Further Reflections…
"As I progressed in recovery, my attitudes gradually changed, and I came to understand that much of what was 'public' before; I preferred to keep 'private.' I learned I didn't have to give my sexuality away to others, but found I could hold it close and cherish it as a beautiful part of me."
Working the S-Anon Program, p. 70

For Today, I Can Let Go

I came to S-Anon to save my marriage. Instead of a detailed list of instructions on how to save my marriage, I found a safe place to talk about my problems and some wonderful tools to use. I didn't experience much serenity for myself until I was willing to surrender my husband, my marriage, and my life to my Higher Power and to let go of the outcomes.

The Third Step says to turn our will and our lives over to the care of God as we understand him. I have found that my serenity is directly proportional to my willingness to work this Step. I have learned I cannot do Step Three only once. Step Three is a daily, One-Day-at-a-Time Step, because life can become overwhelming when I try to handle my whole life at once.

The slogan One Day at a Time is one of the mainstays of my program. For today, I can admit my powerlessness. For today, I can let go of my fears of the future. For today, I can refrain from taking my husband's (kids', boss', friends' and parents') inventory. For today, I can work my program, call my sponsor, pray, and meditate. For today, I can be grateful for what I have. This simple slogan reminds me to stay in the present and surrender everything to my Higher Power.

Further Reflections...
"Step Three suggests that we make a decision to surrender our lives, one day at a time, to our Higher Power, and for most of us this involved both a formal decision and a process."

S-Anon Twelve Steps, p. 36

And the Answer Is...

I had only three questions when I first came to S-Anon: What if...?, If only...? and Why...?. With respect to the first two questions, my sponsor helped me when she said, "The answer to If only...? is that it's too late; it already happened. The answer to What if..? is that it hasn't happened yet, so we won't know until it happens and until God shows us what to do."

These answers made some sense to me, and I was able to start letting go of those two questions. Yet the big question remained – Why...?. I thought that if I knew why he acted out, I would surely be able to figure out how to fix him. My sponsor's answer to Why...? was simply, "Because he's a sexaholic."

Then she said, "A more important question to ask yourself is 'Why am I reacting to his actions?'" With that question, she introduced me to Step One. I began to suspect that I might, in fact, be powerless over sexaholism – over not only the sexaholic's behaviors, but also over my reactions to those behaviors – and that when I do try to have power over sexaholism, my life becomes unmanageable.

Further Reflections...
"We are concerned with two principles in Step One: that we cannot control the sexaholic or his or her sexual behavior, and that because of our attempts to do so our lives have become unmanageable."

S-Anon Twelve Steps, p. 1

A New Lease on Life

I lived with an active sexaholic for 27 years. By the time I came to my first S-Anon meeting, my emotional pain was almost unbearable, and my self-esteem was non-existent. I was unable to share in the group for several months. My shame and pain were too great, yet I knew I wanted the serenity others seemed to have. They were able to laugh and seemed to have peace in their lives. At first the meetings did not seem to help, but someone told me to keep coming back and I did. After a while, I began to notice some changes in my attitude. My self-esteem slowly improved and my pain and anxiety decreased. I was even able to smile a little.

My recovery has given me a new lease on life. Unfortunately, my husband did not choose recovery. That did not stop me from working an S-Anon program. I got a sponsor and worked the Steps. I even attended an S-Anon convention. Sadly, our marriage came to an end. Today with the help of my Higher Power, my friends in recovery and the tools of the S-Anon program, I am slowly rebuilding my life. I am finding the peace and serenity I have always wanted.

Further Reflections...
"Today I will do something that is good for me even if it feels uncomfortable."

[Al-Anon's] *Courage to Change*, p. 227

Adult Child of a Sexaholic

When I first came to S-Anon I heard that sexaholism is a family disease, I didn't think this applied to my family. After a few meetings I remembered a comment my mom had made about my father, (now deceased), having been "obsessed with sex." I went to her and asked what she meant, and my mom shared that after Dad died she had found "stashes" of pornography hidden in the house. Having this light shed on my family life, I began to recall things that indeed made me uncomfortable. I became willing to see the truth about the parents I still love.

In my Fourth Step inventory I became aware of my position in our family accommodating my father's inappropriate sexual comments and jokes in front of children, his use of pornography, and inappropriate books openly displayed. I remembered feeling tension and danger around the topic of sex in our home.

In my Fifth Step I was able to admit the shame I felt about my family life and how my current relationships have been affected. I am grateful to the S-Anon program for giving me a gentle way to discover the truth about my past and begin to heal from its effects.

Further Reflections....
"S-Anon offers help and hope to all whose lives have been affected or are being affected by the disease of sexaholism; there is a solution."

Working the S-Anon Program, p. 76

I Keep Coming Back

Where I attend meetings, I am considered an "old-timer" after nine years of working the S-Anon program. Newcomers sometimes ask why I keep coming to S-Anon since the sexaholic in my life is sober. For me it's simple: by sharing my recovery with others, I get to keep the recovery that was freely given to me. I know I have a daily reprieve, based on my spiritual fitness, from the insanity and chaos that controlled my life before I came to S-Anon.

Early in my recovery I heard someone say, "There is no graduation from this program." I understand that now. Today I know I need this program to help me when life throws me the occasional curve ball, and I grapple with behaviors and attitudes that keep me from experiencing the full freedom that this program offers me.

During a recent S-Anon convention, there was crosstalk in a meeting I attended. While I knew I could raise my hand and offer my observations, I didn't. I felt disappointed in myself for "chickening out." After talking it over with other S-Anons and using the Tenth Step to examine my feelings and motives, I realized that the young girl who still lives within me feared what others would think if I spoke up. So even though I may be an "old-timer," I still can have issues arise from time to time. There is more to learn; God is still healing me.

Further Reflections...
"At its heart, Step Ten is a process of noticing the motives behind our thoughts, words, and actions."

S-Anon Twelve Steps, p. 122

A Life of Honesty

Walking the path of rigorous honesty has not been easy for me. I think of the way I was before recovery—lying when there was no compelling need to do so, not being true to myself, denying my feelings, and unknowingly aiding and abetting my sexaholic husband's double life by my dishonesty. Dishonesty was a way of life for me.

One of the thoughts my sponsor shared was the idea that addiction is about dishonesty and recovery is about honesty. I have learned that living honestly requires several things: that I take the time to understand what I need, and stand up for whatever that is; that I be accountable to another human being, such as my sponsor; and that I practice the Steps and Traditions, even when it is hard and uncomfortable for me. I have not done this alone. My Higher Power has been there every step of the way. God often speaks to me through my conscience, the words of my sponsor, S-Anon members, and remarkably at times through my sexaholic spouse. I have discovered that I do have the capacity to be honest—it is simply up to me to have the willingness to do so.

Further Reflections...
"Honesty is commitment to the truth."
                          Working The S-Anon Program, p. 48

An Ongoing Series of Lessons

At a certain point in my recovery, I noticed I was becoming rather stagnant in my program. I felt I was going through the motions of my program and not fully living it out in my day to day life. I particularly noticed this in my relationships with my sponsees.

After several lengthy conversations about the situation with my sponsor, I realized I had started focusing more on my sponsees' programs and trying to figure out what they needed to be doing, rather than focusing on my own program. My sponsor suggested it might be time for me to work through the Steps again.

I'm grateful for that suggestion, because working the Steps again has been a tremendous boost for my recovery. Focusing on others is a clue that I am being judgmental, as well as avoiding something I need to be paying attention to in my own life. Now I am a lot less focused on what my sponsees should be doing and a lot more focused on what I should be doing. While I have gained many new insights, I will be able to pass on to others when it is appropriate for me to do so. Today I know that I don't have all the answers for my sponsees, much less myself.

Going through the Steps again has reminded me of how respectful and gentle the Twelve Step process is. Working the Steps is the foundation of my recovery and gives me the recovery that I share with my sponsees.

Further Reflections...
"We trust that each sponsee relationship we have – and whatever happens in it – is an ongoing series of lessons, courtesy of a Higher Power."

                                        S-Anon pamphlet, Sponsorship

Labeling

After my first S-Anon meeting, I found myself thinking everyone with whom I came in contact was a sexaholic. When I began attending an exercise class, I noticed the instructor looking at my body. I felt very uncomfortable, fearfully wondering if he was a sexaholic.

I had heard at the meeting how people picked up the phone when they were upset and reasoned things out with another member, so after the exercise class, I did just that. I called someone from the S-Anon group and told her about my situation. I was amazed to hear her perspective. She said she also had taken the same kind of exercise class, and she noted that the instructor needs to look at students' bodies to see if they are in the correct form. I was still somewhat doubtful, but at the next class I noticed that he indeed looked at each class member's body as we worked our way through the various exercises.

This experience highlighted for me how guarded, self-conscious, and fearful I had become while living with a sexaholic. This painful side effect of sexaholism has healed as I have worked my S-Anon program. I have grown in compassion for the sexaholic and in my ability to be comfortable in my own skin and to take care of myself. I no longer feel the fearful need to label everyone a sexaholic.

Further Reflections...
"We may think that all those who we perceive to be addicted or codependent needs to be in Twelve Step recovery. We may be right in theory, but wrong about God's timing for another person. In this case we do well to remember 'Live and Let Live.'"

S-Anon Twelve Steps, p. 128

Becoming Self-Supporting

I used to look to my husband to take care of all my needs, but through my working my program, I have seen that I need to grow up and take responsibility for myself. I have learned to lean on my Higher Power, to surrender my sex-aholic husband, and focus on improving myself. I know we both have a Higher Power with whom we can work and grow. Taking responsibility for me is critical for my health and welfare, because my husband is still active in his sexaholism. I work to keep the focus on myself by applying the principle of self-support from Tradition Seven. I am working at better taking care of my responsibilities such as earning the money I need, paying my own bills, managing my time, dealing with my own frustrations and stress, making recovery connections, and taking care of my physical needs. I am gentle with myself, and I connect with friends in recovery and others who help to nurture me. As a result of being more self-supporting, I spend less time being resentful toward my husband for not meeting my needs.

As I have worked Tradition Seven in my life, I have found that I have lightened up, have reconnected with my creativity and am having more fun. These are some of the gifts I've received by becoming self-supporting.

Further Reflections...
"We failed to see that, though adult in years, we were still behaving childishly, trying to turn everybody – friends, wives, husbands, even the world itself – into protective parents. We refused to learn that over dependence upon people is unsuccessful because all people are fallible, and even the best of them will sometimes let us down..."

[AA] As Bill Sees It, p. 265

Crosstalk Boundaries in Our Meeting

"No crosstalk" as defined in the first S-Anon meeting I attended, consisted of not responding directly to what another person shares – whether by comment or advice. However, when it is my turn to share, I can indirectly address a topic or problem raised by someone else by simply sharing my own experience.

At first, this was very difficult for me to remember. Living with sexaholism gave me the impulse to give advice and fix problems. Additionally, I had spent ten years of intensive training in an academic environment where give-and-take discussions were demanded. Through coming to S-Anon meetings, week after week, I have finally begun to truly listen whole-heartedly without my mind whirling around formulating a response. This is a very liberating gift from S-Anon, one I've started using not only at meetings, but also at home and in my interactions outside meetings.

Further Reflections...
"We just speak from the heart about how we are using or trying to use the tools of the program in our own lives. By honestly describing our own path toward spiritual growth and recovery, we become living proof that the program works."

Working the S-Anon Program, p. 98

Welcoming Newcomers

S-Anon's Fifth Tradition speaks of welcoming newcomers as a part of our primary purpose. One of the ways my group does this is through our telephone hotline. Our recorded greeting is informational and friendly, and we assure callers we will be discreet in returning calls. We then promptly return calls, so they don't have to anxiously wait. We take turns checking the hotline, and because this is important Twelfth Step work, we ask another member to cover our place if we are unable to follow through.

We make a point of introducing ourselves when newcomers walk through our door. We show them the literature, and share with them how it was for us at our first meeting. We explain to them that the meetings have been a safe place for us to share what is going on in our lives, and that each of us has the option of not speaking – there are no rules.

Our group sends around a Newcomers Booklet with our names and numbers for newcomers. We let them know we understand the pain they are going through because we have been there, too. After the meeting we ask for their telephone numbers and get permission to call them in a few days, explaining that sometimes feelings can get stirred up after a meeting.

My S-Anon home group had open arms for me when I first arrived at the door. Now, taking my cue from my group, "welcoming families of sexaholics" is an attitude I try to adopt in all of my interactions with newcomers.

Further Reflections...
"Each S-Anon Family Group has but one purpose: to help families of sexaholics. We do this by...welcoming and giving comfort to the families of sexaholics."
S-Anon's Tradition Five

❖ ❖ ❖

Once Triggered...Now Serene

Before S-Anon, I lived in past memories and sexaholic traumas. For example, I went into obsessive thinking when my partner wore the same clothes as the day before, believing that this meant he hadn't spent the night at his own house. Other obsessive triggers included seeing women of certain ethnicities to whom I knew he was attracted, hearing about movies he had seen and I had not, and listening when he would describe women with whom he had had affairs as "friends," and so on. I seldom experienced peace of mind – I was constantly reacting.

I have steadily worked the S-Anon program for some time now, and I am rarely triggered into reacting anymore. I mind my own business and focus on the things I can change, rather than on the things I cannot control. I no longer participate in conversations with my partner which have to do with his sexual acting out. My sobriety and serenity depend upon my continuing to nurture a primary relationship with a Higher Power who brings me sanity.

Further Reflections...
"We will know peace of mind and feel a stronger connection with the Higher Power of our understanding, and our hope will turn to faith that God is really working in our lives, as we explore the wonders of serenity, dignity, and emotional growth."

The Gifts of the S-Anon Program

Learning to Parent

I constantly wrestle with questions of whether I am a controlling parent or a parent providing structure. When is detachment appropriate with my son and when am I allowing too much freedom? When am I providing too much information about the family addiction dynamics and when am I keeping secrets? What is normal behavior on my son's part and when is his behavior a response to being part of an addictive family?

One day in an S-Anon meeting, I shared my concerns with the group. I am working on finding the balance between "When am I providing guidance and when am I acting out of my own need to control?" Today when I am in the middle of a heated interchange with my son, I take some time out. If I am at home, I read recovery literature on control. If we are in public, I repeat the Serenity Prayer in my head. These things calm me so that I can get in touch with my underlying feelings.

I am a long way from being the kind of parent I would like to be. What I have become is the kind of parent who can admit her shortcomings. Hopefully this will create an atmosphere in my home where things can be questioned and discussed. If my child feels safe doing that with me, I have come a long way toward healing in our relationship.

[Excerpt from *Working the S-Anon Program*, p. 91]

Further Reflections...
"The real issue is often apparent after the emotions I have experienced at the moment have quieted."

Working the S-Anon Program, p. 18

Looking for the Joy

Early this spring, my children taught me a very important lesson. After several beautiful and warm "short-sleeves" days, a cold front came through with a snow-storm. We woke up that Monday morning in early April to three inches of snow on the ground. When I saw the snow, I became grouchy and thought, "It's spring – it's not supposed to snow!" I was still clinging to the belief that I knew best what should happen in life.

Every adult I spoke to that day complained about the awful weather. My children raced to the window and, when seeing the snow, were delighted. They bundled up and went outside to play in it for hours. They not only accepted the snow, they went out of their way to enjoy it! In seeing their example of accepting reality rather than complaining about it, I saw the futility of my own attitude and actions of the day.

Today I try not to view "accepting the things I cannot change" as a burden, but as an opportunity. I am learning to ask my Higher Power not only for the serenity to accept what I cannot change, but also for willingness to look for the joy that is present in all the circumstances of my life, even those I would not have chosen.

Further Reflections...
"I found that 'practicing these principles in all my affairs' became a natural process and resulted in even more awakenings."

S-Anon Twelve Steps, p. 146

Room for the Unexpected

I always liked to figure things out up front so I would have a good idea of what to expect before I engaged in something. While this helped me feel safe and in control, it also meant I spent a lot of mental time and physical energy planning for every possible contingency – even for some things that probably would never happen.

In S-Anon I am learning that when my thoughts go beyond reasonable planning into obsessive circular thinking, I am leaving my Higher Power out of the process. In my obsession I try to control everything – even the uncontrollable. My sponsor says it is O.K. to plan, but to leave room for those unexpected surprises and spontaneous wonders that can happen when God is in the planning. I find that when I do let my Higher Power into my plans, I don't have to expend so much energy arranging my life to "feel safe." The more I let my Higher Power be in charge, the better I take care of myself and the safer I feel, no matter what transpires.

Further Reflections...
"I don't have to control the outcome, but can learn to trust the process. This allows me to be less afraid of the future."
S-Anews, November 1994

No Longer Alone

At my first S-Anon meeting, I felt so uncomfortable just being there that I concluded I did not belong. I made a decision never to return. Sometime later my husband disclosed new incidents of sexual activities outside our marriage. I was devastated. With nowhere else to turn, I realized I needed to return to S-Anon.

This time I found the courage to share the deep burden that was weighing heavy on me. What relief I found! The members validated my feelings – I was not crazy. I discovered my feelings were normal, my situation was not unique, and I was no longer alone. I felt such comfort in that meeting.

I experienced hope as I kept coming back. I heard people say "life does get better" and "you're doing great." These were comforting and encouraging words to my wounded heart, and I was able to press on and "Keep Coming Back." I heard these words from people who courageously worked their program and freely shared from their experience, strength, and hope with newcomers like me. The fog of my obsession and pain began to lift. Now I share with newcomers who courageously have come through the doors of S-Anon. I am so grateful for this program.

Further Reflections...
"Meetings: A chance to let others see us as we really are and to receive unconditional love and acceptance in return."

S-Anon Newcomer Booklet, p. 13

A Loving Gift I Give Myself

Detaching with love and compassion is something I heard about in my first S-Anon meeting. At that point detachment did not seem to offer any great benefit, especially when I considered loosening the grip I thought I had on the sexaholic's life. I thought detaching from my husband's problems might cause him to slide back into his old acting out behaviors. I was overcome by fear and I could not see that detaching would actually take pressure off of me.

I am grateful for receiving a spiritual awakening through doing my First Step work that allowed me to see that I do not want the job of controlling another. After this awakening, I began to detach with love and compassion from the sexaholic's problems to the best of my ability. I found I had much more energy to take better care of myself. I had no idea how much energy it had taken to carry around someone else's burdens!

Practicing detachment has become a loving gift I give to myself. I realize now that using my energy to prop up my husband was more likely holding him back from hitting his bottom. My path is clearer today. Today, I honor the paths that others choose for themselves. I choose to stay on my own spiritual path and trust God to work in all our lives.

Further Reflections...
"Sobriety is not taking other people's inventories and deciding what they should or should not do in their lives."
Working the S-Anon Program, p. 55

Changing the Things I Can

When I was with the sexaholic, I always waited for him to change, and everything I did was geared toward making this happen. Back then, I thought that he was the only one who needed to change in order for me to be happy. In my "wisdom" I also thought I knew exactly how he needed to be different.

The irony is nothing changed until I realized that I was the one who had to do things differently. I had to stop my controlling behaviors and start focusing on myself. So I started setting boundaries for myself to stop my compulsive controlling and gave the whole situation over to my Higher Power.

Amazingly, when I started changing on the inside, change on the outside started to happen as well. It didn't always happen the way I expected, but overall the outcome was for the good. I became healthier and more honest with myself, despite the sexaholic deciding to leave. While I don't have the relationship I had wished for with him, I don't suffer anymore, either. My life is more peaceful and fulfilling now and many good things have come my way since I stopped expecting someone else to make me feel better about myself, and started changing myself instead.

Further Reflections...
"Maybe I am uncomfortable because my prayers haven't been answered the way I wanted them to be – 'make my life better by fixing him.' I have prayed for help, but maybe the answer is I need to make changes in my own life."

Working the S-Anon Program, p. 47

Sexually Transmitted Disease

I have been in S-Anon recovery for a number of years and my husband has a sporadic history of recovery. In spite of this, I thought we had made progress in our relationship. Then I had an outbreak of sores on my thighs and genital area. I immediately contacted my doctor who suspected it was genital herpes. This did not seem possible to me. Why after so many years? My husband was my only sexual partner. I knew he had had several different partners, some prior to marriage and some during marriage, but as long as twenty years ago. I figured it had to have been one of them. After some testing, the diagnosis of genital herpes was confirmed. The Nurse Practitioner assured me that symptoms can show up even many years after exposure.

This experience brought up many old feelings of betrayal, anger, and fear. I took the time I needed to work through these feelings. I was able to find perspective by working the tools of the S-Anon program, along with some outside help. It was also important to share my feelings with my husband. I still have bad days and I feel sorry for myself a times, but I try not to stay there for too long. Instead, I work on my gratitude list and take care of myself, one day at a time.

Further Reflections...
"Sexual contact with others can expose the sexaholic to diseases that are incurable and even fatal; in some cases these diseases can then be passed on to the sexaholic's spouse or partner...ask a doctor for tests for sexually transmitted diseases and follow the doctor's advice on self protection."

S-Anon Twelve Steps, p. xix,xx

The Benefits of Service

I recently served as the chairperson of an S-Anon committee in charge of planning a regional one-day convention called a marathon. I was so excited about what I was working on that I had not considered the gifts I might receive from volunteering in this way. Here are just a few of the gifts.

Doing this service helped me focus on my program, rather than on the sexaholic in my life. I had the opportunity to make contact with the larger S-Anon community outside of my regular meetings. I found that being a "trusted servant," as described in Tradition Two, was a rich and deeply spiritual experience for me. I learned far more from serving on this committee than I had at other occasions when I was in charge. I also learned much about letting go of control and allowing other people to do things in their own way. Working on the marathon was an opportunity to work with recovering sexaholics. This new experience afforded me the opportunity to put into practice what I had learned in S-Anon about communicating clearly and letting go of the results.

There are so many ways to grow in S-Anon, and doing service work in the program has been one of the most rewarding for me.

Further Reflections...
"I do my best to practice what we say at our meeting closing – we share what we have, 'so that we may keep what we have been given.'"

Working the S-Anon Program, p. 21

Seeing the Beauty

By the time I got to S-Anon, I felt unlovable, unwanted, and unattractive from years of living with a sexaholic. While S-Anon members gave me much comfort and support, I also felt threatened by them. I imagined that the sexaholic would be attracted to traits in each of them – traits I didn't have: confidence, humor, long hair, a beautiful face, etc. These were the same comparisons I had been making for years, where I always came up lacking.

As I worked the S-Anon program, I slowly began to see the members of the group in a different way, and I was not threatened anymore. I came to see their pain, their grace, their honesty, and their generosity. It was as if they were transformed before my eyes into the most amazing people. Each time I was with my group, my appreciation for each individual grew and evolved.

Since then, I have begun to appreciate myself, as well. For many years, I had viewed all women, including myself, through the eyes of a sexaholic. In S-Anon I learned to see others and myself as I imagine God might see us. I still have times of struggle, but on most days I see beauty all around me, and, most precious, I see beauty in me, as well.

Further Reflections...
"It is important to remember to be patient with ourselves during this process of being restored to sanity. We are not asked to do all this at once. It takes time to develop faith and to recover. Feeling guilty and having expectations of a quick recovery only interferes with the healing process."
S-Anon Twelve Steps, p. 17

Choosing a Life of Recovery

It has been seven years since my divorce, and I am not in a committed relationship. It is amazing how much pressure I feel from societal expectations by not being in a relationship. This is particularly difficult for me during special occasions or holidays.

My S-Anon program has helped me to put this in a more healthy perspective. Through working the Twelve Steps of S-Anon, especially Steps Four and Five, I began to see how my past holidays and special occasions had been filled with unhealthy expectations and a lack of respect for myself and others. In recovery this is gradually changing. One of the many gifts of working this wonderful program is all the friends I have made. I don't have to be alone if I am willing to ask for what I need.

I am grateful for choosing a life of recovery. I can be serene and experience peace of mind as well as self-love. Relying on my Higher Power and knowing that my fellow S-Anon members will be there to support, encourage, and help me on this recovery path is very comforting.

Further Reflections...
"Sobriety is knowing and owning all of my own behavior and choices."

Working the S-Anon Program, p. 54

Bountiful Challenges

I entered S-Anon and my husband entered his recovery program several years ago. Thankfully, there has been steady progress. My husband has recently had difficulties with sexual impotence. I have gained the gift of being open to many options from the support of other S-Anon members, and I am able to see the unexpected gift of his condition. Our Higher Power must believe we are ready to explore, on a deeper level, how to apply the principles of our programs, in light of this new challenge. We clearly have been given a gift to learn how to enjoy and have emotional intimacy in our marriage — without the sexual relationship we once had.

Having learned early in my life to "stuff" my feelings has made this a big challenge for me. As a result, I've become more aware of how the disease of sexaholism affects me spiritually, emotionally, and physically. My husband's impotence may not improve, but we are learning there is more to life than sex, and we are experiencing a richer companionship because of it.

There have been bountiful amounts of struggles, and some positive outcomes have resulted from working through this situation. My anger and frustration have bubbled to the surface, and I had the opportunity to work through my desire to blame him for his past behavior. I can now appreciate his good qualities, and I know I am becoming a better person. I am learning patience, compassion, and how to respond differently.

Further Reflections...
"Today sex is optional, and I don't have to use it to get intimacy."

Working the S-Anon Program, p. 66

"Breathe... Easy, Easy, Easy"

Busy, busy, busy! That was who I was before S-Anon. I am still a very active, energetic person with many interests, but since beginning my recovery, I am learning not to over-plan my days. A large part of my overdoing was a defense I used to not feel my painful feelings. Slowing down felt scary, but I discovered it allowed me to feel and heal the painful feelings of growing up in an alcoholic home, then living in a sexaholic home.

I now take more time for rest and relaxation, including walks alone in nature, daily meditation time, and periodic spiritual retreats. This is all still fairly new to me, but I am noticing I feel calmer, more peaceful, less anxious, and less rushed than I used to feel. It is also helping me to become a more punctual person. My new replacement motto for "busy, busy, busy" is now "breathe... easy, easy, easy."

Further Reflections...
"Some of us misused drugs, alcohol, or food, and others kept so busy with activities that we didn't have time to feel our emotions. We often neglected our health, our jobs, and our children. No matter how we tried to struggle against it, deny it, or minimize its effects, the failure of our efforts to cope with sexaholism brought us to the point of despair."

The S-Anon Problem (short version)

Free to Be Me

I have kept secrets all my life. I understand now that keeping secrets was a way for me to try to avoid the shame and embarrassment I was feeling. Secrets gave me a way to deny that anything was wrong within my family, as well as relationships with most everyone I knew. What was most damaging about my keeping secrets was how I was able to fool myself for far too long. This left me feeling lonely and isolated. I felt like an outsider in relationships that meant so much to me.

When I first came to S-Anon, I heard "We are only as sick as our secrets." Truly understanding how this applied to my own life took me awhile. I kept coming back and took direction from my sponsor and others. I learned I had a place where I could share my secrets without the fear of being judged, criticized, or ostracized. In S-Anon, I came to find that I could leave the secrets behind and be my true self, striving each day to be the person I was always meant to be, no longer feeling like an outsider among those I care about. I am finally free to be me.

Further Reflections...
"We isolated ourselves from those closest to us in an attempt to keep our secrets. We suffered fear, anxiety, depression, guilt, loneliness, rage, and a lack of energy and motivation... As we begin to devote ourselves to Twelve Step recovery... we learn we are not alone in facing the problem of sexaholism... we find hope."

S-Anon Twelve Steps, p. 2-3

Answered Prayer

The program is working. The glimmer of peace is there, sometimes feeling like a mirage, sometimes like a wonderfully palpable bliss. I pray for peace of mind, peace of heart, and peace of spirit. When the peace comes, I am at peace with the world and that peace shows through me. For instance, today, someone asked me, "What are you smiling about?" I said, "I didn't even know I was smiling."

I can occasionally still visit a state of mind where I am in knots – that state of mind where I used to live, spending my days obsessing. In that state, my face is pinched and my stomach and back are tense. I feel afraid and alone. In those times, I pray to open myself to my Creator, and I thank God for the many answered prayers I've already experienced. Then I find strength to pick up the telephone and make an S-Anon connection. I am given creative ideas to face my life and wait through the uncertainties – sometimes through music or art or a project. I find peace that God is with me and I am never alone.

Further Reflections...
"I give credit to my Higher Power for lifting my bitterness and resentment. I'm not sure when it happened, and I know I didn't plan it. I thought I had good reason to be angry for the rest of my life, but found that I am not hurting inside anymore."

Working the S-Anon Program, p. 38

Learning to Release and Let Go

When I first started coming to S-Anon, we had a special meeting about trusting God to take care of our worries and deepest hurts. We were asked to write down our worries and cares on strips of paper, tie them to helium balloons, and let them go, symbolizing releasing them to God. As we watched them rise, one person's balloon got stuck in an oak tree. The frustrated person grabbed her keys and threw them at the balloon, which shook free and began to rise again – but the keys remained in the tree!

This reminded me of my years before S-Anon and before I had come to rely on the slogan "Let go and Let God." When I came to S-Anon, God showed me there were still times I tried to control what I had surrendered. For instance: sometimes I would let go of my worries, but then tell God what to do with them.

Today when I let go, I visualize God releasing the "balloon," knowing He receives whatever it is I surrender at the point of release. In my visualization, God is in control of where the balloon lands. This means God is in control of the outcome.

Further Reflections...
"Simply having faith in a Higher Power is not enough. We have to surrender our will and our lives over and over again. Now, in all times of emotional disturbance and indecision we can pause, get quiet, and in that stillness let go of our problems and worries. We can have the confidence that we have an ever-present help in times of need."
S-Anon Twelve Steps, p. 29

Leaving the Outcome to God

I realized I needed to work Step Three after I began a relationship with yet another sexaholic. I discovered he was not sexually sober, despite attending a recovery program for sexaholism. I found myself experiencing familiar feelings; anxiety, depression, and hopelessness about the future of our relationship. I doubted my ability to make good choices for myself.

I called an S-Anon friend, and she read the first three Steps to me. Hearing those Steps again, especially Step Three, made me realize I hadn't really turned my will and my life over to the care of God. This became apparent when I thought about the sense of panic and insecurity that had been plaguing me. I had been invested in my own agenda for how my life was supposed to be and the fantasy of how I wanted this relationship to turn out.

Answering the Step Three questions listed in *S-Anon Twelve Steps* has been the true beginning of surrendering my agenda and my fantasy. Day by day, I am learning to leave the outcome of my life to God. My responsibility is to do the footwork needed to have a deeper and more honest relationship with myself.

Further Reflections...
"Now we can let go of our dependence on the sexaholic, let go of our illusions of control over other people and outcomes, and, most important, let go of desperately trying to play God in our own lives."

S-Anon Twelve Steps, p. 36

Accepting Myself Honestly

When I first came to S-Anon, I thought I had all the answers. I quoted from books and told others how to deal with their problems. I did not realize I focused on everything except my own thoughts and feelings. One day a fellow member shared on "getting real" about her life. She realized she had been dishonest and had put on a front so that her life would look better to others than it really was. She said she feared what others would think if they knew the truth. I was terribly uncomfortable hearing this and then realized I recognized myself in what she was saying.

After listening to other people speak honestly, I discovered that I had a lot to learn about myself. I had not been real or truthful with others or myself. I became willing to accept that I do belong in S-Anon, that Step One applies to me, and that I am teachable. Accepting myself honestly allowed me to feel safe to share truthfully with other S-Anons recovering from the effects of sexaholism. I no longer isolate myself by thinking I am alone in my problem and better than others. I have choices today and I am grateful for the S-Anon program.

Further Reflections...
"I see that being committed in a relationship doesn't mean giving up myself, it means being honest about who I am, and being courageous enough to share the reality of myself with someone else, regardless of what they're going to say."

Working the S-Anon Program, p. 63

Daily Progress

How wonderful God's timing is! Right before a special family celebration, the topic at my S-Anon meeting was "progress not perfection." Many people shared how before S-Anon they desired to do things perfectly and how they were now learning to accept themselves and others just as they are. In my sharing I noted how I had frequently acknowledged the dangers of my perfectionism and what a toll it took on me, but here I was back trying to make everything perfect for entertaining so many family members in my home.

That meeting was exactly what I needed. One more time I recognized that I was exhausting myself to have everything just right and to anticipate all my family's needs and wants. This in spite of all I had learned working my program.

It was good to be reminded that my family celebration would come, whether or not I had my house and food perfectly in order. Again, I was reminded that the daily progress — not perfection — of my program is sufficient.

Further Reflections...
"We always want to aim for the best, even though we know that we cannot be perfect. We accept ourselves, as we travel at our own pace towards spiritual growth."

S-Anon Twelve Steps, p. 64

Dabbling in S-Anon

While I was thinking about what a speaker had said regarding denial and pride at a recent S-Anon meeting, my Higher Power gave me a helpful image. Fear, denial, and pride are like false friends sitting on my shoulders, whispering lies into my ear. They were something like Cinderella's stepsisters, who kept her from going to the ball.

I began to see that my own denial and false pride had kept me from "attending the ball," that is, from truly enjoying my life. Denial and false pride kept me stuck in the role of a frustrated, selfish, helpless victim. In that victim role, I was neither humble enough to seek help, nor responsible enough to take action for myself. Denial and false pride fueled my continuing self-criticism and being judgmental. The result was I felt free to give advice to other people, while not taking it myself. As a result, I only dabbled in S-Anon, taking half-measures rather than truly working the S-Anon program.

Today, I more readily can recognize when I am listening to denial and pride, those false friends on my shoulders. I surrender them as quickly as I can, giving them less time to take up space in my head, so I can truly work the S-Anon program and enjoy my life.

Further Reflections…
"[Our defects] were our defenses against the world… We must admit the old ways haven't worked very well. We are now ready to let them go."

S-Anon Twelve Steps, p. 64

My Opinion Has Value

One of the hallmarks of my unhealthy thinking and behavior is my tendency not to express my opinion. I often go along with the other person's opinion instead of considering what I believe. S-Anon helped me to see that having no opinion does not necessarily relieve me of the responsibility of a decision made. When I do not participate in the decision process, I leave myself open for resentment when things do not turn out my way. Working this program has allowed me to make progress in clearly speaking my opinion and letting Higher Power guide the outcome.

Tradition Two reminds me of the importance of taking the time to have a considered opinion and to express that opinion appropriately. When I practice this, I am actively participating in the group conscience—whether it is in an S-Anon meeting, at work, or with family. I believe that God gave me a unique personality and point of view. When I do not take part in the group conscience, I am not being true to myself and I am not helping the decision-making process. It is as if I cease to exist! S-Anon has shown me that I am a worthy person capable of making a contribution. When I do so, everyone benefits.

Further Reflections...
"A decision that is discussed thoroughly by as many members as possible and is guided by a Higher Power is an expression of the group conscience."
Working the S-Anon Program, p. 30

True Colors

I learned in school that leaves are only green because of photosynthesis. Their true colors come forth in the fall when the light is reduced and photosynthesis ceases. This image from nature is helpful in understanding my recovery in S-Anon.

When I did my Fourth Step, I found out that I often believed what other people said about me. I went along with other people's ideas and didn't really think for myself. As I grew in recovery, I started to learn who I was and to see my true colors. I also became able to accept other people's colors and didn't have to see everyone the same. This increased honesty has provided a much more interesting life than my previous existence.

It is exciting to appreciate that God has created each one of us with beauty and individuality. I want to be willing to observe and honor it.

Further Reflections...
"As I connect at deeper levels with my Higher Power's love for me, I feel a greater ability to be honest, to know myself, and to let myself be seen and heard by others."
Working the S-Anon Program, p. 49

Letting Go of Old Memories

Before recovery, I felt anger was not something a spiritual person should experience. So I rationalized my anger away and made excuses for other people. Today, with several years of S-Anon recovery, I understand it is healing for me to identify and feel my emotions.

This weekend I remembered an incident between my sister and me from years ago. I was surprised by the fury that flooded through me as I recalled the incident, even though it occurred over seven years ago. Perhaps the memory surfaced because I had not allowed myself to experience anger during the actual event. The memory continued to come up over the weekend, bringing anger with it each time. I acknowledged that I had had the right to feel angry about the incident, but I also had to ask myself, "Am I going to continue to be angry every time I remember this incident and others like it?" I suddenly had an insight: my Higher Power does not hold onto my shortcomings, but forgives me. What a freeing thought that I could do the same!

I decided to let go of the anger immediately. I visualized holding the memory in my hands. In my mind's eye, I saw myself washing my hands and letting the water wash the angry memory away. This visualization might not work for everyone but it worked for me!

Today, I realize it is part of my recovery to acknowledge the painful past – and to realize it is the past – and to take steps to move toward a serene future.

Further Reflections...
"As we begin to recover in S-Anon, we learn how to manage our lives in a way much better than ever before."
S-Anon Twelve Steps, p. 3

Abstinence...A Healing Journey

Abstinence has led my sexaholic spouse and me on a healing journey. It started after his first Sexaholics Anonymous meeting, when some old timers suggested that he consider a 30-day abstinence from sexual relations with me as a way of "drying out" from his disease. He was desperate for recovery and I was desperate to fix him, so I readily agreed. At the end of 30 days, he was not ready. Less enthusiastically, I agreed to another 30 days. Again he was not ready. Now I was angry. I called another S-Anon member and complained, cried, and criticized for an hour. She brought me back to reality by saying: "You know, if sex was not the most important sign of love for you, this would not be that big of a deal. After all it's only 30 days, not forever."

I started considering my thoughts and feelings about sex rather than simply thinking of it as a barometer of my husband's love. At the end of this period of abstinence, I was the one not ready!

Since then we have had a number of abstinence agreements, each offering important lessons. Sometimes my lesson was about our relationship, but most of the time it was about me and my fears. Today I thank God for the tool of abstinence and the opportunity for growth in my program that it provides.

Further Reflections...

"Many couples agree upon a period of time for the abstinence and a time to renegotiate or end the abstinence period. When discussing our desire for abstinence with our partner, it is best to choose a calm time and to speak in terms of our own needs and feelings."

Working the S-Anon Program, p. 68

❖ ❖ ❖

"...We Tried to Carry This Message..."

Step Twelve says, "...we tried to carry this message..." To me this use of the word "tried" implies I am not in control of the outcome. I am practicing the spirit of Step Twelve when I focus on my Higher Power's will for me, rather than delude myself with the illusion that I know what is best for another. How I work Step Twelve is a personal measure of my emotional sobriety. Am I attempting to fix, control, or manipulate another person when I carry the message or am I humbly sharing the message of my recovery with no expectations?

For me, successfully carrying the message depends on surrendering the outcome. When I carry the S-Anon message to the newcomer, I make a conscious effort to let go. I remember it is not my business what the newcomer decides for him or herself. Step Twelve simply directs me to try to share how S-Anon has helped me and has given me hope.

Actions ultimately speak louder than words, and I know that my attitude and behavior are vital parts of my Twelfth Step message, too. After all, how I am there for the newcomer when I share the message is a reflection of how well I work the program in my daily life. I can't transmit what I don't have.

Further Reflections...
"We need to learn to give up expectations about outcomes and catch ourselves when we are trying to fix anyone. We look to find a balance between taking care of ourselves and helping others; we can be available to those we want to help without taking on all their burdens."

[Al-Anon] Paths To Recovery, p. 120

Respect

The gifts of the S-Anon program include regaining self-confidence, independence of spirit, and the courage to be true to myself. I am so pleased that working the program is giving me those gifts.

Today I have choices about how to respond to a co-worker who disrespects me. In the past, the only option for me was taking on the victim role and defending myself by attacking the other person. Today I know I don't have to attack anyone, or keep the peace at the price of my self-worth and dignity. Working with my sponsor, I take small steps to retain my dignity and self-worth. I am choosing to get to work earlier now and spend a few moments in prayer, putting into the God Box on my desk my written prayer that my co-worker be in his Higher Power' hands for the day. That God Box on my desk is a reminder that I do not have to take my co-worker's sarcasm personally.

I ask my Higher Power, on a daily basis, for the courage to continue taking small actions of faith like these. I know I am not alone in my efforts – I have the help of S-Anon and my Higher Power.

Further Reflections...
"But as we shed old ideas that made us feel isolated or unworthy, we began to understand new and hopeful spiritual concepts. We grew in the faith that a loving and caring Higher Power would guide and protect us."

Working the S-Anon Program, p. 24

The Gift of Healing

During a recent difficult illness, I was aware that there wasn't anything I could do to ensure my recovery from the illness. I could not speed up the healing time or make the illness go away. All I could do was eat well, get plenty of rest, and try to have a positive attitude through talking with others and with God. While I could do those things and cooperate with the doctor's orders for balancing exercise and rest, the actual recovery was something I could not make happen.

This experience has reminded me of the nature of my S-Anon recovery. Sometimes my recovery is slow and painful and the progress seems hardly measurable. Other times the pace and rewards of recovery are swift and evident. Either way, healing happens in God's grace and time. Healing is a gift.

Further Reflections...
"I don't have to control the outcome, but can learn to trust the process. This allows me to be less afraid of the future. I am learning to accept change and not automatically see it as the end of the world or negative, but rather an opportunity for growth."

Working the S-Anon Program, p. 42

The Power of Words

I have found that words can carry tremendous power, yet often little thought is given to how they are expressed. Careless, hurtful words can crush a spirit, and gentle, kind words can heal.

Words brought me into S-Anon. First there were the carefully considered words of a friend on the phone who suggested I look at some issues. Next there were the words of *The S-Anon Problem* read by the person who answered the phone line when I first called for help. Then there were the welcoming words read at the first meeting I attended and at every meeting since. Finally there were the words I read in the S-Anon literature I took home that first night.

The literature used in S-Anon meetings and available from the S-Anon World Service Office is conference approved, meaning it is carefully and thoughtfully written, revised, considered, edited, and evaluated by dozens of experienced S-Anon members. This process ensures that our literature reflects the S-Anon principles accurately and that no one person speaks for S-Anon as suggested in Tradition Twelve.

I am grateful for the growing awareness of the power in words – spoken and written. It is my prayer that my words will be useful in carrying a message of hope.

Further Reflections...
"...it was in our S-Anon Literature that I found similar experiences that really hit home with me. It consistently focused on the solution rather than the problem, and the solution was what I really needed, not further analysis of the problem."

Working the S-Anon Program, p. 16

Sharing the Message

If my Mom was to get the Mother's Day book and card I had prepared on time, it had to be at the post office before 5:00 p.m., just before I was to meet my S-Anon sponsor for Step work and dinner. I rushed to finish.

In my haste, I inadvertently placed my S-Anon "blue book" into my Mom's envelope with the Mother's Day card, and dropped it in the post office's mailbox. As I drove off, I glanced at the seat to make sure my Step notes were with my S-Anon book. I was horrified – instead of my "blue book" and notes, there was my Mother's book!

I rushed back to the post office. Slipping through the doors just before they were locked, I begged the postal clerk to retrieve my mistaken mailing. She was understandably reluctant. I decided to be honest with her, and explained that I had erroneously mailed my S-Anon Twelve Steps book rather than my mother's gift book. As she dug through the mail, she asked what S-Anon was. I explained briefly about S-Anon. As she handed over my book, she thanked me for being so honest and for the information. She explained that her sister in another state just had called with the news of her husband's affairs. "Now I have something helpful I can share with her," she said.

I walked out of the post office, thrilled to have my S-Anon book back and glad that God could make use of my hasty error in such a fortunate way.

Further Reflections...
"In S-Anon, we learn to place the focus on ourselves and our own recovery, and that's what I share with others."
Working the S-Anon Program, p. 96

Grateful to Be Married to a Sexaholic

When I lead a newcomer's meeting, I share I am grateful to be married to a recovering sexaholic. I tell them that I am not being sarcastic or trying to diminish the pain they are experiencing. Rather, my gratitude arises out of my awareness that sexaholism brought me to S-Anon, which has given me many gifts.

One of these gifts is a relationship with myself. Before S-Anon, I acted how I thought others wanted me to act. I would change my opinion on a topic to avoid another person's anger. In recovery, I came to think of my pre-recovery persona as "the chameleon-velcro woman" – stick to whomever and mimic them. Through S-Anon I have discovered who I am and have developed the courage to be myself, regardless of what others think or say. What a gift to truly like myself today!

Another gift has been learning to take the focus off my husband and put it onto myself. For years I tried to change my husband and got nothing but frustration. Coming to S-Anon has allowed me to enjoy him for the person he is.

Discovering I was married to a sexaholic was my worst nightmare. S-Anon has given me the gift of a better life. For that I am truly grateful.

Further Reflections…
"We will find the courage to be true to ourselves."
The Gifts of the S-Anon Program

No Longer God's Supervisor

I had been struggling with Step Three, so my sponsor suggested that I read Step Three stories in our Conference Approved Literature (CAL). Over and over I read how turning our will over to the care of a Higher Power can be such a benefit. I was especially interested in how difficult this could be, since I tend to "bombard" my problems with willpower, trying to fix the messes in which I have often found myself.

"Bombarding" described what I was doing in all aspects of my life. I would attack people, places, and situations that did not agree with my agenda. Based on the belief system that was modeled for me while growing up, I was under the illusion that this was the responsible way to live. I constantly felt uncomfortable with how my life was going, however, and I became "full of myself," denying that God could handle the situation.

Working the S-Anon program shines a spotlight on who I am, and how I operate in this world. I am learning that it is necessary to crack open the mold I thought I had to live in, and then to restructure my beliefs. Humility, honesty, acknowledging the truth – these are the things that have helped me to stop "bombarding" situations with my self will and to deflate my being "full of myself." As a result of working Step Three, my Higher Power is now in charge. I still do the footwork, but I am only God's assistant now, not God's supervisor.

Further Reflections...
"We found that surrender was no longer a dreadful prospect; it was our freedom from mental and emotional slavery."

S-Anon Twelve Steps, p. 36

Tradition Seven

For several years, I chaired an organization within my profession. The job sometimes required printing and shipping materials, for which I incurred copying and mailing costs. I routinely did not request reimbursement for those expenses, even though funds were budgeted for them. I told myself that it didn't cost that much, that it was embarrassing to ask for money and that the organization was small and needed to conserve its funds

I have grown in my S-Anon recovery, and today I see my behavior differently. S-Anon taught me that taking care of myself is just as important as not caretaking others. When I paid for company expenses out of my personal funds, I actually was falling back into an old family pattern of not asking for anything for myself. I also was choosing to be a martyr by caretaking the organization's pocketbook, despite their already agreed-upon budget. Today I know it is respectful and healthy for me to allow my organization to operate on its own, without my unasked-for contributions.

The Seventh Tradition underlies my self-care. Tradition Seven helps the S-Anon fellowship remain healthy through practices ranging from financial guidelines at the World Service Office, to paying rent at the facilities where we hold our local meetings. It also helps in relationships and my personal life, as well. The more I practice Tradition Seven, the better I feel about myself.

Further Reflections...
"[Tradition Seven] teaches us — as individuals, as groups and as part of the worldwide fellowship — the importance of the self-supporting concept. We can also use Tradition Seven as a model for healthy relationships in many other groups — families, jobs, community — just about anywhere."   *[Al-Anon] Paths to Recovery, p. 196-197*

❖   ❖   ❖

Getting to Know Myself

I have discovered that the longer I work the S-Anon program, the better I get to know myself. For example, every winter I find that I hibernate. I still go to meetings and hang out with friends, but I spend more time meditating, painting, and writing. After a few years of this, I noticed that my hibernating sometimes turns into isolating. By doing the Tenth Step, I was reminded that before program I did a lot of isolating. I spent a lot of time hiding in my apartment and avoiding life in general. This was rarely productive time, as I would drink, use drugs, and brood over the choices I had made in my life.

Now I see that isolation is a way I disconnect from my Higher Power and divert myself from my own "primary spiritual aim." I am still capable of isolating; however, I have the choice not to stay in isolation for long. S-Anon helps me break unhealthy cycles like hibernation becoming isolation. Using the tools of the S-Anon program: meetings, writing, service, calling my sponsor, and more – helps to put my day-to-day life back in perspective. When I have a hard time taking care of myself, S-Anon gets me out of the house and among people who genuinely care about me.

Further Reflections...
"We isolated ourselves from those closest to us in an attempt to keep our secrets. We suffered fear, anxiety, depression, guilt, loneliness, rage, and lack of energy and motivation."

S-Anon Twelve Steps, p. 2

Life Became Simple and Peaceful

After reading Step One in *S-Anon Twelve Steps*, I listed where I had been powerless as a result of trying to exert power over others. Topping this list were situations where I feared being emotionally abandoned.

I learned very early to connect with people who had difficulties, because they inevitably needed help with their problems and consequently would not leave me. Unfortunately, my fear of abandonment tormented me into becoming whatever they wanted. So I stayed with my sex-aholic partner, even though his behavior threatened my health.

S-Anon helped me see that my fear had led me to abandon myself through having no boundaries. So I began setting boundaries and taking care of my emotional well-being, and, in response, my spouse began to physically and emotionally distance himself. I was terrified he would leave, but I had learned to ask myself, "Must I tolerate sexual and emotional abuse in exchange for maintaining a relationship?" The answer gradually came: to stay with my husband meant accepting things that were unhealthy and intolerable for me, physically and spiritually. I had to risk his abandonment in order to heal.

When I finally accepted I would be in the care of my Higher Power no matter what others chose to do, I was able to let go of the fear and let go of my marriage. Amazingly, my life became so much more simple and peaceful.

Further Reflections...
"...and I realized that my Higher Power really is loving and caring. After all, He provided all the wonderful people in S-Anon and S-Ateen who have shared their experience, strength, hope, support, and courage."
Working the S-Anon Program, p. 79

❖   ❖   ❖

Seeing with Eyes Wide Open

When I came to S-Anon, it was as though my eyes were opened. For the first time I was able to see the depth of how I had been affected by the sexaholic's lying, dishonesty, and duplicity. My husband had been so convincing, and I so wanted to believe him. In my first meeting, I felt relieved and validated when someone said, "When sexaholism is active, this sets up a cycle of lies and deceit."

It wasn't easy to see how I had participated in this disease process – how I had enabled his lying, and how I had lied to myself and others about what was really happening in our home. I had been so afraid of feeling the pain and seeing the truth of living with active addiction, that I fooled myself into believing that living a lie would be so much easier.

My spouse is still active in his sexaholism, but I no longer depend on him to be honest. Instead, I am learning to take better care of myself by setting healthy personal boundaries and depending on my Higher Power. I know now that sexaholism is painful and a dreaded way to live. I pray that God will help my husband find recovery. I am grateful that I am living my life in recovery today. I can take whatever action is necessary to take care of myself. S-Anon gives me a place where I can hear the truth.

Further Reflections...
"The old tools may have included denial, obsession with the sexaholic, covering up the problem, isolation, rage, and manipulation. In letting go of the old tools, we were able to try new, more effective ways to aid us in recovery."
Working the S-Anon Program, p. 1

Willingness to Serve

Taking the example of my sponsor, I got involved in service work early in my recovery. I became active in our local S-Anon convention where I helped with behind the scene duties.

Being a perfectionist, I prepared extensively so the convention would go smoothly. As we got closer to the closing meeting, I heaved a sigh of relief. Just before the last meeting was to start, the convention organizer informed me that they were without an S-Anon speaker and would I be willing to fill the gap? I was stunned. What would I share? I had nothing prepared! Would I look the fool? I would probably cry!

My sponsor had encouraged me to share if asked, so I took a moment to practice the Third Step. I turned over the willingness to speak in front of the group to my Higher Power, and I asked God's help in what I would say. This was my prayer: "Please God, help me not to worry about how I appear, but to say what will be helpful for those who are listening." When I got to the podium, I simply told my story. I did choke up, but a voice within said, "You're okay. Just take a deep breath, and wait until you can speak again." I did. That day, I took a "leap of faith" by turning my will and my life over to a Higher Power, and it worked!

Further Reflections...
"Until now, we may have believed that the sexaholic and our compulsive concerns were the only things we needed to turn over to God. Now we are called upon to surrender our will and our lives, to surrender ourselves completely."
S-Anon Twelve Steps, p. 27

Topic Meetings

Twice monthly, my home group holds a "topic" meeting. Sometimes a member has an issue weighing on his or her mind, so that selection of a topic is nearly instantaneous. Other times, we need to search for a topic of discussion, so we each pick up a piece of Conference-Approved Literature (CAL) and peruse the contents or index for something that "jumps off of the page." Once a topic is agreed upon, we spend several minutes reading out loud on that topic before sharing. There is always plenty of food for thought.

I recently realized that holding these topic meetings is a good example of adherence to Traditions Two and Four. In these meetings there are no self-appointed leaders dictating our agenda, and each member can help decide the direction of the sharing. The process of choosing a topic offers me opportunities to practice letting go of the control of my need for things to go smooth, and also to practice speaking up in a healthy way with my opinion. These are healthy behaviors I get to practice with the people in my meetings.

A topic meeting is a great way for me to sort out my thoughts and feelings on an item "pressing" for me and to get input from others' experience. Each time we've had a topic meeting, I've been amazed to discover that I do have something to share, even those meetings when I first thought the topic didn't really apply to me.

Further Reflections...

"Meetings are opportunities to identify and confirm our common problems and to share the experience, strength, and hope of recovery."

Newcomer Booklet, p. 14

Fear, Courage, and Strength

Eight months ago I discovered my spouse was having an affair. The initial shock and pain lasted three or four months. Just as I was beginning to have hope that this anguish was ending, I realized I was living with a daily fear and dread of it happening again. Then the "what ifs" began: What if I got a divorce, how would I ever get through it? How would I survive the grief? Even though my spouse was going to SA meetings, I was now ill at ease in groups: at church, with friends, family, or strangers.

I recognized I was powerless over this obsessing and fear and that it was ruining my life. I cried out to God for relief. At an S-Anon meeting I heard the words that the courage and strength would come if and when I needed it. It sounded so simple, but I couldn't get it when I was grasping and filled with fear and questioning. Gradually, it began to sink in — although I am powerless over the sex-aholic and his disease, I am not alone, I can be okay no matter what, and that I have a Higher Power I can lean on. Peace was restored to my life.

Further Reflections...
"The only solution to my fear, my desire to control, and my feelings of victimization has been to live one minute at a time and to act as if I trust God, even when I don't."

Working the S-Anon Program, p. 39

"Yes," "No" or "Oh"

I used to get my needs met in indirect ways because some members of my family could not tolerate direct discussions of problems — theirs, mine, or ours. So I manipulated, seduced, whined, bargained, ignored, denied, and lied about my problems. That indirect communication resulted in terrible resentment when others didn't "get it." My resentment and anger at home with my family, in turn, caused me to bully and berate others outside my home – and even myself sometimes. With S-Anon, I am learning a better way.

I am finding when I believe in myself, I can ask for what I need from a position of quiet strength. I do not have to fall into old self-defeating behavior just because someone else is behaving inappropriately. I have many choices that can leave me feeling good about myself, even if a situation ultimately doesn't go my way. For example, I can refuse to accept the unacceptable, I can walk away until the situation evens out or I can simply respond with a "yes," "no" or "oh" and go my own way.

All this takes a lot of daily practice, of course, but it's worth it because I am experiencing more peace and serenity than I thought possible.

Further Reflections...
"When we approach the process of recovery with honesty, open-mindedness, and willingness to apply the principles of the Twelve Steps to our lives, we will soon begin to see the rewards. We will become able to surrender our self-defeating behavior."

Gifts of the S-Anon Program

The Amends Process

For some time, I have prayed and talked with my sponsor about how to make amends to my husband for my failings in our relationship. It has been difficult to contemplate because interactions between my husband and me over the last year have shown that I clearly struggle being kind to him, most likely because of a pattern of defenses I developed to avoid recurring pain in our relationship.

Recently, I agreed to start going to S-Anon couples' meetings and to participate in sessions with his therapist. A benefit of this has been finding safe and healthier environments in which to communicate. I am learning to make "I" statements (rather than "You" statements) and to be courteous and more respectful. I can now ask him to clarify certain statements I perceive as half-truths or outright lies. I have realized that I, too, have not been totally honest with him. How wonderful to discover that I do not have to relinquish my truth to my husband's truth, nor make excuses for him anymore.

My sponsor recently said that since I began these actions, I had already begun the amends process without realizing it. She noticed I am taking better care of myself by not ignoring or excusing omissions, half-truths, and lies. She has heard me be more courteous and respectful of my husband. She said I am a more kind and caring person and less defensive today. When I really started working the program, the program started working me.

Further Reflections...
"Was our behavior toward the sexaholic really above reproach, or do we have some amends to make for rage-filled attitudes, words, or behavior?"

S-Anon Twelve Steps, p. 86

Relationship Fantasies

Before recovery, I fantasized about my relationships. I fantasized about others acknowledging all I did for them. I imagined their delighted expressions of surprise and their words of gratitude. Those fantasies drove me to write "meaningful" letters, seek "perfect" gifts, prepare "memorable" meals and plan "magazine cover" holidays.

In my early S-Anon recovery, I still did a lot of fantasizing. When I thought about calling someone in the program or talking to God, I imagined in vivid detail what I would say and what they would say. By the time I finished fantasizing, I no longer felt the need actually to call or pray! Yet staying in my head kept me isolated and alone.

The disconnected relationships I had witnessed in my childhood couldn't teach me how to have mature, emotionally intimate, and respectful relationships. I relied on fantasies of what relationships "should be." Thankfully, I discovered through my Fourth Step work that fantasizing drives my self-centeredness and perpetuates disconnection in my relationships.

Today, I know when I engage in relationship fantasy, I avoid true intimacy. With the help of S-Anon, I can be in a relationship now, rather than just think about it. Today, I ask God to show me how to walk humbly with others, rather than impress them or ingratiate myself with them. I have surrendered my fantasies, and the reward has been intimacy with God and others.

Further Reflections...
"...It came to me that I had a relationship with God... I began to feel that I was spending time with my very best friend and it was a sweet experience for me. An added bonus was the growing knowledge that God wanted an intimate relationship with me, too."

S-Anon Twelve Steps, p. 133-134

❖   ❖   ❖

Changing My Own Behavior

After a long, two year process, I finalized my divorce from my sexaholic spouse. My husband did not want the divorce, and he attempted to exploit my sense of sadness and guilt in an effort to get me to reconcile. My conscious contact with my Higher Power and the tools of S-Anon helped keep me grounded during the divorce process, and I was able to get through it with my dignity intact.

The concept of detaching with love and compassion became a very important standard by which I rarely strayed. My husband would frequently attempt to engage me in re-evaluating "what went wrong in our marriage and who was at fault." Detaching with love and compassion helped me to recognize this "hook" and not take the bait. I would gently, but firmly, say to him that I could not discuss this with him or that he was entitled to his opinion and I was entitled to mine. As I detached from potentially pointless arguments, I felt stronger rather than be dragged down by them.

It has now been many months since the divorce, and I have a sense of relief and serenity that I have never known before. Because of my recovery in S-Anon, even after the divorce, my co-parenting relationship has been strengthened. I now know from experience that changing my own behavior can positively affect the outcome of a situation.

Further Reflections...
"Today when we have difficulty in our relationship, inevitably what's going on is me bumping up against my old ideas of how things 'should' be."

Working the S-Anon Program, p. 73

❖ ❖ ❖

Keep It Simple

After about a year into recovery, I decided to leave my marital home and divorce my spouse. I was fortunate to be in a very good financial position; so many options were open to me. I obsessed about those options, particularly where to move to find the perfect, larger new home. Questions raced through my thoughts. What school district should I live in? How much square footage would be adequate? Could I really live without a fireplace? How much larger of a kitchen would I need?

After I thought I had it all figured out, I approached my then three year-old son and asked him how he would feel about us moving to a nice, big new house. He looked at me and replied, "Mom, will the ice cream truck still come there?" His innocent question abruptly brought me back to reality and reminded me to Keep it Simple – things didn't have to be big or breathtaking to be wonderful. I was humbled, and I let go of my obsession over "bigger and better."

So often my Higher Power speaks to me through the mouths of my children. S-Anon is teaching me to be still enough to listen.

Further Reflections...
"...the more I came to meetings and began working the S-Anon program, the more I saw the real wisdom in the simple sayings. 'Act as if...' and 'Keep it Simple' are surprisingly practical and helped me through difficult, emotionally-draining situations."

Working the S-Anon Program, p. 51

The Three A's

All my life I have been a problem solver; in fact, I thought I was pretty good at it. When I became aware of a problem, such as a character defect in myself, then the logical thing was to do something about it. I would decide what change to make, and think, "Well, do it! Quit fooling around."

This is how I responded when I learned of my husband's sexaholism, but my attempts to solve that problem were futile. I got impatient and frustrated, and I became condescending and resentful towards my husband.

Learning about "The Three As" (Awareness, Acceptance, and Action) made me realize a very important step was missing in my problem solving. I consistently jumped from "awareness" of a problem to "action" without taking the time and effort for the middle step of "acceptance." I am learning that before I can take any action to make needed changes, I must come to an acceptance of the situation-- acknowledge what is. Sometimes it takes a while to accept something, which really slows down my pounce-on-the-problem impulse. In the time it takes me to reach acceptance, I see that the only things I can change are my attitudes and actions.

Only by experiencing awareness and acceptance, can I achieve the perspective needed to take appropriate action, to solve the problems that are actually mine to solve.

Further Reflections...
"...we are relieved of the burdens of our overly self-reliant past and our unmanageable circumstances. We are freed to learn better ways of thinking and acting."

S-Anon Twelve Steps, p. 81

What I Need, When I Need It

My spouse asked me what he could get for me for an upcoming special occasion. I said I wanted flowers. When the special day arrived, he proudly presented me with an African violet in full bloom. It was beautiful, but I felt disappointed. I had wanted cut flowers, not something I would have to take care of.

When the violet started to drop its flowers, I decided to just let the poor thing die. My disappointment and displeasure continued to simmer, even as I ignored the plant's need for care. Then the unexpected happened: the violet began to flourish. It just wouldn't die. I needed something green in a corner of my bathroom, so I watered the plant and stuck it in there, once again expecting it to perish within a few weeks. I paid no attention to it. Again, it thrived. The flowers bloomed, and it looked as splendid as it did when I first saw it.

That plant has been in that corner of my bathroom for over a year now, blooming and resting, blooming and resting. I have to say I never have had as much pleasure from flowers as I've had from this living plant. My experience with the plant reminds me that I don't always know what is best for me. When I keep an open mind and trust my Higher Power, I find I get just what I need, just when I need it.

Further Reflections...
"Hungry for recovery, we gradually began to identify and surrender our urges to say 'Yes, but...'"
Working the S-Anon Program, p. 50

This Process Helps Me Surrender

Sometimes my day begins with worry and fear over something I'm not able to control. I've learned that this is the time to let God take care of whatever is robbing me of my serenity.

Throughout my day, when that urge comes to fix the sexaholic or whatever person or situation is bothering me, I say the slogan "Let Go and Let God." I then ask myself, "Is there anything I realistically need to do about this situation?" If the answer is "no," I find that saying this slogan again helps me let go and proceed with my morning. At mid-morning, I stop and reflect on how I am feeling. If whatever is troubling me has come back into my head, I again surrender my thoughts and the situation to God.

Every few hours, I check in with myself and repeat the process of Letting Go and Letting God. I find this process helps me surrender matters to God until I am clear about what God's will is for me. I am so grateful that I have this tool to lighten my load on any given day.

Further Reflections...
"I wish I could just surrender my fears once and for all. I think I have let go of a concern or fear and a few moments later realize I'm trying to figure it out again. So I breathe the slogan again – Let Go and Let God."

Working the S-Anon Program, p. 12

A Place to Blossom and Grow

When I came into this room of S-Anon "strangers," I was miserable and in pain. As I sat listening to the readings I began to wonder, "How do these people know about my life?" After all, most friendships involve months of time, even years, prior to sharing intimate details of one's life.

After these S-Anon "strangers" shared their own painful stories, I risked sharing my own, and deep meaningful friendships emerged in my life. From sharing my most horrible secrets with this group of "strangers," I received healing unparalleled by any therapy I ever had tried. The people sitting in the rooms of S-Anon know more about me now than my closest childhood friends know.

My S-Anon friends offer healthy empathy, because their understanding comes from truly experiencing what I have experienced. Not only do they share their history, but also the strength and hope they have found by using the tools of the S-Anon program. The safe, caring group of S-Anon friends accepted me at my most vulnerable, and that has given me the tools and support with which I have been able to heal, blossom, and grow.

Further Reflections...
"...meetings assured me that my feelings were real and that I wasn't alone."

Working the S-Anon Program, p. 4

Character Defects

My Higher Power often shows me my character defects in the ordinary circumstances of my life. I am not a strong person. My doctor has advised me not to strain my muscles as I have back problems. In spite of this, I loaded two boxes of books into the car to donate to the library. There was a traffic tie up, so I decided to park in the back of the library and walk the books around, rather than wait a minute in traffic. I walked one box around and realized what I was doing.

That day I recognized some tangible character defects: impatience and impulsiveness, because I didn't want to sit in traffic, but rather get the job done; resentment, because these were mostly my husband's books and I was doing this because he wasn't; and disregard for my needs, because my back and strength were not really up to carrying a box full of books around the library. I was thankful to my Higher Power for pointing it out to me. The next day, while resting my sore back, I finally took Steps Six and Seven seriously. I became willing for God to remove all these defects of character — as well as the pain in my back.

Further Reflections...
"It was very clear to me at the time that this particular character defect needed to be removed. Other times I don't have that clarity, but through working the Steps I have come to a place of willingness where I try to notice the shortcomings in myself that separate me from God and others. "

S-Anon Twelve Steps, p. 78

Character Strengths

Volunteering for service opportunities in S-Anon helped me discover some of my character strengths, such as being able to sit quietly with someone as they share their pain. Recognizing that strength has helped me take better care of myself when uncomfortable situations arise at home. Through service, I learned I can experience hope when I stay in the moment and just work on the task at hand. Answering our local telephone hotline and welcoming newcomers are opportunities for me to share this hope with others.

Taking the focus off my troubles and finding healthy ways to offer my help to others has deepened my recovery. Helping others through service has allowed me to step back and have a clearer perspective on my own troubles. Sometimes service is putting the chairs away after a meeting, or filling in for the group secretary. Each time I am of service to members or to the group as a whole, I become more connected with the S-Anon fellowship.

Today, sharing my experience, strength, and hope has become the heart of my S-Anon program. Participating in S-Anon service work has become a wonderful opportunity for me to share with newcomers the skills and hopeful perspectives I have developed by working the program.

Further Reflections...
"Service helps us to be responsible, to connect, and to begin making progress in recovery."

Working the S-Anon Program, p. 20

Self-Focus through the Tenth Step

Taking a daily Tenth Step inventory has helped me see that even in recovery I still want to control my husband. For example, in a recent Tenth Step I observed that I had superimposed the map of my recovery onto him and made comparisons: I am doing a better job at recovery; I am "ahead" in my Step work; I am more vigilant at prayer; I am doing more group service; I have more sponsees; and on and on. Discussing this observation with my sponsor helped me see my "best thinking" has caused a division in my marriage.

S-Anon tells me it is important to focus on myself rather than the sexaholic. Taking a daily written Tenth Step helps me recognize when I am heading into unhealthy thinking or unhealthy behavior with my partner and gives me the option of behaving differently. So when I notice I am checking up on my husband to see if he is working his program the way I think he should, I can call my sponsor, put the results in God's hands, and get on with my day. Daily Tenth Steps help me to have a healthier and more realistic relationship with my husband, as well as a stronger connection with God.

Further Reflections...

"When I stop taking inventory, I become blinded to the ways I cope with life that are wrong, painful, and harmful to my relationships."

S-Anews, March 1998

Detaching from and Attaching to

Sexaholism existed in my family as far back as my great-grandfather. He sexually abused my mother and many of her siblings and cousins. His wife, my great-grandmother, overdosed on pain pills shortly after he was caught molesting a neighbor's child. These topics were taboo and rarely discussed.

Not surprisingly, I chose many sexaholic partners before I found the help of S-Anon. When I look at my history, I can see that I was groomed for these relationships; sexaholism is a family disease. I had been surrounded by the effects of sexaholism as well as other forms of addiction such as; alcoholism, self-mutilation, anorexia, food addiction, attempted suicide, and a lot of resentment and isolation.

That environment had seemed "normal," and I must now work to let go of the disease and the problems it has caused for me and my relatives. I am learning that it is not my job to carry the shame and pain of other family members. In recovery, I can detach from the role of taking care of others and I attach to the safety of my meetings and my Higher Power. I am choosing a "recovery family." These new relationships are a healing gift of the program – a bigger gift than I possibly could have imagined when I started the process of recovery.

Further Reflections…

"…so we commit ourselves to our own recovery. With the loving help of other S-Anon members and the God of our understanding, we take positive action to make our lives more serene and fulfilling."

Keys to S-Anon Recovery (short version)

Plan A? Plan B? Or Plan C?

Here is my experience with a great sharing I heard at a meeting. It went something like this:

- Sharing: You know, I always come to God with 'Plan A' – what I really want.
- Experience: God, I would really like the sexaholic to show me affection the way I think she should.
- Sharing: But I know that God may have something else in mind, so I come prepared with 'Plan B', too.
- Experience: OK, God, if I can't have the affection I want from my wife, could you at least get her to spend more time with me?
- Sharing: What I forget is that God has a much broader point of view than I do, and generally has a 'Plan C'– a wonderful plan I could never have dreamed of – tucked away in his back pocket.
- Experience: So what happened was… I got out of my wife's way, called my S-Anon sponsor and went to a lot more meetings. I stopped being so demanding.

I was able to Let Go and Let God. A few weeks later she left me a note saying, "Went to my meeting. Be back soon. I would like to have some time with you. I made a special dinner, please provide the flowers."

Further Reflections…

"…letting go by placing the situation in God's care is not the same as giving up…it is placing my concerns in God's care and surrendering to God's will."

Working the S-Anon Program, p. 13

Sexual Intimacy

I ignored my own sexuality for years through obsessing about the sexual lives of men in my life. Even when I thought I was thinking about my own needs, I was more focused on what my partner thought, wanted, or needed. Focusing on others' thoughts helped me avoid achieving a comfortable and enjoyable sex life for myself.

I now understand I need to build emotional intimacy before developing sexual intimacy. Through applying the principles of the program, I now have let go of trying to prove anything through sex. I let go of trying to impress my partner, to keep up with him, to control him, to keep him faithful or interested or whatever mental "tape" I'm playing at that moment.

Today, when I am emotionally and physically close with my partner, I focus on what is comfortable and healthy, and I ask for what I need. By using the tools of S-Anon, I can enjoy my partner for who he is – a separate and unique person with different needs and wants than mine. I want my partner to cherish me as a special individual person, and I now can cherish him, as well. Just for today, I can let go of my fantasies of a perfect relationship and interact in a detached yet loving way with my partner.

Further Reflections...
"I had no concept of my own sexuality as separate from the demands or desires of my partner... [but] ...today I accept that in order for me to achieve 'healthy' sexuality, I will have to continue to look at myself and share what I see with my partner."

Working the S-Anon Program, p. 64-65

The Gifts of Twelfth Step Work

When I was new in the program, service work meant "carrying the message" in small ways. For example, one way I gave back to my group was providing tissues for the meeting.

As my recovery progressed, I ventured into new areas of Twelfth Step work. I developed the confidence to "put myself out there" and be available to others through sponsorship. In the group, I learned a sense of self-respect and a sense of shared responsibility that taught me to be a team player. I also learned that I am good at leading. I learned how to work with others diplomatically and how to look for and discern common ground instead of forcefully pursuing my own agenda.

Gratefully, service work keeps me coming back, even during the periods when I think I don't need a meeting. I work together with other members to help the meeting stay healthy and grow so there will always be a place for the newcomer to go.

These are just a few of the gifts I have received from S-Anon Twelfth Step work. What valuable contributions it has made to my recovery! Truly, I have received much more help than I have been able to give. The rewards of service work in S-Anon are as individual as we are, but in my experience, they are priceless.

Further Reflections...
"We gain so much for our own recovery when we share our experience, strength, and hope with others."
Working the S-Anon Program, p. 103

Identifying My Emotions

I grew up in a sexaholic household where the atmosphere was thick with anger and resentment. A perpetual cloud of tension hung in the air. Consequently, anger has always been a "comfortable" emotion for me, one that I easily experience and "use" whenever problems arise. Needless to say, the discovery of sexaholism in my marriage has given me plenty of opportunity to express anger. Yet my over-reliance on anger as an all-inclusive emotion means that I do not experience other emotions nearly so readily. This has diminished the quality of my life.

I am grateful that the tools of the S-Anon program helped me learn to identify my other emotions and to respond appropriately to problems, rather than just get angry. Working with my sponsor helped me see that my anger often masked other, more painful emotions such as sadness and fear. I use writing as a tool to explore my emotions on a deeper level when problems arise. Another tool I use is prayer, asking my Higher Power for the courage to feel a range of emotions and to respond appropriately to situations.

The S-Anon program has helped me find a healthier way to live.

Further Reflections...
"The tools of the S-Anon program are actions we take, principles we use, and attitudes we develop."
Working the S-Anon Program, p. 1

Change

Growing up, I heard that change is what life is about and that the only constant thing is change. Yet for me to take "a leap of faith" and actually make decisions that might alter my life in a profound way can feel like jumping off a cliff or diving into the unknown. This is especially true when the change concerns my relationships.

Change seems to involve an ending to something, and endings always bring up fear and grief – two emotions I have tried to avoid most of my life. Sometimes I avoid those feelings by staying in a holding pattern and not taking necessary action. For example, after taking the Third Step with my sponsor, I avoided writing my Forth Step for as long as I could. I've come to see that when I don't take action, I start feeling stuck, and, when I feel stuck, I go back into fear and want to put the brakes on my recovery.

It really helped me to hear an S-Anon member share in a meeting how she "took the leap and the net appeared." Little by little, I am taking that leap, and I am changing. Sometimes the change is subtle and sometimes it is noticeable, but I am changing and I am grateful to be in recovery.

Further Reflections…
"Step Four is an action step….It leads to self-understanding, which can help us to make great changes in our thoughts and behavior."

S-Anon Twelve Steps, p. 39

The Doors Are Open to All

When I heard about S-Anon, I was afraid that it was a religious organization. I feared that I would have to "conform" to get help. Happily, at that first meeting, I saw that my concerns were unfounded. S-Anon is open to all who want help with the effects of sexaholism.

I heard that message of openness in the S-Anon Preamble to the Twelve Steps, in words taken from S-Anon's Third Tradition; the only requirement for membership is that there be a problem of sexaholism in a relative or a friend. I was not required to look or talk a certain way, contribute a specified amount of money, pray the way others did, or even believe in God. What relief I felt!

As I attended meetings, I began to see that the concept of anonymity, as laid out in the Twelve Traditions, ensures that the help of S-Anon is available and open to all. For me, Tradition Twelve means that it doesn't matter who we are outside (or even inside) the rooms of S-Anon. When we come together to solve our common problems, each of us is able to give and get help based on the principles of our program, and each of us can receive help whether we are newcomers or seasoned members.

Further Reflections...
"S-Anon is a fellowship of people who share their experience, strength, and hope with each other so that they may solve their common problems and help others to recover."
S-Anon Preamble to the Twelve Steps

Traditions – Maintaining Unity at Home

For years in S-Anon I focused only on the Twelve Steps. I did not give much thought to the Twelve Traditions. I saw their value in maintaining unity without conformity in meetings, but that was all.

An S-Anon couples meeting* with the Traditions as a topic changed my mind. A couple shared how they applied the Traditions to their family life. They described how they applied the Traditions to the purchase of a new home. They used Tradition One as their guiding principle, equally considering the needs and desires of each family member, including their children. I listened in amazement as the wife described how her personal choice was overruled by family consensus. In my family of origin, children's opinions were seldom considered or respected. The couple ended by saying the house they chose was perfect for their family needs. Their unity had been upheld and strengthened in the process.

That was a turning point for me. Now I consciously apply the Traditions to my daily life at home and work. I have found that whenever I am puzzled by a situation that involves others, the answer is inevitably found in the principles of the Steps and Traditions. Life is easier when I utilize the entire program.

Further Reflections...
"...we do well to consider the needs of the family, our coworkers, or the S-Anon group as a whole, as well as our individual needs and desires, when making decisions or taking actions."

Working the S-Anon Program, p. 30

*For more information about S-Anon couple's related-meetings, please contact the WSO.

Something That Affects Our Whole Family

Looking back, I now see many obvious signs that pointed out my need for help in coping with the effects of my spouse's sexaholism. Life had changed in our home. In the earlier years, life was filled with friends and family outings. Our children had friends over to play and sleepovers on the weekends. Gradually, all that changed, and my days became filled with worrying and angry outbursts. I spent countless hours plotting and scheming to make him see how much he was hurting us. I made every effort to keep up appearances that we were a happy family.

Finally, I discovered my husband's pornography. Suddenly, finding help became more important than keeping family secrets. I actually did Step One that day without realizing it: I admitted in my heart that I was powerless and that my life was overwhelmingly unmanageable.

I came to S-Anon ready for help. I learned to be responsive rather than reactive in our home. I used the S-Ateen literature to help our teenaged children and assure them that they were not alone.

Now I understand this is not just my husband's illness, but something that affects our whole family. I am grateful that as I am healing, our family relationships are becoming stronger, healthier, and happier. There is laughter in our home again. Thank you, S-Anon, for showing me the way.

Further Reflections...
"Growing up in a sexaholic home will influence many of our life choices, including our choice of a partner, unless we identify and address our own unhealthy beliefs and behaviors that we have learned through living with the disease of sexaholism."

Keys to S-Ateen Recovery

❖   ❖   ❖

One Day at a Time

It seems to me that the 24-hour day is a unit of measure that God created to help us learn to deal with our problems and pleasures. The slogan "One Day at a Time" reminds me of this daily rhythm. Within the time period, framed by sunrise and sunset, I face the toil and pleasures of life. Then there is rest, as I temporarily let go of my problems and lay to rest my mind and body to replenish my reserve.

I find this daily rhythm echoed within the Twelve Steps. I work the S-Anon program as hard as I can, share in fellowship and do service "Just for Today." Then I can rest and let go of unfinished business through working Step Ten, trusting God to hold it for me while I slumber. Upon awakening, I work Step Eleven and renew my awareness that, for this day only, I will have the ability to tackle all the day will hold, with God's help.

S-Anon has taught me that I need not be overwhelmed if I employ the tools of the program. Recovery in my day-to-day tasks and interactions is one of my greatest rewards.

Further Reflections...
"Today, I feel free to experience more and more of life as I live it one day at a time, increasingly free from the effects of sexaholism."

Working the S-Anon Program, p. 17

Connecting with Reality

My first S-Anon meeting was enlightening – I was not alone! I had thought I was the only person living with so much fear and anger. It was reassuring to find out that there were others just like me, others who had also grown up with a parent who was an addict. It was reassuring to find others who had feelings and thoughts similar to my own.

I found I was not the only one who believed that sex was the most important thing in a relationship. I was not the only one to believe I could control the people around me through my words and actions. I heard others who also had thought, as children, that it was our fault that our parents fought. We had thought as teens, that sex would bring love and affirmation, instead it brought complications to our lives. Here were others who also thought that if we provided pleasure through sex, the other person would like and accept us. I found others who also had experienced doubts about God's existence, who also had thought that even if God did exist, he surely would not help us since we weren't worthy of his care and forgiveness anyway.

Coming to meetings helped me stay connected with reality and let go of these old beliefs. Hearing others share their experiences helps me to cope with my own, because I get information that I can adapt to my own situation. If I miss meetings, not only do I lose contact with the people I have grown to love, I also get bogged down in my old unhealthy thinking. Meetings help keep me sober in S-Anon.

Further Reflections…
"We attend as many meetings as we can…"
                              Keys to S-Anon Recovery (short version)

❖   ❖   ❖

Coming to Appreciate the Traditions

I came to S-Anon from another Twelve Step fellowship. I immediately noticed that S-Anon emphasized the Twelve Traditions much more than my other fellowship. All the talk about the Traditions frustrated me. I was suffering and uncomfortable and had come to S-Anon to get help, answers, and solutions, not to dissect the Traditions.

As time went on, I grudgingly became accustomed to my group's monthly, in-depth, Tradition review meeting. While I inwardly groaned as the Tradition of the month was introduced at those meetings, I inevitably came away with a new idea or fresh perspective. After many months, I realized I actually had come to appreciate the Traditions and those Tradition meetings. It became clear to me that the group's ongoing study and practice of the Traditions had created a safe place to find solutions for the problems we face due to the effects of living with sexaholism. I came to see that safety is important because there can be so much shame associated with sexaholism.

Today, I understand that I can apply the Traditions not only to my S-Anon group, but also to every relationship in my life. By applying the principles of the Traditions to my life, I am improving my relationships with co-workers, family and friends, and even the sexaholic. The Traditions have produced a firm foundation in my relationships, one that is stable, solid, and consistent.

Further Reflections...
"The Traditions evolved from the experience of AA and Al-Anon groups in solving their problems of living and working together. S-Anon adapted these Traditions as group guidelines, and over the years members of our fellowship have found them to be sound and wise. Without healthy groups, there would be very little individual recovery."
Working the S-Anon Program, p. 29

Different Experiences of Love

Iused to look for a love that seemed to exist only in my imagination. Then I came to S-Anon and learned of many different kinds of love. I am grateful for the work I have done with my sponsor, which has opened my heart to a love that is indescribable.

I have experienced the love that exists through the S-Anon program. This began when I learned to trust a sponsor and to trust the power of the Steps and Traditions. I experienced the love of my Higher Power, and I learned more about being present to others, forgiving myself and having compassion. I also found the joy of helping and of being of service to others. I've learned about being honest and that saying "no" is not only an option, but is sometimes a loving service to another human being. I have learned to love myself by taking the time to know myself better and not abandon myself and my truth.

These experiences of love in my S-Anon program have led to new experiences of love in my life. I have learned I no longer have to take over another person's life for that person to feel loved. Likewise, I do not have to be totally taken care of by the other person. Instead, I can share the love I have in my heart with that other person and trust that we can remain individuals even while in our love relationship.

Further Reflections...
"Our ability to give and receive love will expand tremendously..."

Gifts of the S-Anon Program

Only as Sick as Our Secrets

At my first S-Anon meeting I felt a huge relief at hearing the stories of other S-Anons. For the first time I understood I was not alone. I had lived through many years of secrets and lies in my relationship with the sexaholic. It took me a long time to find the willingness to face the truth of my partner's sexual secrets, especially infidelity. Something that was very helpful to me was a saying that I heard in one of those early meetings: "We are only as sick as our secrets." This gave me the courage to share the shame I felt as a result of my partner's behaviors. It also helped me face the shame of my own secrets such as jealousy, violating my partner's boundaries, and disrespecting his feelings and needs.

I cherish those early recovery meetings where I started to speak up and shine the light on secrets I had been keeping, even from friends who were in other Twelve Step programs. I now understand that secrets cannot sustain their power over me if they are exposed to God's light. I believe God knew my secrets all along and gave me the S-Anon program so I could share my shame and heal. I now have the opportunity to pass on what I have learned to others who want what I have. The truth has set me free!

Further Reflections...
"In time, we learned to recognize the truth ourselves and to accept reality."

Working the S-Anon Program, p. 49

Sponsorship

Initially, I was afraid to be a sponsor. I thought "I don't know everything I need to know yet. What if I mess up another person's life by saying the wrong things?" My sponsor lovingly reminded me that I don't have that much power. After all, I am not God. She said that all I need to do is be available, to share my experience, strength, and hope. I remember thinking, "I can do that." The funny thing was that as soon as I decided I was ready and willing to sponsor, a newcomer asked me if I would be her sponsor.

Sponsoring others has taken me to the next level of my recovery. I see how it helps me remember to look at my own behavior and attitudes, because I can't very well suggest that a sponsee do something I am not already doing myself. Often, what I tell a sponsee is exactly what I need to hear. I am so grateful for the S-Anon program and for tools like sponsorship. It never fails that when I give, I get back so much more.

Further Reflections...
"When anyone, anywhere reaches out for help, let the hand of S-Anon and S-Ateen always be there, and let it begin with me."

Sponsorship in S-Anon Pamphlet

Accepting Reality

"I've been doing this for a year now and nothing is better," I muttered to myself as I trudged from my car to the S-Anon meeting room. I was angry and I wanted the pain to be over and the stress to be gone. I wanted to find some peace in my marriage and in myself.

The topic of the meeting that night was acceptance. As I listened to the sharing, I found my anger dissipating and my clarity growing. It occurred to me I had been trying to move ahead with my marriage, rather than facing my pain and the lessons it had for me. I had not fully accepted the reality that the trust in the marriage had been broken and needed to be rebuilt with honesty.

When it was my turn to speak that evening, I shared some of these thoughts. I also shared that the hardest part of acceptance was admitting I was not in control, and that the anger that continued to plague me was really anger at God because I was not in control.

Since my awareness at that meeting, I have tried to slow myself down and to make sure I come to acceptance before I take action on any issue. Regarding my marriage, I pray for "the serenity to accept what I cannot change, courage to change what I can, and wisdom to know the difference." I trust that the correct course of action will be clear when the time is right. The S-Anon fellowship reminds me that I can already have serenity if I am willing to trust the process.

Further Reflections...
"Acceptance has been the answer to my marital problems."

Alcoholics Anonymous, p. 450 (3rd ed)

Gratitude for CAL

Reading Conference-Approved Literature (CAL) is something I do to stay connected to my recovery. In my day-to-day life, S-Anon literature directs me to stay in the solution, not in my problem. Our S-Anon literature is unlike other material available commercially, because it is written by S-Anons sharing their personal experiences. These experiences give me great hope. I have found that CAL is a great reminder to me of my faith in a Higher Power, and it directs me back to the importance of having an "attitude of gratitude" every day.

Reading the experiences of others who have lived with the family disease of sexaholism and who have found recovery in S-Anon lights my path and encourages me to try new ideas. I do not have to agree with everything I read, but I do find that reading S-Anon literature has become a mental exercise that helps me to practice honesty, open-mindedness, and willingness to grow.

I used to walk the journey of life alone, but not anymore. The experience, strength, and hope of other S-Anon members accompany me on my way. I cherish the S-Anon literature. Reading it is a commitment to my program and me.

Further Reflections...
"I have grown to love the literature that our fellowship continues to develop. I grew up in a sexaholic family, dated sexaholics, and now am married to a sexaholic. The S-Anon literature speaks to that experience like no other literature."

S-Anews, March 1999, p. 3

S-Anon Is There for Me

My adult daughter disclosed to me that my husband, her stepfather, had molested her from the time she was five (soon after we were married) until she was fourteen. I then discovered that he had also molested his own daughter. I felt as though I was walking around in a stunned nightmare. I was outraged by his violation and became extremely fearful, not only of what the future might bring, but of facing my pain about the truth of my life and the choices I made.

Eventually I turned to S-Anon, where things started changing in my life. I began to see how important it is to take care of myself, so that I can be emotionally present in my own life. Now I am better able to support my daughter, as she continues to heal through the betrayal and pain of being molested by my husband. I am also aware, on a deeper level, how important it is for me to put myself and my family into God's hands.

I began to concentrate on my Step work, and I continued to check in with my sponsor and others regularly. I have much to work through, and I am still a bit shaky at times, but I am beginning to experience some relief. I am grateful that S-Anon is here for me in my home town — that S-Anon is open to all who are affected by another's sexual behavior — and that the spiritual principles of the Steps and Traditions continue to guide me. IT WORKS!

Further Reflections...
"...Now we are beginning to fear pain less. We see that pain paves the road to many new realizations about ourselves, others, and God. Listening to people in S-Anon, we grasp the reality that despair and failure can be transmitted into hope and success."

S-Anon Twelve Steps, p. 74

Live and Let Live

Many of my self-defeating behaviors are related to the ways I do not take care of myself. For example, I sometimes catch myself consumed by thoughts of another person. I might think obsessively about that person, project my anger on them, or compulsively express my anger about that person's behavior. In these times, I am taking energy away from myself, energy that is wasted and cannot be regained. When I waste my life's energy, I am not taking care of myself.

The slogan "Live and Let Live" helps me recall that other people have a right to live their lives as they choose. Using that slogan helps me take action to bring the focus back to myself physically, emotionally, and spiritually. For example, taking a hot bath or working out makes me more aware of my body. Reading S-Anon literature or writing in my journal brings me in touch with my emotions. Engaging in prayer and meditation exercises my spirituality, especially if I pray for the person I am trying to change or control. These are steps I can take to "live and let live."

Further Reflections...

"We realize we cannot find serenity for ourselves if we continue to focus on someone else's recovery, so we commit ourselves to our own recovery. With the loving help of other S-Anon members and the God of our understanding, we take positive action to make our lives more serene and fulfilling."

Keys to S-Anon Recovery (short version)

Coincidences or God Incidences?

Recently my husband and I went to see our daughter perform in her school's talent show. We sat side-by-side excitedly anticipating her performance. Within minutes, the row in front of us began to fill up. It was then that I found myself at a mental and emotional crossroads that I have faced time and again, in my S-Anon recovery. Directly in front of my husband, a young woman sat down…just the type of woman that I believed could be a trigger causing his lust addiction to kick in.

In the past, I would have spent the rest of the evening feeling anxious and watching to see if he was focusing on her. I would have been unable to relax and enjoy our daughter's performance. Thanks to working the program, I was able to make a different choice and find humor in the coincidence that, of all the empty seats in that auditorium, this girl chose the seat right in front of my husband. He could choose whether or not to work his program, and more importantly, I could choose to not focus on him and work mine! I was able to relax, enjoy the evening, and focus on the love I felt for our daughter that night.

Further Reflections…
"…our hope will turn to faith that God is really working in our lives, as we explore the wonders of serenity, dignity, and emotional growth."

Gifts of the S-Anon Program

Surrender and the Answers Will Come

Before S-Anon, my prayers were often filled with bargaining and demands of "Why?" and "Why me"? Then sexaholism hit — the discovery, the denials, my disbelief – my prayers changed. It was as though sexaholism pulled the rug out from under me, and all I had left was God. I couldn't do anything but cry out in pain. Would God hear me and answer? Amazingly, the answers would come. I prayed for freedom from the pain. I was given peace in the midst of chaos. I prayed for a miracle. I was given S-Anon, to begin to recover from the effects of sexaholism.

All I had to do was surrender my pain, my fear, and my terror to God. I practiced the Third Step and surrendered trying to control my life, my sexaholic, my marriage, kids, church, business, everything, one day at a time. It's not easy, but I have learned not to be afraid of God's answers. I offer my prayers in honesty and transparency, and wait for the answers that always prove best.

Further Reflections...
"When we surrender to God, we connect with a Higher Power and become whole persons. We discover that we do receive guidance for our lives to just about the extent that we stop making demands upon God to give it to us on order and on our terms."

S-Anon Twelve Steps, p. 28

I Pray Again

Step Eleven suggests we "improve our conscious contact with God, through prayer and meditation." Members of my group have encouraged me not to wait until I formally get to Step Eleven to do this. So, as I work my way through the Steps toward Step Eleven, I am trying to pray and meditate regularly.

My talks with God are intensely personal. When I pray, I mostly tell God about the concerns in my heart and those worries that whirl around in my head. When I do this, I find release. Sometimes I take my concerns back, but my life inevitably becomes unmanageable when I try to control others. I pray again.

Being so new to S-Anon, I am still shy about sharing openly in the group. Perhaps my upbringing influenced my tendency toward being extremely private. Then again, maybe it is just another example of guarding against the intimacy of being truly known.

As I see how other members flourish by speaking up, I am encouraged that I will do the same. I am praying that God will grant me the courage to follow the example of these members.

Further Reflections...
"The regular practice of prayer and meditation rewards us with emotional balance, a sense of belonging and knowing that God watches lovingly over us... As we gain small glimpses of God's reality, we know our path will continue to lead us to greater knowledge of His will."

S-Anon Twelve Steps, p. 129

A Breath of Fresh Air

When I came to S-Anon, I had no faith in God and distrusted organized religion. At my first S-Anon meeting, my reaction to the references to God and a Higher Power was to wonder if I had stumbled into some kind of "religious cult." I wanted to leave, but I had been asked to try six meetings before making a decision on whether or not S-Anon was for me. I came back.

By the sixth meeting, I realized that no one was going to preach or tell me what type of relationship I should have with my Higher Power or even what that Higher Power should be for me. It was like a breath of fresh air. I could see for myself that other people were being helped by a Power greater than themselves. The people and their problems were diverse and complex. That gave me hope. For the first time in my life I started to hope that there could be a Power greater than myself who could and would help me.

I am now in the process of getting to know God for the first time in my life. I am finding this process wonderfully joyful and comforting. The more I trust in God, the more I receive. I am grateful to S-Anon for opening the door to this relationship. I know with my history of negative experiences in organized religion, I would not have found God in a church. Today, I am grateful for the opportunity to discover my Higher Power in my own way, and in my own time.

Further Reflections...
"Our program is designed to help us regardless of our various beliefs. Let us not defeat our purpose by discussing any particular denomination."

Obstacles to Recovery

❖   ❖   ❖

Anonymity

I was married to someone who had a respected position in our community and who was also a sexaholic. My regular S-Anon meeting was held at a small church with a somewhat hidden parking lot. One evening I parked my car and was hurrying across the lot to the building when a man who knew my spouse and me came out and spoke to me. I hurried on inside and hoped he would not know what I was there for. I was nearly panicked as I feared that our horrible "secret" might be discovered and my husband might lose his job.

That evening, I left the meeting quickly; as I drove home I was obsessed with this encounter as this man was also quite prominent in the community. I imagined that he was there attending some other event at the church. Then I began to realize something: this is a small church, the only activity going on that night was Sexaholics Anonymous and S-Anon meetings-he was one of us! What a shock! I had a sigh of relief knowing that if he was one of us, then he would know about protecting someone's anonymity. But I also needed to keep my responsibility and not tell anyone, not even my husband, that I had seen him at the meeting site. Eventually, on other evenings when I saw him, I felt more comfortable knowing that our mutual anonymity was respected.

This experience has taught me two things about the Twelfth Tradition. Social position is not important in recovery, and anyone can come to a Twelve Step recovery meeting.

Further Reflections...
"My meeting became one place where I did not feel paralyzed by fear of other people's expectations and impressions of me or my family."

Working the S-Anon Program, p. 43

❖ ❖ ❖

Reaching Out and Making a Connection

My head is a dangerous neighborhood to go into, so I shouldn't go there alone. — Anonymous

Once I finally admitted that I truly was powerlessness over sexaholism and that I could not solve my problems alone, I became willing to pick up the telephone and connect with other S-Anon members. Before that point, I tended to just stay in my head, trying to work out my problems on my own. Today, when I sponsor someone who struggles with making program phone calls, I suggest something that was recommended to me when I struggled to make calls: just call your sponsor every day and tell her what you are cooking for dinner. The point is this daily ritual offers practice in reaching out and making a connection.

For me, this simple calling ritual was important because developing the habit of daily phone calls when things were going well made it much easier to pick up the phone to discuss a problem when things were not going well. I often have heard my Higher Power speaking through my S-Anon friends on the phone. When someone calls me for support, I ask my Higher Power to help me listen with compassion and to provide me with the right words to say.

Further Reflections...
"Talking with someone who understands and can suggest some direction in working the Steps is so helpful."

Working the S-Anon Program, p. 7

Believing I Will Make It

I work in the world of the Internet. I know there are dangerous and explicit sites out there, but I never dreamed those sites would be viewed in my home.

When I met my husband, he was not a fan of the Internet. I never suspected that my husband's strong stance against the Internet was (I later found out) actually an attempt to wean himself from his addiction to viewing pornographic sites.

I knew he occasionally viewed pornographic magazines. I learned over time, that pornography itself was only a symptom of what was causing so much strain in our relationship and the unhappiness my spouse exhibited. Over time I learned about his addiction to lust. As my husband's sexaholism progressed, our emotional and sexual intimacy disappeared.

We started going for counseling. Eventually, I started attending S-Anon and my spouse started going to his recovery program. I started facing my own feelings around our relationship and my husbands' disease. I've discovered my own powerlessness, and just how difficult it is to face my enabling and other unhealthy behaviors. In time, my healing began. I am sustained by the hope I'm finding in S-Anon. Whether or not my marriage makes it, I am beginning to believe I will make it.

Further Reflections...
"[It] does not mean that my life will be free of difficulties – it does mean that I will have what I need to face them and will not have to face them alone."

Working the S-Anon Program, p. 40

Forgiveness and Serenity

Growing up, I thought forgiveness was something I had to feel all the time, so forgiveness seemed impossible for me. Working the S-Anon Steps, I not only found forgiveness, but also the serenity that can come with forgiveness.

Seven years after my first husband, a sexaholic, died, I still visited his grave each year. By his graveside, I would remember and relive the hurtful betrayal I felt during our nineteen years of marriage. This year when I visited his grave, I felt a peace that hadn't been there before. In the months leading up to my visit, I had been working Step Nine, which had helped me understand I had never forgiven my husband for his infidelities in our marriage, and I still had been holding onto the past. I also had realized I had not forgiven myself for my role in our misery together.

Today I choose to let go of past hurts and I offer my experiences to others to help carry the message. I pray for people who have harmed me, which has helped me to let go and begin to heal. I ask God to forgive me for my part and for the willingness to forgive. If I need to make direct amends, I do so promptly. When the matter returns to my mind, I pray, "God bless that person," instead of replaying the incident in my mind. As a result of these ongoing Step Nine and Ten actions, I am enjoying the peace and serenity that come with forgiveness.

Further Reflections...

"We now take the list we made in Step Eight and make direct amends to those people we had harmed. We are ready to take responsibility for our past and the hurt we caused others."

S-Anon Twelve Steps, p. 99

❖ ❖ ❖

A God Box in Notebook Form

Journaling is a powerful tool for me, a healthy way for me to work through uncomfortable situations in my life. I also use it to pray, meditate, and work through my obsessive thinking.

Sometimes I pray through writing letters to God, sharing my pain, experiences, gratitude, and feelings. Praying through journaling helps me to focus and keep my thoughts from wandering. As a result of this kind of prayer, I've gained a deeper intimacy with my Higher Power. Other times I read from one of our Conference Approved books or other inspirational readings and write on what I have read. I am constantly amazed at how many insights I have gained by doing this.

In working through my obsessive thinking, I use journaling as a "waste-basket" to dump my thoughts so they don't continually clutter up my head and obscure my thinking. Journaling gives me something I can do when I am feeling frustrated, kind of like using a "God Box" in notebook form.

When I use the "God Box" of journaling, I find that I gain more serenity and a healthier prayer life. I gain deeper insights regarding my feelings, my shortcomings, hopes, and dreams.

Further Reflections...
"I find it helpful to write down my worries, cares, and impossible situations on slips of paper and physically place them in a God Bag (I've also heard of God Boxes and God Jars). It helps me to symbolically put into God's care the things I don't need to carry around."

Working the S-Anon Program, p. 19

Breathing Again

Before recovery, it was as though I was walking around in a fog, not really seeing where I was going — constantly bumping into one painful situation after the next, always holding my breath. I would react and try to remedy my feelings by focusing on every detail, staying in denial about reality. I wanted change, but I thought it had to come from something outside of myself.

I was stuck in the "what if's" and nothing seemed to make a difference—until I attended S-Anon. At first all I could see was everyone else's pain and I wanted to fix the people in my meetings. At some point I realized that I could not manage taking care of other people, my marriage, spouse, children, and home, and take care of myself at the same time. I had hit my S-Anon bottom.

This is when I understood the meaning of powerlessness and unmanageability and I found my Higher Power. I started to see that a Higher Power was working in the lives of S-Anon members. I wanted what they had. Nothing else had worked—but here was this very simple program, which asked nothing of me but my attendance and willingness to be open to whatever truth my Higher Power had for me. Life began to slow down long enough for me to see that there was hope for change, and I felt myself breathing again.

Further Reflections...
"There is a relaxation and peace, and we find serenity and dignity within ourselves."

S-Anon Twelve Steps, p. 3

The Light of Hope

After attending S-Anon meetings for a few months, I started to let down the thick wall I had spent years building around my heart. I had constructed that wall strong enough to ride out the stormy seas and ferocious winds that had seemed constant in my life. I had done all this without help from anyone.

By working Step One and finally admitting I was completely powerless over the disease of sexaholism, my protective wall started to crumble. Small rays of sunshine began to shine through the cracks, giving me a better view of my past and shining the light of hope on my future. That light revealed the endless hours I had spent planning and scheming in hopes of controlling my sexaholic spouse. I saw that I had given nearly everything of myself away, and, because of this, I was spiritually and physically empty. Although I attended church regularly and prayed daily for the craziness to go away, I finally saw I had not been completely willing to surrender and turn my life over to God. While I did give God little bits and pieces, I had held on tight to my fear and pain.

Today, I am slowly building a strong foundation for my spirituality, my heart and my marriage. Although there are still fragments remaining of that wall, the light of hope has found its way to my heart. I truly know that by having God first and foremost in my life, I will be okay. I also know that someday I will find that the remaining fragments have disappeared.

Further Reflections...
"Letting go is...placing my concerns in God's care and surrendering to God's will."

Working the S-Anon Program, p. 13

The Project of My Life

My Higher Power opened my eyes to the fact that I love a "project." The project can be managing my daughter's diabetes, buying a new house or planning a vacation. I love to focus my attention on a problem and use all my energy to solve it. Of course, other people's problems have always been particularly attractive projects to me.

Since beginning to work the S-Anon program, I have let go of my need to manage other peoples' lives. I find that there is still one big project on which I can focus my attention and receive great benefit. It will keep me busy for a lifetime. That project is my own life!

I actually have found serenity knowing that taking care of myself is a full-time job and worthy of my attention. I needn't look elsewhere for any other challenges. This revelation has helped me with several aspects of my recovery. I am better able to connect with my Higher Power. I find it is easier to stay out of other peoples' business, which helps me keep my own side of the street clean. My life has lost an underlying negative edge, because I am more focused on the solution than on the problem.

With the help of Step Eleven, I still am enjoying having a project, and I like that the project is me.

Further Reflections...
"I have prayed for help, but maybe the answer is that I need to make changes in my own life."

Working the S-Anon Program, p. 47

I Am Where I Belong

Early in recovery, I often wondered how I ended up in S-Anon. There was no question I was qualified – I was married to a sexaholic – but why did I choose to marry a sexaholic in the first place? Unlike so many of my friends in S-Anon, my family of origin seemed fairly healthy, with no addiction or abuse present. I puzzled over the question for a long time, and even felt a little bit like an outsider in S-Anon because my family of origin didn't seem like that of anyone in my group.

I found this missing piece when I completed a thorough First Step. I have an older sister who is mentally handicapped, and the dynamics of my family were very similar to those of a family living with active addiction. Our lives centered around my sister and the challenges of caring for and living with her. This resulted in many fears and other emotions that were never discussed openly. I realized, even though my story may be unique, my feelings and behavior are still similar to that of other S-Anons.

Now I know it does not matter how I got here, only that I am here! Tradition Twelve reminds me that while what brought each of us here may be unique, we are here for a common purpose and the S-Anon principles can be applied in all our lives. I am where I belong.

Further Reflections…
"Today, when I say 'Keep coming back!' to newcomers, I wish for them the hope and help that I have found in S-Anon."

Working the S-Anon Program, p. 4

Trusting the Process of Recovery

During those first months in recovery, when my life seemed so chaotic, I was sharing with an S-Anon friend when I used this metaphor to describe how I was feeling. I was blessed with her wise response.

The metaphor: "I feel as if I'm in a little boat, out in the middle of the ocean. I'm adrift with no rudder, no sail, no motor, and no oars. I'm terrified and just want to put my arms over the side and start paddling."

Her response: "Well, you could do that, but you might paddle away from the current. Perhaps you just need to lay back and wait to catch the current that will send you where you need to go."

My friend's response helped me to regain a sense of calm even in the chaos and pain of that time. She reminded me that I am powerless over the reality of the present moment, but that I can have faith in my Higher Power. If I put myself in God's hands I will probably find that I have more options than the ones I am considering. My friend's gentle response helped me to surrender and to trust the process of recovery.

Further Reflections...
"For many of us who thought we could only trust ourselves, the concept of surrender seemed truly frightening."
S-Anon Twelve Steps, p. 35

No Longer Waiting to Live

One of my first spiritual awakenings in S-Anon was that I had been "waiting to live." I took lots of photographs, prided myself on a keen memory, and stored away the experience of my life for later. I would smile or put on my sad face at the appropriate times, but my heart was not in the moment. My heart had been sealed away to avoid the pain of life. I was too afraid to live fully in the moment. I got so far down the road of waiting to live that I became numb to the experiences of my life as they actually occurred.

Releasing denial shattered my stuffed treasure chest and three years of grieving followed. I grieved the addiction and the pain it left in its wake, but I also had to grieve my unlived life, as well. I could not go back and hold my son as a baby, I couldn't go back and feel my first kiss, I couldn't go back and feel myself as a bride in all those photographs. The grief of my missed life was keen.

Today, my recovery goal is to live fully in the moment: to cry today's tears, to laugh today's laughter, and to no longer wait to live.

Further Reflections...
"When I focus on my recovery journey, I honor my thoughts and feelings and pay attention to what they have to tell me regarding my path. I attend to the spiritual meaning embedded in the minute-by-minute details of my life. As I keenly notice the changes I undergo when I stretch myself spiritually by using a slogan, Step, or Tradition, I stay in today."

[Al-Anon] Hope for Today, p. 153

Discovering Fellowship

I lived with a sexaholic and for years I considered going to S-Anon, but I stayed away, fearing that no one would understand. Then a co-worker revealed to me her newly-discovered situation with her husband – he was a sexaholic. She said she was going with a friend to an S-Anon group. I felt an emotional tug, and I offered to go along with my co-worker, thinking I would "support" her.

That first meeting was enlightening – I could really relate to what was said! I saw that in S-Anon I could openly share my issues and concerns with the other members, because they knew exactly how I felt. They had experienced the same feelings and had many of the same concerns. They really understood. What freedom to know someone understood the secrets with which I had been living! The relief and sense of belonging I felt were indescribable. My journey of truth-telling began that day, and the shame and denial I had experienced about my husband's acting out began to fall away.

While I enjoy that sense of fellowship most of the time, I occasionally start to feel that I'm alone and no one can understand – that I'm not a part of, but rather apart from the group. Then I remind myself that I can share even those feelings with my S-Anon group, and they will understand. The truth is that I never have to be alone with my fears and misgivings again – I truly belong.

Further Reflections...
"Most of us came into S-Anon feeling deeply lonely... When we reached S-Anon we found ourselves among people who really understood, and a sense of belonging began to grow inside."

S-Anon Twelve Steps, p. 52-53

Fear of Failure

During the early days of my program, my friends in S-Anon would suggest that I consider practicing the slogan "Easy Does It." As far back as I can remember, I do not think I ever took anything easy. It was difficult for me to learn how to read and to know where I fit in with friends at school. It was difficult for me to grow up in a house with a rage-aholic. Life was not easy. To move through my life I worked hard, learned to focus, motivated myself to do more, and ignored my physical limits to perform better and faster. The idea of taking it easy seemed to equal failure based on my previous experiences.

My fear of failure continues to challenge me and I am aware that I have more healing work to do. However, in S-Anon I am having new experiences that include God. I no longer feel I have to prove anything to anyone. I am actually finding that working hard is okay, but it is so very important that I also take time for myself and enjoy my recovery.

Further Reflections...
"'Easy Does It' reminds me to be good to myself and let a Higher Power lead me."

Working the S-Anon Program, p. 14

I Only Need to Take Care of Myself

My husband was required to make a court appearance as a consequence of some phone sex calls he had made. I chose to attend court with him that day. After my husband was sentenced to supervision, my husband, his lawyer, and I went to a room for my husband to sign some papers. After the lawyer took the papers from my husband, he looked at me and said, "You can take care of him now." I stood there seething. My gut instinct was to rant and rave and tell the attorney that my husband and his behavior were not my responsibility! Gratefully, I did not act on my impulse to rage, knowing it would not be productive.

As I left the courthouse, I had calmed down enough to feel sad that the attorney had no idea about the nature of the family disease of sexaholism. He did not understand the role care-taking and enabling play to keep the disease going. At the same time I was very grateful for my awareness that I wasn't responsible for the sexaholic's behavior. There was nothing I could do to change or control his actions. The freedom that I felt in knowing that I only need to take care of myself was such a relief!

Further Reflections...
"As I grew... it became clear that my true responsibility was to care for myself. I began to see how my caretaking and controlling actually hurt others, possibly cheating them out of an opportunity to learn and grow."

[Al-Anon] *Hope for Today,* p. 41

What Is a Slip in S-Anon?

Working the Steps has helped me discover so much about myself. Because of this, I am better able to define for myself what an S-Anon slip is. For example, there are times when I have done things with unconditional love for the sexaholic, others, and myself. There were no doubts about my motives. I felt clean, because my motives were kind and caring.

On other occasions I have done something similar, but I was motivated by character defects like fear, selfishness, or people-pleasing. Inevitably I experienced pain, guilt, disappointment, resentment, or depression – unmistakable fruits of unhealthy motives. When I react out of any one of these defects, I have slipped in my S-Anon program.

Therefore, what usually determines whether or not I have "slipped" is not what I did, but why I did it. A tool I have found useful for taking a look at my motives is the Tenth Step. I take the time to make an honest inventory of my actions and turn over what I find to my Higher Power. Then I am better able to identify my motives. I am learning to recognize where I am headed in advance, check my motives, and not take the action before I slip.

Further Reflections…
"Sobriety [in S-Anon] is knowing and owning all of my own behaviors and choices."

S-Anews, Winter Issue, 1994, p. 4

Terminal Uniqueness

As I walked to my commuter train on a recent morning, my thoughts were of my father-in-law, 400 miles away, struggling with the effects of cancer treatment. Walking down the train station's platform I observed other commuters and wondered how many of them were also dealing with a loved one's illness or if they, too, were struggling with illness, loss, or even addiction.

As I took my seat on the train that morning, I became aware that I was feeling compassion and concern for others. How different from when I first came to S-Anon many years ago! At that point I was so focused on fixing my spouse's sexaholism and my own pain that I had little awareness of the pain of others. I did not understand how similar everyone's experiences are, simply by virtue of our common humanity.

I have lost my "terminal uniqueness," that sense that no one can truly understand my personal pain because it seems different or greater than other people's pain. Through working the program, I have gained appreciation and compassion for my fellows, including the sexaholic. Today I am able to focus on the similarities that unite me with others rather than the differences that divide us.

Further Reflections...
"Talk to each other, reason things out with someone else, but let there be no gossip or criticism of one another. Instead, let the understanding, love, and peace of the program grow in you one day at a time."

S-Ateen Meeting Closing Reminder

Stepping Off the Roller-Coaster

I used to live with an active sexaholic, believing I had absolutely no choices in my life. I spent five years waiting for him to marry me – five years that felt like a continuous roller-coaster ride. He constantly threatened to leave, and often did, although always returning. I put my life on hold at great cost to my health and well-being. I was so consumed with hoping the sexaholic would be someone different than who he was, I lost awareness of who I was. I felt powerless to be anywhere or do anything else.

I rode the emotional roller-coaster until coming to S-Anon. In S-Anon I spoke freely about my fears and concerns and was not judged. People loved me even when I could not love myself. At meetings, I heard the truth, over and over again. S-Anon program provided me with a map (the Steps and Traditions) and a compass (the literature, the fellowship, and my sponsor) to find my way off the roller-coaster.

It took some time and heartache to fully grasp the slogan "Let Go and Let God." I asked for guidance from my sponsor, said lots of prayers, and focused on my Step work. When I was ready, I ended my relationship with the sexaholic and even wished him well. Today, I am grateful to be stepping forward into my new life, trusting that my Higher Power will guide me.

Further Reflections...
"We cannot know for sure that our relationship with the sexaholic will ever be what we might have wished for, but we do know that we can learn to trust a Higher Power and the process of recovery."

Working the S-Anon Program, p. 59

Permission to Stretch My Wings

I remember telling people there were only two things that were truly mine: my coffee cup, which was off limits to the rest of my family, and my annual solo week of vacation at my mom's house with no children or husband. Now as I look back, I can see my old statement was a great example of how I consistently placed the needs of others above my own needs.

While I outwardly embraced the ways I sacrificed for others, on the inside I was angry that I had to be the one who always was doing things for others. I felt like the victim of my circumstances and trapped by my inability to do anything different for myself.

S-Anon gave me permission to stretch my wings and try new things. I learned to take better care of myself and my needs. I learned to listen to my body when I was tired or needing special care. I learned to occasionally purchase something I wanted for myself, rather than wait for someone else to get it for me. I learned to take time to relax and play.

Thanks to my work in the S-Anon program and the support of my S-Anon friends, I now enjoy making decisions that are as considerate and thoughtful of me as those I make for others. This is one of the many gifts of the S-Anon program for me.

Further Reflections..
"I thanked God for the gift of the S-Anon program and for giving me release one day at a time from fear, control, and over-responsibility."

S-Anon Twelve Steps, p. 116

Putting the Steps into Practice

I was exhausted, lonely, and at the end of my rope when I stepped through the doors of S-Anon. I wanted the serenity I felt in that room, so I worked hard to put the Steps into practice and, as a result, so much has changed.

I feel joy, which is not dependent on my circumstances. The spiritual principles I found in S-Anon, especially in Steps Two and Three, helped me recover that feeling of joy. I am grateful for my life. I have come to believe that no matter what is going on; I can trust my Higher Power is in control. I am serene. I saw evidence of my progress when my recovering sexaholic spouse acknowledged a relapse, and I was able to maintain my serenity.

I have changed because I learned to focus on myself and to put the Steps into practice. Learning to focus on myself and experience serenity have not come easily. It was difficult to become vulnerable enough to reveal my problems and weaknesses. However, the joy I now feel makes it all worth it, so I will continue to do what has worked: diligently work the Twelve Steps, get support through attending meetings, work closely with my sponsor and, above all, trust God.

Further Reflections...
"When I am disturbed, it is because I find some person, place, thing, or situation – some fact of my life – unacceptable to me, and I can find no serenity until I accept that person, place, thing, or situation as being exactly the way it is supposed to be at this moment. Nothing, absolutely nothing, happens in God's world by mistake."
Alcoholics Anonymous (4th ed), p. 417

The Common Cold – An S-Ateen Story

When I think about going to S-Ateen meetings, I don't like to think about being sick and needing help because it sounds so harsh. Instead, I like to think I'm curing my emotional common cold.

I got the cold from my dad, a sexaholic. I don't have the same symptoms as my dad, but I still have a cold. Some of my cold symptoms include denial, anger, and self-abuse. The cold continues spreading until someone stops it. I feel that every time I go to a meeting, I'm healing my cold, and I am not alone in my healing process because the cold we have is common! When I began my Step work, I felt as though I got a teaspoon of cough syrup, and the symptoms began to fade.

It has become clear to me that the only way to be "cured" of this cold is to work the program, go to meetings, read S-Anon literature, and follow the Steps. It is the way to a healthier me.

Further Reflections...
"With the loving help from other S-Ateen members, our S-Ateen sponsors, and the God of our understanding, we take positive action to make our lives more serene and fulfilling. We attend as many meetings as we can, get support from other S-Ateens, and begin to apply the Twelve Steps to our lives. We use the telephone, S-Ateen Conference Approved Literature, and the S-Ateen slogans."

Keys to S-Ateen Recovery

Opportunities for Growth

My sponsor taught me about the importance of service work in S-Anon. She suggested that I stay open when asked to do service. If I was asked to speak, it was an opportunity to share my experience, strength, and hope. When someone asked me to sponsor them, it was a chance to return the gifts that I had been freely given. Each new service experience taught me something about myself. Through interacting with others, I better learned how to put the spiritual principles of this program into action. My sponsor's encouragement helped me become the person I am today.

The service of sponsorship has taught me many things. Most of us come to this program broken in some way, and participating in service work is not something everyone feels comfortable doing right away. While most of my sponsees follow up on my encouragement to accept the gifts of service, one of my sponsees refused to do any service work. This became an opportunity for us to do some Step work together. She shared her fear with me, which was based on childhood experiences of never being recognized for doing anything right and the consequences she faced as a result of those experiences. I saw that my sponsee was taking the time she needed for healing.

In time, she took baby steps toward service – setting up chairs and helping to clean-up after the meeting. I had the privilege of being a witness of this shy, fearful woman grow and finally allow herself to take the risk of offering her help in many ways since then. I love the way this program works.

Further Reflection...
"Part of sponsorship is modeling how to put the Steps into practice 'in all our affairs.'"

Sponsorship in S-Anon Pamphlet

❖ ❖ ❖

Surrendering My Pain

Prior to coming to S-Anon, my husband disclosed to me that he had been sexually involved with many other women, with one affair lasting three years. My husband's sexual behavior involved huge sums of money, including the financial support of one of these woman and her children. I was devastated to learn this information and to deal with the magnitude of the impact sexaholism had on my life and marriage.

I felt so alone and overwhelmed. I knew I could not handle this myself, but I didn't know anyone to whom I could turn. At a total loss, I fell to my knees and asked God to help me with this unbearable pain.

I felt God answered my prayer by making me aware of S-Anon a short time later. I have attended meetings for a short time, and I am beginning to contemplate Step One, I have started to write daily, and in my writing, I ask my Higher Power to help me with my sadness, fear, anger, and grief about being powerless over my husband's addiction. I ask God for help with the unmanageability of my life. The meetings are helping me realize I am not alone. With the help of other S-Anon members, I now feel the beginning of hope in my heart.

Further Reflections...
"Some of us came to the program feeling an anger bordering on rage, and at the same time feeling weak, defeated, and hopeless. Only later did we realize that reaching out for the help of S-Anon had taken a great deal of courage, and that it was the beginning of our recovery."

We're Glad You're Here; Information for the
Newcomer Booklet, Welcome

More Than My Emotions

After I came out of denial and faced the reality that my beloved partner was a sexaholic, I experienced terrible emotional pain, especially fear. It seemed like much of the time I felt so overwhelmed by those emotions that I actually became the fear and pain.

I have found that to calm myself, it helps to first acknowledge my pain and fear. Just noticing my emotions gives me some space from those awful nagging feelings. This distance helps me see I am not just a lump of pain or fear – I am more than my emotions. As one of our S-Anon slogans says, "This Too Shall Pass." In thirty minutes (or a day or week), I may well feel better.

I also focus on observing my breathing as a method of detaching from my obsessive thoughts and overwhelming feelings. By focusing on my breath and following the rising and falling of my abdomen, I actually slow down my racing thoughts and I am released from obsession. Focusing on my physical body gently brings me back to key realities: I am a living, breathing being, and I am on a path led by my Higher Power.

I need not give in to despair or painful emotions. I can find relief in the present moment when I breathe, acknowledge the feelings, and remember that they are not permanent.

Further Reflections...
"...feelings aren't facts. I am a complex, fascinating human being with a wide range of emotions, experiences, and thoughts. There is more to my identity than one feeling or another, one problem or another. I am a wealth of contradictions. I can value all of my feelings without allowing them to dictate my actions."

[Al-Anon] *Courage to Change*, p. 339

❖   ❖   ❖

Hope for Today

Working the S-Anon program has renewed my hope. I have found hope through a wonderful sponsor who works with me. Even though it seems that I am taking forever to finish my Fourth Step inventory, I feel grateful to have a sponsor, who has been very gentle and patient with me, telling me, "don't push the river; it flows by itself."

My hope also comes from attending our International S-Anon Conventions and our regional S-Anon marathons. At these gatherings, I learn more about working the S-Anon program from members from other parts of the country and the world. As they share their experience, I learn hopeful new ideas that help me become able to take better care of myself. I become aware of new insights into my behavior and my character defects.

The experience that gives me the most hope is the relationship I am developing with my Higher Power. Not only does my serenity depend on that relationship, but also through that relationship I truly have re-discovered myself in a way I could never have imagined. This re-discovery is illustrated by a photo I have of myself at about two years of age. That picture shows a joyous, smiling, golden-haired little girl who has hope and love in her face. I know that God is within that little girl, and God is within me as an adult, too.

Further Reflections...
"S-Anon is a Twelve-Step program of recovery, and can be a source of hope and help for those affected by the sexual behavior of a family member or friend."

Information for Professionals Pamphlet

Self Worth

One specific change I can see in myself is a great improvement in my self worth and self confidence. I frequently looked for validation outside of myself. If there was a vote, I'd wait to see how everyone else voted, before adding my vote. If I had a struggle with some action I needed to take, I would ask someone "What should I do?" or, "What would you do if you were me?" Well, the fact is, no one is "me".

As I rediscovered who I was, by listening and talking to others, and working the Twelve Steps with a sponsor, I realized I carried much shame. Many of my behaviors reflected the shame and sickness of the disease of sexaholism. As healing occurred, I realized I was capable of making decisions for myself, with the help of a Higher Power. I am so grateful for my program!

I can have compassion for myself and know that today, because of my program; I have choices regarding my actions. The answers do come when I trust my process and when I am patient with myself.

Further Reflections...
"There seemed to be no me! As I connect at deeper levels with my Higher Power's love for me, I feel a greater ability to be honest, to know myself, and to let myself be seen and heard by others."

Working the S-Anon Program, p. 49

Gratitude for Literature

The S-Anon meeting I attend has a different topic every week, selected at the discretion of that evening's leader. The leader's topic is usually either a personal current recovery issue, or the group's consensus on a topic. In either case we usually find some information and reflection on the topic in one the books we have of Conference Approved Literature (CAL) before we move into the discussion time. I am so grateful for our CAL, because it provides me with a broad base of experience, strength, and hope from across the S-Anon membership. I lean on the wisdom of others who have gone before me and find great hope in reading how their Higher Power has worked miracles.

I have broadened my use of CAL to my quiet time at home. I try to read something every day and reflect on its message to me. When I am unable to get to a meeting, I like to read CAL with an S-Anon friend over the telephone or by myself. I feel my Higher Power uses CAL to teach me about living in the solution rather than in the problem.

Further Reflections…
"S-Anon Conference-Approved Literature represents the S-Anon point of view regarding our recovery and the problems that arise from another person's sexaholism. Our literature is written by S-Anons for S-Anons and offers the best experience about recovery from the family disease of sexaholism."

Working the S-Anon Program, p. 15

The Antidote to Complacency

Sometimes, while wrapped up in everyday life, I find myself getting complacent in my S-Anon program. When I am not in emotional pain or enduring some crisis in my life, it somehow seems easy for me to forget that I am part of the family disease of sexaholism. When I am complacent, I allow life's distractions to interfere with making and returning phone calls, journaling, and meditating. It is usually at this time that I start judging my performance as a sponsor and start thinking I "should" be doing a better job. At this point I am reminded that it is time for me to get back to work on my program.

Again and again, my Higher Power has shown me that when I become complacent I am capable of making personal choices that can lead me to slips in my S-Anon program and ultimately, to more emotional pain. It is in these times of complacency that I most need to be with newcomers in S-Anon. Spending time with newcomers reminds me of the turmoil of my past. I receive the gift and reminder that the effects of sexaholism are real, and that I have been given a program to heal from the pain. In listening, I realize I have something to give. However, to keep what I've been given, I need to recognize my complacency when it arises and be willing to get back to work.

Further Reflections...
"We will not regret the past nor wish to shut the door on it."

Alcoholics Anonymous, p. 83

God Has a Plan

Life has a way of working out. Before S-Anon, I often felt that I was waiting for the "other shoe to drop." I expected problems, and that is exactly what I got. From one crisis to another, the world seemed unsafe and unfair. My negative thoughts and attitudes darkened my heart and my vision of reality. I even drove as if my anxiety was keeping the car from breaking down! I didn't know that there was another way to exist and thrive.

Since I have been working the Steps, Traditions, and Concepts, I have come to realize that my anxiety was an attempt to have control. My negative attitude was my way of dealing (or not dealing) with my pain of having an unmanageable life. My work in the program has shown me that my spiritual growth is the surest way of instilling hope and gratitude in my life.

Recently, I experienced a life-threatening illness, my insurance changed and there was fear in my mind that the new insurance company wouldn't allow me to see the doctor who had seen me through the illness. As my anxiety rose I feared the worst. Because of the tools of the program, I finally surrendered the outcome, and accepted God's will for me. I am so grateful it all worked out. Again, I learned the lesson that God has a plan and life has a way of working out!

Further Reflections...
"As we grow in our understanding of these spiritual principles, we thank our Higher Power for our defects, which continually remind us of our humanity and the need for God in our lives. We finally understand 'Thy will, not mine, be done.'"

S-Anon Twelve Steps, p. 70

The Formula for Serenity

Early in my recovery, my intense feelings of hurt and betrayal fed my rage and consumed me. I often felt rageful toward my partner and wanted to shame and hurt him as deeply as I had been hurt. I wasn't sure I could control my actions.

In S-Anon I learned that when I felt like this, I had lost my serenity and needed to use my program tools. My thoughts often raced so rageful that I couldn't speak, so I didn't call a program friend or my sponsor, and I usually didn't think to pray for guidance. My out-of-control emotions blocked everything out.

I finally found a formula that works for me. When I started feeling enraged, I removed myself from the sexaholic's presence and retreat to a quiet place. I read Conference Approved Literature until I regain serenity. I read stories of strength and courage that gave me hope. As I read, I am reminded of key principles: sexaholic's are sick people, not bad people; I am powerless over this disease, but not over my own actions. The anger gradually dissipates and I start to feel compassion for both myself and the sexaholic.

No matter how angry, hurt, or depressed I feel, this formula helps me regain serenity. Once that intense anger subsides, I can call my sponsor and my program friends for their strength and encouragement. At this point I am usually able to start making a connection with my Higher Power. I can take charge of my life and not look to a relationship as the source of my serenity and happiness.

Further Reflections...
"...there is no situation to difficult to be bettered, and no unhappiness too great to be lessened."

The S-Anon Welcome

I Have Choices

Before recovery I focused on my problems, thinking I had to figure out and resolve each one. Looking back, I realize that I often made others' problems my own. I wasted a lot of time and energy attempting to fix what was not mine to fix. I chose to make problems my main focus, and I generally missed the good in my life.

S-Anon has helped me see that I have choices. I can choose to enjoy the day and look for the good that is there. I can enjoy my daughter sharing her day with me. I can feel my Higher Power's love for me through the gentle actions and words of others, a smile from a stranger in response to one of my own, kind words, and the blessings I feel from being kind.

I am glad recovery has given me choices, including the choice of where to put my focus each day. I'm beginning to trust that my problems will be resolved in due course, so they don't have to be the object of all my time and energy. Instead, I can choose to be happy and joyful today, despite my problems. Thank you, S-Anon, for helping me see the choices that are always there for me.

Further Reflections...
"...we begin to see our problems in a new light, and the awareness dawns that we do have choices concerning our own actions."

Keys to S-Anon Recovery

Forgiving Myself

In addition to forgiving the sexaholic, I am finding I need to forgive myself. I made choices and acted in ways that I regret. I paid bills knowing that they were for inappropriate sexual activities. Then I became angry, wondering why the sexaholic didn't show any appreciation for me. I went on cleaning sprees, organizing and throwing away stuff, thinking I could accomplish an orderly, peaceful life. I realized that my frenzied activity was a cover for wanting to have control over something – anything – since it was evident I couldn't control the sexaholic. I refused going out with my kids because I thought I needed to be home and "watch" the sexaholic, thinking that maybe with my help, sobriety would happen.

My thinking and behavior were not helpful to me or others, yet I kept on trying. Changing seemed as difficult for me as it was for the sexaholic to change. I saw that I was as sick and in need of Twelve Step recovery. Realizing this helped me have compassion for myself and the sexaholic. We each needed to mind our own difficult business a day at a time. I have a big job ahead of me and with God's help and support of the S-Anon program I am willing to begin.

Further Reflections...
"Do I realize that forgiveness can begin with me? Do I understand that a choice not to take the time necessary to work through feelings and forgive can be a choice to reject freedom and remain a victim?"

S-Anon Twelve Steps, p. 95

My Role

When my husband told me of his sexaholism and his new-found recovery, I downplayed it and basically denied the impact it had had on my life, and my daughter's life. Then the day came when he told me he had relapsed. I was petrified he would be arrested, worried about how it would affect our daughter, and concerned about my ability to cope. I anxiously stayed up all night waiting for the police to ring our doorbell. The police never came, but as a result of the experience, my husband admitted himself to a psychiatric hospital for severe depression. Because of his willingness to understand his powerlessness, a miracle happened that changed my life forever — the hospital referred me to S-Anon.

At my first meeting I heard about the three C's: I didn't Cause it, I can't Control it, and I can't Cure it. It was helpful to hear I didn't cause it, but it was very difficult for me to understand that I couldn't control or cure it – particularly cure. Since childhood, I had taken on the role in my family as the "fixer," taking care of others' problems. I thought being the "fixer" was a good thing, so it was hard to swallow that I couldn't cure my husband's sexaholism.

I understand now (through working the Steps) that sexaholism has had a significant impact on both my daughter and I, and I have relinquished my role as the family "fixer." While I still have a long way to go, I am grateful when I experience moments of peace and serenity.

Further Reflections...
"Even when we try hard and fail, we can be glad, knowing that the pain of failure is transformed into experience, strength, and hope with each attempt at growth. Pain is the touchstone of all spiritual progress."

S-Anon Twelve Steps, p. 115

❖   ❖   ❖

Heal My Heart

I have to admit that sometimes letting go feels more like chest-wrenching pain than a gentle detachment with love from the actions of another person. Through using the principles of the S-Anon program, I have done all I can to stay safely in my relationship with my sexaholic partner. It has become clear that it is no longer safe to remain in the relationship, and I know I must now face my fear and let go, but my chest hurts when I do. I decided to offer that feeling to God and to invite God to do "heart surgery."

This is my prayer: "God, if it is your will, please open my chest and heal my heart. You have opened the door for me to separate from the sexaholic before, but today please give me the courage to walk through the door. Not without sadness. Not without pain. Not without hope. Not without help. Please remove all the hurt and pain and heal my heart."

I am grateful for the willingness to work an S-Anon program, for the support I have from family and friends in my meetings and for new opportunities that lay ahead of me. Thank you God, for answering my prayer.

Further Reflections...
"It has been difficult to take steps of faith and to develop a more hopeful perspective on life. In fact, it is often painful....Listening to people in S-Anon, we grasp the reality that despair and failure can be transformed into hope and success."

Working the S-Anon Program, p. 74

The Here and Now

Being present is just that – being fully aware of myself and the situation in the here and now. Before working an S-Anon program, I worried too much about the future to be in the moment. Now I practice the slogan Easy Does It by slowing down. When I experience myself jumping into future fear, I breathe and breathe again. I can accept that I am exactly where I am supposed to be in this moment.

Being in the moment is still new and unfamiliar. Old habits are hard to break, yet I am so ready to be in the moment and eager for new experiences. I am finally able to surrender and willing to be teachable. I am building new strengths. There are so many beautiful things surrounding me now. There is so much for which to be grateful, yet if I do not slow down and just observe and relax, I miss them all. When I remember to live in the here and now, I am happy. Rarely am I sad when I am in the moment. When I realize I am exactly where I am supposed to be and who I am supposed to be in this moment, I am content. Today I am on my path.

Further Reflections...
"One day while watching small children play, I realized they were the healthiest, most sane people I knew. They knew how to live life in the present."

S-Anon Twelve Steps, p. 19

Let Go and Let God

After a painful argument about the use of internet pornography, my spouse decided to sleep in the car that night. I was pleased with the idea and hoped he would think more clearly the next time he was tempted to use our computer in that way. In the morning, I kept checking out the window hoping he would come in the house before our children woke up.

I became obsessed with trying to conceal the problem from our children. I also wanted to hear some assurance from him that he loved me and we were going to be okay. My discomfort in trying to control his problem and keep the family secret was nearly unbearable.

I'd heard in my S-Anon meetings the slogan "Let Go and Let God," as well as examples of how others had worked the Third Step. I decided this was a good time for me to put this spiritual principle to practice. I prayed and turned over the situation to God. I continued with my decision to let God handle it. It was difficult for me, but I was able to pull myself away from the window and focus on making breakfast.

Within minutes, it began to hail! I had to laugh at God's timing and sense of humor. The sound of the hail hitting the outside of the car woke up my husband. I try to remember this situation when I'm tempted to orchestrate my husband's recovery. God can communicate in ways I haven't even imagined.

Further Reflections...
"One of the fruits I've gotten from the program is to just look for the doors to open naturally...'or God to open the door.'"

Working the S-Anon Program, p. 100

 ❖ ❖ ❖

Forgiveness and Acceptance

I was raised in an alcoholic, sexaholic family and I married a sexaholic. Over many years of my life, I experienced an extraordinary amount of shame, blame, and anger. My painful life experience affected my perceptions of relationships, myself, and others. It also affected my perceptions of forgiveness.

When I first came to S-Anon, I had a hard time believing that I might actually forgive those people who had abused me. My perspective changed over time as I continued with my S-Anon Step work. My sponsor guided me to see where I could forgive others and myself.

My Fourth Step inventory and my Fifth Step work led me to see that forgiveness ultimately means accepting that every human being, including myself, is flawed on some level. While I can judge whether or not a person's behavior is acceptable to me, I can do so without judging that person as a human being. My sponsor helped me understand I could also extend forgiveness to myself through the gift of self-acceptance.

Through S-Anon, I have come to see that non-judgment is the essence of acceptance and that acceptance is the essence of forgiveness.

Further Reflections...
"Under very trying conditions I have had, again and again, to forgive others – also myself. Have you recently tried this?"

[Alcoholics Anonymous] *As Bill Sees It, p. 268*

Applying Tools to Dating

When I finally started dating after my divorce, I was concerned that I again would choose someone who was an addict and that I might not be able to take good care of myself. I wondered how I could use the tools of the program to enjoy healthy dating. I shared about my anxiety in my meeting, as well as with my sponsor. My S-Anon friends reminded me about something I had learned early in my recovery to listen to my feelings.

To stay in touch with my feelings, I have to take care of myself mentally, emotionally, and physically. The slogan H.A.L.T. – a simple check-in to see if I'm too hungry, angry, lonely, or tired – has been a terrific tool to maintain my sobriety and listen to myself. When I am not paying attention to my mental, emotional, and physical state, I become vulnerable to old patterns of thinking. When I take care of myself, I can get clear as to what my choices are and what the next right action is.

Taking care of myself with H.A.L.T. has been a valuable tool as I explore dating again. I am finding I can trust the recovery process, and my Higher Power. I am learning to take care of myself in relationships.

Further Reflections...
"Trust is a process over which I have some control. I don't have to form relationships any faster than I'm ready."
[Al-Anon] Hope for Today, p. 198

God Provides for Me – Just in Time

There is a concept in business called "Just In Time" manufacturing. The idea is to save money and increase efficiency by receiving raw materials "just in time" to be manufactured, rather than expensively storing them at the factory until they are needed.

It occurred to me one day that my experience with God is quite similar to this "just in time" concept. I used to face challenging situations feeling empty-handed and unequipped. Through working the Steps, and practicing using the many tools of the program, I have come to see that when it is the right time to act, my Higher Power supplies just what I need in each situation. This happens when I ask for clarity to make healthy decisions, when I need an answer or an opportunity to be revealed, when I stay open to new ideas for help regarding my finances, and when I am in need of a program phone call. And sometimes the provision comes without me even realizing I needed it. God provides for me "just in time."

Through many years of having these "just in time" experiences, I have learned that I can trust my Higher Power to supply whatever I truly need when the time is right. Today I don't have to see the resources up front to know that they will be there "just in time."

Further Reflections...
"Turning my will and my life over to my Higher Power is the only tool I know that has saved me at times when I was at my lowest and didn't know where to turn next."

Working the S-Anon Program, p. 61

Changing the Channel in My Brain

For a long time I constantly obsessed about the sexaholic's behavior. Vivid pictures ran through my head like a grainy, X-rated film. Unfortunately, my obsession was like pouring salt on an open wound – over and over again.

After several meetings and learning to apply the tools and principles of the S-Anon program to my life, I was able to go a few days without constantly focusing on the sexaholic. I started replacing my obsessive thoughts with working Steps One and Two, and with making outreach calls. After a few more months of meetings, I found I could go a week at a time without brooding over the past. I had a sponsor, who I called regularly, and also spoke with whenever the old images and thoughts popped into my head. Reaching out helped me redirect my thinking and my behavior. My sponsor suggested that when the images and thoughts came to my mind, I turn them over to my Higher Power and visualize placing the sexaholic in God's hands.

I am powerless over whether or not the obsessive thoughts come, but when the images come into my head, I now have the tools necessary to change the channel in my brain. I can pray to my Higher Power, ask my sponsor for help and guidance, and write about my feelings and share them with another program member. I don't have to have obsession and pain; I can have serenity.

Further Reflections...
"Through working the S-Anon program, many of us have overcome powerful feelings, which are not ours to carry,....Our solution depends on keeping focused on our own personal path of recovery and allowing the sexaholic to do the same."

S-Anon Twelve Steps, p. xix

Now It's My Turn

In my first months of recovery, I spent almost every meeting in tears, feeling deep pain and hopelessness. One evening, the leader for the meeting brought treats for the group to celebrate her S-Anon birthday – another 365 days of working her S-Anon program. She shared how grateful she was to be a part of this fellowship and how happy she was to be celebrating her birthday that evening among fellow S-Anons.

I found myself in tears again, but this time it was for the hope she gave me. My S-Anon birthday was over eight months away, but I thought if I could feel happiness at my one year S-Anon birthday, then that could be something to hope for and work towards.

Over the months, my hope for happiness became a reality. It is now my tradition to bring treats for the group on my S-Anon birthday. Because of the program, I can rejoice in my new life and freedom that I have received through working the Steps and being part of this fellowship. Now it's my turn to pass on encouragement, strength, and hope.

Further Reflections...
"It has been painful at times, but I have learned how to find serenity, healing, and love in my life. Today, because of S-Anon, I know a freedom and joy in living that I would have never thought possible."

Working the S-Anon Program, p. 80

Surrendering "Good and Bad"

When my S-Anon group was studying the Seventh Step in the S-Anon Twelve Steps, I was struck by the prayer quoted from Alcoholics Anonymous, which begins…"My creator, I am now willing that you should have all of me, good and bad." At first I thought "good and bad" alluded to how supportive I was of my husband's recovery. I thought recovery was about my being a supportive, trusting wife, and squashing my own feelings about all the craziness of sexaholism that had been brought to light. My thinking was, "If I just do this relationship right, I'll get what I need and want." I came to realize that surrendering "good and bad" had nothing to do with how well I managed the relationship, but rather with my "good and bad" as an individual. I realized recovery was about dealing with reality and making healthy choices, to help deal with my emotional responses.

I started looking at me – the good and bad aspects of my life. I saw one of my "bad" characteristics was self-pity, which led me to blame others for my unhealthy choices. Another "bad" was my need to control, which came out of my fear of experiencing more pain. I'm still learning to appreciate the "good" in myself, but I definitely know one "good" has been my willingness finally to be honest with myself about the effects of sexaholism on my life. As I have surrendered my life – the good and bad – to the care of my Higher Power, I have gained some peace and serenity. I thank God for this program.

Further Reflections….
"The more I get to know God, the more I trust His love and care for me."

Working the S-Anon Program, p. 42

Voicing Concerns about Internet Access

I used to think I had to go along with behavior that felt uncomfortable because it was somehow important to seem carefree and agreeable. I did not like being the one who said "no" or who questioned someone else's opinion. S-Anon has helped me begin to change, but I still struggle at times.

Recently my husband mentioned he would like to have a cable modem installed in our home to access the Internet faster. At first I swallowed my concern and said nothing. In my old pattern I did not think I should object—faster is better, right? I dismissed the fact that I was already uncomfortable with having Internet access, let alone a faster and more expensive access. I disregarded my concern that my husband was recovering from an addiction to pornography and his number one delivery system had been the Internet.

Thankfully, my S-Anon program kicked in and I was able to voice my concerns. It was not easy, but after much discussion and placing the results in God's hands, my husband and I agreed to remove all Internet access in our home. I know this might not be necessary for every family recovering from the effects of sexaholism, but it turned out to be best for us. I am grateful that I had the support to find the courage to have an open discussion with my spouse. I thank God for recovery.

Further Reflections...
"True honesty for me only comes when I concentrate on myself. I try to determine what I think and feel, and I'm learning to express it, even if I know my spouse may not agree."

Recovering Together: Issues Faced by Couples
(Revised Booklet 2007), p. 10

Just How Far I Have Come

When I discovered my supposedly sober husband's stash of pornography, I felt as if the carpet had been pulled out from under me. Now with this new, ugly knowledge, I questioned everything I believed as I looked back over the events in my past.

But even in that hole of confusion and despair, it was important to remember what I already had learned in S-Anon: that I did not cause his relapse or bring it on. This betrayal was the result of my husband's sickness. I was pleased that I did not beat myself up with thoughts of "if only I was skinnier, younger, prettier…." or "if only I wasn't such a nag and so boring…" as I had done before I came to S-Anon. Instead, I reminded myself that this is his illness. My part in the illness was active if I believed the lies and manipulations and continued in denial. I told myself that I was a lovable, beautiful, worthwhile person, no matter what his actions were – and I believed it.

With those thoughts I was aware of just how far I have come in my recovery.

Further Reflections…
"As devastating and shameful as the disease of sexaholism can be, it does not compare to the richness of the continual spiritual awakening, renewal, and healing that God has brought into my life. I am astounded by God's ability to free so many of us by His message of truth, as He weaves our healing with that of those around us when we follow His lead and carry the message."

S-Anon Twelve Steps, p. 148

Recognizing Insane Behavior

At four, I already knew my role: the cute one in the family. To this day, I do not know why I was selected for this part. If given the choice I would have selected the artistic one or the smart one. Yet it was settled – child number four was the cute one.

I remember a time from childhood when my church was to go on a camping trip. My Mom, as usual, felt compelled to sew an entire new wardrobe for me to take to that dusty campground, while we six children, between 10 years and 10 months, spent our time unsupervised. As usual, Mom's hard work paid off: everyone fussed over my sexy, pre-school-sized clothing, Mom got lots of accolades – "How does she manage to find time to sew with all those children?"

I never gave my experience much thought until I was in recovery. One day I was pulling clothes out of my young child's dresser to take camping. I selected sturdy, worn, I-don't-care-if-it-gets-ruined outfits. I was on my knees sorting through the pajamas when I suddenly wondered, "Why did Mom dress me up like a miniature adult?"

I called my sponsor to share my realization: "It's not sane to get dressed up to go camping!" "Yep," was all she said.

Further Reflections...
"Also, like other addictions, sexaholism affects the whole family."

S-Anon Newcomers Booklet

No – A Healthy Option

It is difficult for me to disappoint someone and say "no." Yet, I am learning that it is necessary for me to be able to do so. Setting limits is a challenge, but I am making progress. S-Anon has taught me that I do not have all the answers, nor do I have to be the solution. Sometimes this means that I step back and do not take direct action or any action at all. This is hard for me on many levels, because I do not like the feelings that are stirred up when I say "no." In the past I would rather feel the physical exhaustion of doing something I am too tired to do, than feel the emotions that come with saying "no."

Setting limits for myself is particularly difficult with family members, especially with my mother, the sexaholic in my life. If she has a want or need and I am clear that it would be unhealthy for me, then saying "no" becomes a healthy option. I no longer want to take on her responsibilities. I visualize placing my mother in her Higher Power's hands. I then give her the space to find another way to take care of her needs. Likewise, I am learning that this works in reverse. My mother has the right to say "no" to me, also. Today I can say "no," knowing that God is taking care of others, as well as me.

Further Reflections...
"Learning to listen to our hearts and to honor our feelings takes time and work."

Working the S-Anon Program, p. 49

Secrecy vs. Anonymity

When I first came into S-Anon, I appreciated having personal anonymity; I was angry and ashamed, and I did not want anyone to know about what was happening in my family. Yet in my anger and desperation, I did not believe the sexaholic had any right to anonymity. After all, the secrets he had kept and all the lies he had told had destroyed our family. Now he was in recovery, and I could not understand why he was allowed "anonymity." Wouldn't that be license to continue to lie and to keep secrets?

What I came to understand though prayer, meditation, and the help of my sponsor was that I had equated "secrecy" with "anonymity." Working my program helped me realize that secrets keep me sick, but anonymity creates an environment where healing can happen. I came to see that anonymity respects the right of each person to disclose his or her own story. I finally understand why anonymity is the spiritual foundation of our fellowship: it creates a safe, non-shaming place to identify and share with others who have experienced similar situations. Our respective fellowships gave my partner and me the chance to heal from the very secrets we were both keeping.

What is the difference between secrecy and anonymity? Secrets kept me sick while anonymity helps to keep me safe... one day at a time.

Further Reflections...
"Anonymity is the spiritual foundation of all our Traditions, ever reminding us to place principles above personalities."

Tradition Twelve

Overcoming Fear

I have come to believe that the best way that I can carry the message is sharing with other people in a meeting. I was more familiar with going into a group and blending into the woodwork. I was afraid of saying the wrong thing, hurting someone's feelings, or making a fool of myself. My thoughts were always focused on how other people were seeing me, so sometimes the best approach was just not to speak.

At my first meeting I thought, "I don't know how I'll ever be able to do this." But someone told me, "If you want to get better, you have to raise your hand. You have to share what's going on with you." So I did, and I do. It really does work.

Further Reflections...
"By sharing, we take part in the fellowship, coming out of the isolation that is common among us."
Working the S-Anon Program, p. 6

Choices vs. Victim Role

When I feel victimized, it is because I have forgotten I have choices. Remembering I have choices helps take me out of the victim role. I believe God has given me free will, so at any given time I have many options available to me. When I cannot see my options, I read some S-Anon literature, discuss things with my sponsor or other S-Anon friends, or pray to my Higher Power. The important thing is that I choose to take responsibility for my choices, rather than choose to be a victim by default.

Through working the Fourth and Fifth Steps around my feelings of victimization, I became aware that I am capable of harming others. For example, at times I have treated my children and co-workers poorly, and I know I have spoken cruelly to punish the sexaholic when she has hurt me. Through the Fourth and Fifth Step, I understand that when I do take responsibility and make good choices for myself, I am less likely to hurt others.

Further Reflections...
"We discovered that we were the source of much of the pain for which we had blamed others."

S-Anon Twelve Steps, p. 39

Islands of Retreat

I look forward to my meeting each week and enjoy seeing the familiar faces I have come to know. When I am away from my weekly meeting, the rhythm of my life feels greatly interrupted. Upon returning to my meeting I find that I again feel a sense of joy and connection. My S-Anon meeting is the place I go to be heard, to hear others, and to connect with my Higher Power. I hear the victories others are experiencing as they practice the principles of the program. I also see people come in one day with troubles burdening them, only to return the next week with the weight lifted off their shoulders. This gives me great hope.

The relationship I have with people in the fellowship also extends beyond meetings. We go out for coffee after the meeting or meet for dinner or lunch during the week. This time gives each of us an opportunity to share further about what is going on in our lives.

I am given islands of retreat through my weekly meetings and fellowship. These retreats are filled with people who are walking along side of me on the path leading each of us to a healthier way of life for our families and ourselves.

Further Reflections...
"Meetings are a vital part of the S-Anon program, providing us with the opportunity to identify and confirm common problems and to hear the experience, strength, and hope of others."

Working the S-Anon Program, p. 3

I Am Never Alone

Occasionally I find myself in a great deal of pain because of the sexaholic's acting out. That is when I try to remember that I am never alone, and I don't have to handle it all by myself. Left to my own thinking, I would try to handle it myself. S-Anon has taught me that trying to rely on myself usually just ends up extending my suffering as I muddle my way through the painful feelings.

So I say a prayer and turn it all over to my Higher Power. I call my sponsor or another S-Anon member for some helpful reminders: I am powerless over what another person does and no matter how bad it is right now, "this too shall pass." I read the literature and remember to focus on myself. I go to a meeting.

When I reach out for help, my Higher Power and the strength of the S-Anon program carry me through whatever is troubling me. I don't have to do it all alone. That is a gift of this program.

Further Reflections...
"We learn we need not face our problems alone. Instead, we learn to turn our will and our lives over to the care of God. As long as we placed self-reliance first, a genuine reliance upon a Higher Power was out of the question."

S-Anon Twelve Steps, p. 72

All I Did Was Work My Own Program

One evening, my husband (a recovering sexaholic) and I were discussing the concerns we had about the behavior of a friend and how that behavior was affecting the friend's family. I shared with my husband something I had learned in S-Anon: if one family member is willing to make changes and seek recovery, other family members see the changes and sometimes become willing, too.

At that point, it occurred to me that I didn't know if that had been true in our situation. So I asked him, "How much did my going to S-Anon meetings influence your decision to go into your own recovery program?" His reply: "It had a huge role." He said as he saw me beginning to change, he knew he would lose me if he didn't do something, too.

The amazing thing was I hadn't asked him to go into a recovery program. All I did was work my own program to recover from the effects of living with sexaholism. I worked the Steps with a sponsor, attended meetings, and read our literature. S-Anon taught me to take care of myself and Higher Power will take care of the rest. I am very glad I put that principle into practice.

Further Reflections...
"Today, with the help of this fellowship and the Twelve Steps, I am happy. I am grateful to have this program and to be in this relationship with a recovering sexaholic."

S-Anon Twelve Steps, p. 9

A Day Filled with Gossip

I came home from work one day feeling angry and ashamed about my behavior. At my job I had gossiped about four people: my supervisor, the covering supervisor, and two of my co-workers. While other people may have started the gossiping, I had contributed by adding my two cents.

I previously had done a Fourth and Fifth Step; however, my habit of gossiping had not come up in that work. After sharing with my sponsor about all the gossip I had participated in, she suggested I do some writing. I dreaded the process, but I dreaded even more the shame I knew I would feel if I did not take the steps to change my gossiping habit.

My writing was revealing. I had started gossiping during my school years and had continued it into adulthood. I was indiscriminate; it didn't matter whether or not I liked the people about whom I gossiped. I gossiped about my spouse and his family, and I gossiped about people I didn't know personally. What was consistent about my gossiping was the neediness that seemed to underlie it. I wanted to be liked and accepted, even at the expense of others and my own self-respect.

I was ready to let go of gossiping and people-pleasing. On my knees, I asked God to remove those defects and to help me to know how to make amends. I am grateful God is removing those defects, and today I can look my coworkers in the eyes.

Further Reflections...
"As I reflect on my Sixth Step, what shortcomings can I bring to my Higher Power? What are some positive characteristics with which God might replace the defects?"

S-Anon Twelve Steps, p. 83

Letting Go of Shame

Prior to S-Anon, the shame I felt from being sexually abused had tremendous power in my life. Since joining S-Anon, the love, acceptance, and support of the group and my Higher Power have helped change that. One night, the voice of my shame awakened me and instead of denying the shame, as I usually did, I prayed to my Higher Power about it. I affirmed that nothing – not even shame – could or would separate me from the love of my Higher Power. Then I allowed myself to feel the shame. I wept and wept until a great relief and peace came over me.

Looking back, I realize I experienced Steps One, Two, and Three that night. I admitted my powerlessness over shame – it was clear I could not keep shame under control by sheer will power. Knowing that my Higher Power loved me enough to restore me to sanity allowed me to feel the painful feelings of shame rather than trying to escape or control them. I was able to surrender my will and my life to the care of God. I trusted that God would not let the shame overwhelm me. I felt relief and peace from again finding that God can be trusted to do for me what I cannot do for myself.

Further Reflections...
"When I did share the truth about myself with my Higher Power, I finally started to have a real relationship with God. It was a turning point in my recovery."

S-Anon Twelve Steps, p. 54

Fully Self-Supporting

When I first came to S-Anon, I viewed the Seventh Tradition solely in financial terms. Over time, I have broadened that view to include many other aspects of self-support in relation to our group. All members can contribute service, time, and ideas, as well as money to make our group fully self-supporting.

I have also extended this spiritual principle to my relationships. In my disease I often found myself doing for others what they could do for themselves and expecting others to take care of what I could do for myself. Applying Tradition Seven to my family situation stops me from taking on others' responsibilities as my own. Tradition Seven reminds me to allow the people in my life to be fully self-supporting, without unnecessary contributions from me. Tradition Seven also encourages me to take action on behalf of my own needs, without expecting someone else to come to my rescue. There is a balance in being responsible that I am learning through working the S-Anon Program.

Further Reflections...
"'Fully self supporting' can, however, refer to more than just financial support. Each member of the group has an opportunity to support the group by taking a turn in a service position, such as chairing a meeting, answering local hotline calls, leading newcomer meetings, or volunteering at a convention or open meeting. Similarly each family member can be encouraged to strive to be physically, emotionally, and spiritually self-supporting to an appropriate extent."

Working the S-Anon Program, p. 34

The Twelve Steps of S-Anon

Working the Twelve Steps of S-Anon, that is putting the principles of the Steps into practice in our lives, brings about our recovery from the effects of living with the sexaholism of a family member or friend.

1. We admitted we were powerless over sexaholism—that our lives had become unmanageable.

2. Came to believe that a Power greater than ourselves could restore us to sanity.

3. Made a decision to turn our will and our lives over to the care of God *as we understood Him.*

4. Made a searching and fearless moral inventory of ourselves.

5. Admitted to God, to ourselves, and to another human being the exact nature of our wrongs.

6. Were entirely ready to have God remove all these defects of character.

7. Humbly asked Him to remove our shortcomings.

8. Made a list of all persons we had harmed, and became willing to make amends to them all.

9. Made direct amends to such people wherever possible, except when to do so would injure them or others.

10. Continued to take personal inventory and when we were wrong promptly admitted it.

11. Sought through prayer and meditation to improve our conscious contact with God *as we understood Him*, praying only for knowledge of His will for us and the power to carry that out.

12. Having had a spiritual awakening as the result of these Steps, we tried to carry this message to others, and to practice these principles in all our affairs.

The Twelve Steps of Alcoholics Anonymous: 1. We admitted we were powerless over alcohol - that our lives had become unmanageable. 2. Came to believe that a Power greater than ourselves could restore us to sanity. 3. Made a decision to turn our will and our lives over to the care of God *as we understood Him*. 4. Made a searching and fearless moral inventory of ourselves. 5. Admitted to God, to ourselves, and to another human being the exact nature of our wrongs. 6. Were entirely ready to have God remove all these defects of character. 7. Humbly asked Him to remove our shortcomings. 8. Made a list of all persons we had harmed, and became willing to make amends to them all. 9. Made direct amends to such people wherever possible, except when to do so would injure them or others. 10. Continued to take personal inventory and when we were wrong promptly admitted it. 11. Sought through prayer and meditation to improve our conscious contact with God *as we understood Him*, praying only for knowledge of His will for us and the power to carry that out. 12. Having had a spiritual awakening as the result of these Steps, we tried to carry this message to alcoholics, and to practice these principles in all our affairs.

(The Twelve Steps reprinted and adapted with permission of Alcoholics Anonymous World Services, Inc. Permission to reprint and adapt the Steps and Traditions does not mean that AA is affiliated with this program. AA is a program of recovery from alcoholism – use of this material in connection with programs which are patterned after AA, but which address other problems, does not imply otherwise.)

The Twelve Traditions of S-Anon

The Traditions guide the growth and health of our groups and our world wide fellowship. Each time we read the Traditions in a meeting, we are reminded that "our group experience suggests that the unity of the S-anon Family Group depends upon our adherence to the following Traditions."

1. Our common welfare should come first; personal progress for the greatest number depends upon unity.

2. For our group purpose there is but one authority — a loving God as He may express Himself in our group conscience. Our leaders are but trusted servants — they do not govern.

3. The relatives of sexaholics, when gathered together for mutual aid, may call themselves an S-Anon Family Group, provided that, as a group, they have no other affiliation. The only requirement for membership is that there be a problem of sexaholism in a relative or friend.

4. Each group should be autonomous, except in matters affecting another group or S-Anon or SA as a whole.

5. Each S-Anon Family Group has but one purpose: to help families of sexaholics. We do this by practicing the Twelve Steps of S-Anon, by encouraging and understanding our sexaholic relatives, and by welcoming and giving comfort to the families of sexaholics.

6. Our S-Anon Family Groups ought never endorse, finance, or lend our name to any outside enterprise, lest problems of money, property, and prestige divert us from our primary spiritual aim. Although a separate entity, we should always cooperate with Sexaholics Anonymous.

7. Every group ought to be fully self-supporting, declining outside contributions.

8. S-Anon Twelfth Step work should remain forever non-professional, but our service centers may employ special workers.

9. Our groups, as such, ought never be organized; but we may create service boards or committees directly responsible to those they serve.

10. The S-Anon Family Groups have no opinion on outside issues; hence our name ought never be drawn into public controversy.

11. Our public relations policy is based on attraction rather than promotion; we need always maintain personal anonymity at the level of press, radio, TV and films. We need guard with special care the anonymity of all S-Anon and SA members.

12. Anonymity is the spiritual foundation of all our Traditions, ever reminding us to place principles above personalities.

S-Anon's Twelve Concepts of Service

S-Anon's Twelve Concepts of Service illustrate that Twelfth Step work can be accomplished on a broad scale. The Concepts are guidelines for the World Service Office staff, the Board of Trustees, standing committees, and World Service Conference members to relate to each other and to groups.

1. The ultimate responsibility and authority for S-Anon world services belongs to the S-Anon groups.

2. The S-Anon Family Groups have delegated complete administrative and operational authority to their Conference and its service arms.

3. The Right of Decision makes effective leadership possible.

4. Participation is the key to harmony

5. The Rights of Appeal and Petition protect minorities and assure that they be heard.

6. The Conference acknowledges the primary administrative responsibility of the Trustees.

7. The Trustees have legal rights while the rights of the Conference are traditional.

8. The Board of Trustees delegates full authority for routine management of the S-Anon headquarters to its executive committees.

9. Good personal leadership at all service levels is a necessity. In the field of World Service, the Board of Trustees assumes the primary leadership.

10. Service responsibility is balanced by carefully defined service authority, and double-headed management is avoided.

11. The World Service Office is composed of an Executive Director and staff members.

12. The spiritual foundation for S-Anon's World Services is contained in the General Warranties of the Conference, Article 12 of the Charter.

The General Warranties of the Conference

In all proceedings the World Service Conference of S-Anon shall observe the spirit of the Traditions:

1. That only sufficient operating funds, including an ample reserve, be its prudent financial principle;

2. That no Conference member shall be placed in unqualified authority over other members;

3. That all decisions be reached by discussion, vote, and whenever possible, by unanimity;

4. That no Conference action ever be personally punitive or an incitement to public controversy;

5. That though the Conference serves S-Anon, it shall never perform any act of government; and like the fellowship of S-Anon which it serves, it shall always remain democratic in thought and action.

Other Available S-Anon Publications and ISBN Listings

Books:

S-Anon Twelve Steps (P-1) 0-9676637-0-9

Exploring the Wonders of Recovery: A Companion Guide to the S-Anon Twelve Steps (P-5) 0-9676637-2-5

Working the S-Anon Program (P-4) 0-9676637-1-7

Booklets and Pamphlets:

Information for Professionals about S-Anon and S-Ateen Family Groups (L-10)

Recovering Together: Issues Faced by Couples (RA-2)

We're Glad You're Here-Newcomers Booklet-Helpful Information for the Newcomer (P-3) Spanish Version (P-3s)

Service Literature:

S-Anon/S-Ateen Service Manual (P-2)

S-Ateen Literature:

S-Ateen Meeting Format & Readings (P-2ST)
S-Ateen Checklist (L-8)

A complete listing of our literature can be found on our website: *www.sanon.org*

INDEX